The Illustrated Encyclopedia of
HUMAN DEVELOPMENT

NEW YORK

Academic Advisors:
Professor Ian MacDonald, M.D., D.Sc., F.L., Biol.,
Professor of Applied Physiology,
Guy's Hospital Medical School, London.

Dr. F. A. Chandra, B.Sc., M.B., B.S., Ph.D.,

Editors:
Michael Bisacre
Richard Carlisle
Deborah Robertson
John Ruck

© Marshall Cavendish Limited 1978—84

First published in the USA
1984 by Exeter Books

Distributed by Bookthrift
Exeter is a trademark of Simon & Schuster, Inc.
Bookthrift is a registered trademark of
Simon & Schuster, Inc.
New York, New York

Printed and bound in Italy by New Interlitho SpA.

ISBN 0-671-07039-8

This volume is not to be sold in Australia
or New Zealand

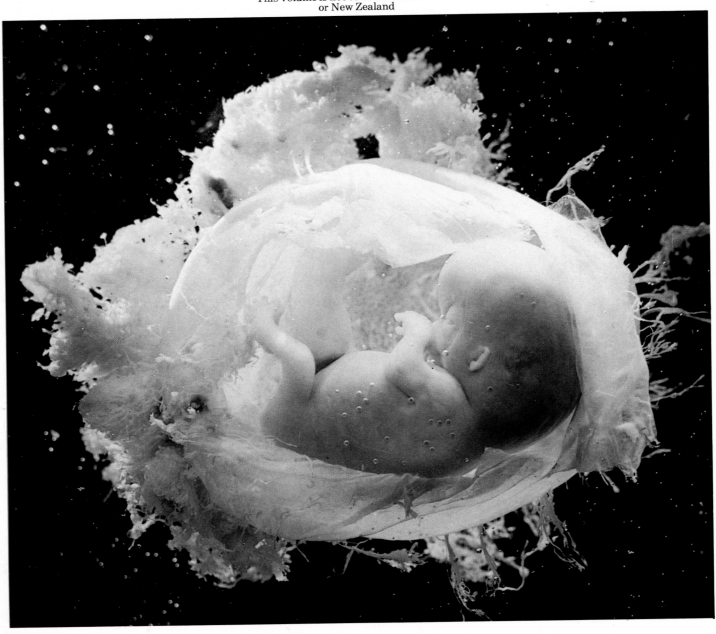

Contents

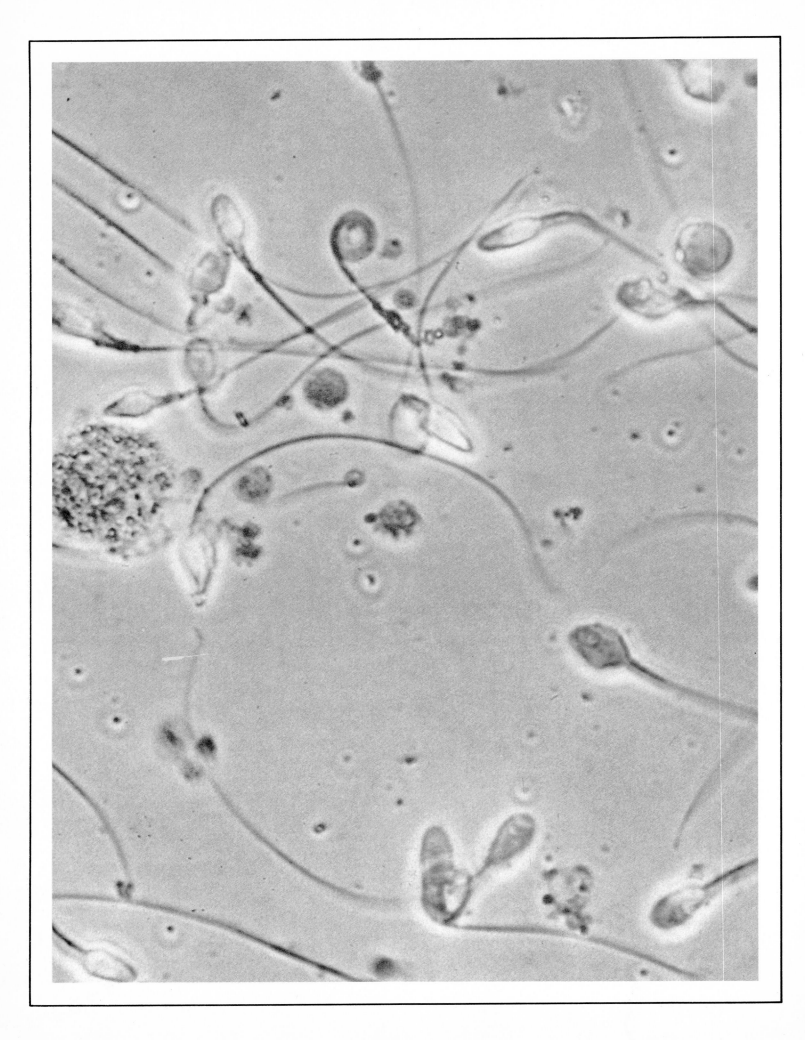

Human Life

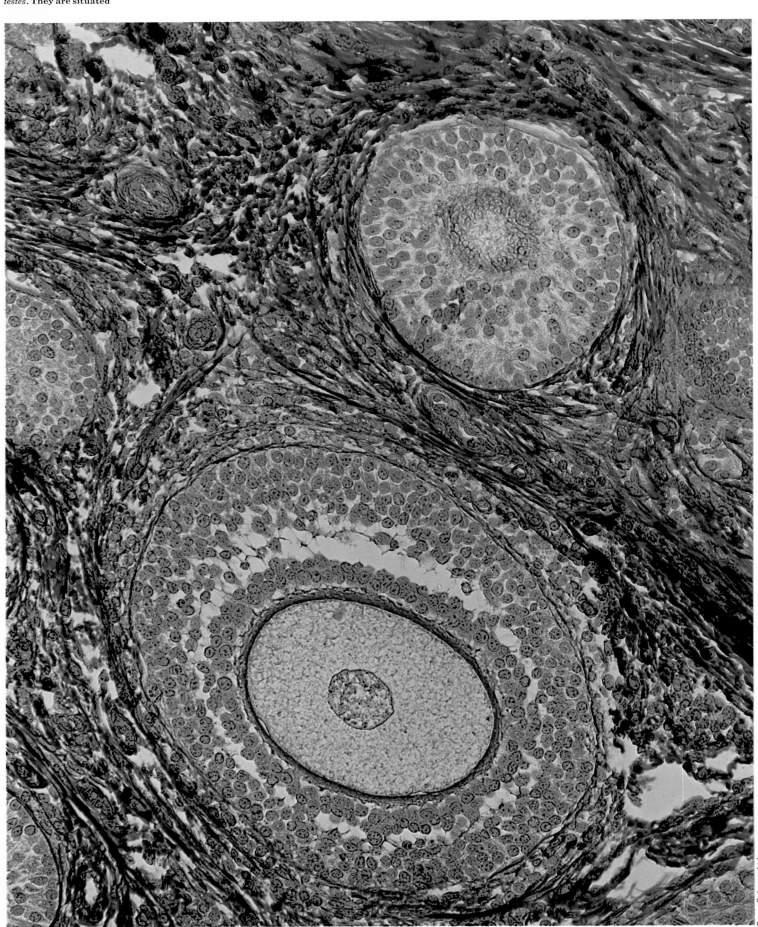

Conception

The birth of a new individual has always been regarded as a highly significant event, but not until the beginning of the nineteenth century was an accurate understanding of the reproductive process achieved.

All mammals, including man, produce offspring by a process of sexual reproduction involving the union of male and female. During the seventeenth century the celebrated Dutch microscopist, Anton von Leewenhoek, invented a microscope which enabled him to see that *semen*—the male fluid emitted during intercourse—contains tiny tadpole-shaped cells, the male sex cells or *sperm*. But not until 1827 did Karl Ernst von Baer—the pioneer of embryology—observe the corresponding female sex cell, the *ovum* or egg. Until this discovery, the role of sperm and ovum were hotly disputed. Some believed that the sperm contained the *homunculus*, a miniature, but perfectly formed, human which was merely nourished by the ovum. Rivals contended that the role of the sperm was to activate a preformed human in the ovum. We now know that homunculi do not exist: complex organisms are built by the division of simple cells, each containing genes which control the development of the whole. This explains how both sperm and ovum are equally important in reproduction and also why children share the characteristics of both parents.

The development of the sex cells

The first stage of reproduction, *conception*, involves the development of sperm and ova in the *gonads*—the primary reproductive organs—of the male and female and the joining together of these cells in the body of the female.

Both sexes possess two symmetrical gonads. The *testes*, the male gonads, are two oval bodies about five cm (two in.) long, suspended in a sac outside the body to maintain the lower temperature necessary for efficient sperm production. Each testis is divided into about 250 small lobes filled with tubes called *seminiferous tubules*. Within these tubes, cells known as *spermatagonia* are constantly developing and during the process of *spermatogenesis*, which lasts several weeks, they become mature sperm.

Spermatagonia, like normal body cells, contain 23 pairs of *chromosomes*. They carry the characteristic determining genes. The formation of both sperm and ovum must involve a reduction of this number by a half, to 23 single chromosomes, so that the new cell produced by their subsequent union will have a normal complement of 46 chromosomes. This is achieved by a specialized process of division known as *meiosis*. The spermatagonium which has matured to the point where this process may start is called the *primary spermatocyte*: chromosome pairs separate, one member of each pair moving into each of the two new cells formed by the division. These new cells, the *secondary spermatocytes*, now contain only 23 chromosomes and each of them undergoes a second meiotic division. The strands of each chromosome divide, half going to each spermatid, in which they then develop into complete chromosomes.

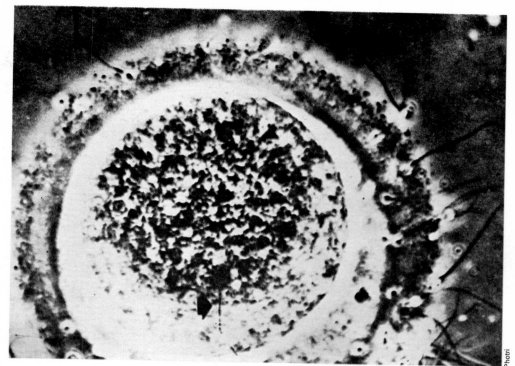

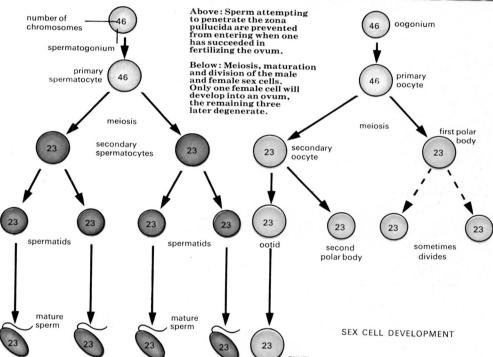

Above: Sperm attempting to penetrate the zona pullucida are prevented from entering when one has succeeded in fertilizing the ovum.

Below: Meiosis, maturation and division of the male and female sex cells. Only one female cell will develop into an ovum, the remaining three later degenerate.

number of chromosomes — 46

spermatogonium

primary spermatocyte — 46

meiosis

secondary spermatocytes — 23 | 23

spermatids — 23 | 23 | 23 | 23

mature sperm — 23 | 23 | 23 | 23

46 oogonium

46 primary oocyte

meiosis

secondary oocyte — 23 | first polar body — 23

ootid — 23 | second polar body — 23 | sometimes divides — 23 | 23

ovum — 23

SEX CELL DEVELOPMENT

Up to this point, the spermatids are round and must undergo many physical changes to become fully fledged sperm with head, mid-piece and tail, specially adapted to transmit their genetic material to the ovum. They are aided in these changes by *Sertoli*, or nurse, cells, large pyramidal-shaped cells which project from the edge to the centre of the seminiferous tubule. Each spermatid embeds itself in a Sertoli cell. This helps it to reduce the cytoplasmic material which normally surrounds the chromosomes, and this densely packed genetic material will form the head of the sperm. The head is elliptical in shape, slightly flattened and acquires a covering cap known as the *acrosome*.

A tail is formed from cylindrical fibres which eventually propel the sperm by contracting in length—first on one side of the tail then the other—and producing whip-like movements. These make it move in a forward direction. The spermatidal mitochondria, containing enzymes which break down food to provide energy for the mature sperm, migrate to a position where they will form a mid-piece between head and tail. The sperm detaches itself from the Sertoli cell and moves to the *epididymis*, a convoluted tube lying along the back of the testis, where final maturation occurs and the entire sperm is then covered by a cell membrane. They can wait here for up to three or four weeks before they are used but after this period they will be reabsorbed.

The mature sperm is invisibly small: van Leewenhoek was certainly not far wrong when he asserted: 'I judge a million of them would not equal the size of a grain of sand'. Powerful electron microscopes

Photri

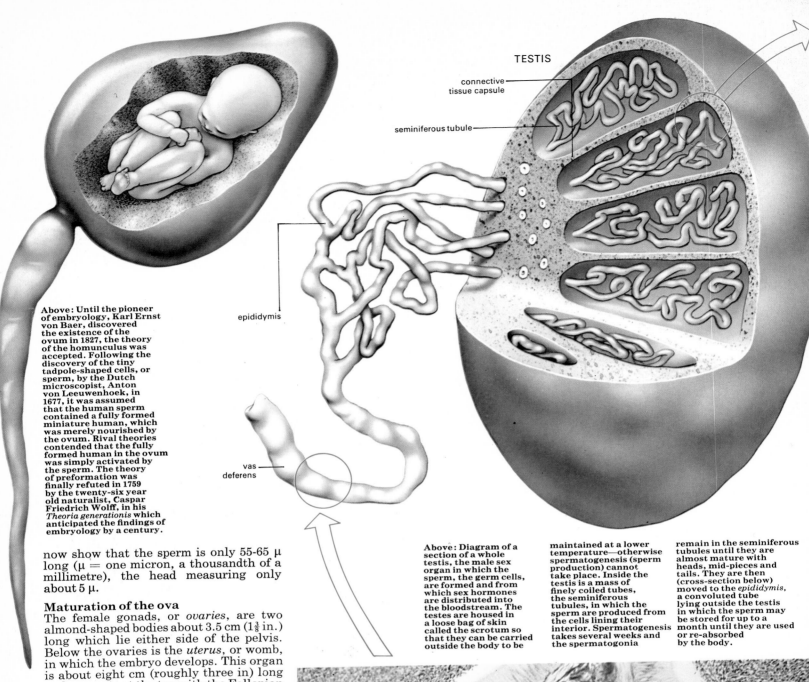

TESTIS

connective tissue capsule

seminiferous tubule

epididymis

vas deferens

Above: Until the pioneer of embryology, Karl Ernst von Baer, discovered the existence of the ovum in 1827, the theory of the homunculus was accepted. Following the discovery of the tiny tadpole-shaped cells, or sperm, by the Dutch microscopist, Anton von Leeuwenhoek, in 1677, it was assumed that the human sperm contained a fully formed miniature human, which was merely nourished by the ovum. Rival theories contended that the fully formed human in the ovum was simply activated by the sperm. The theory of preformation was finally refuted in 1759 by the twenty-six year old naturalist, Caspar Friedrich Wolff, in his *Theoria generationis* which anticipated the findings of embryology by a century.

now show that the sperm is only 55-65 μ long (μ = one micron, a thousandth of a millimetre), the head measuring only about 5 μ.

Maturation of the ova

The female gonads, or *ovaries*, are two almond-shaped bodies about 3.5 cm (1⅜ in.) long which lie either side of the pelvis. Below the ovaries is the *uterus*, or womb, in which the embryo develops. This organ is about eight cm (roughly three in) long and connects at the top with the Fallopian tubes. These are narrow ducts, about 10 cm (four in) long. Their wider open ends are near the ovaries. At the lower end of the uterus is its *cervix*, the neck, which contains a narrow opening and projects into the *vagina*—the wider channel which connects the reproductive system with the outside of the body.

The *oogonia*, the female equivalent of spermatagonia, are not produced continuously. A baby girl possesses about a half a million potential ova which do not multiply. Many of these never develop further but degenerate, a process known as *atresia*. In a woman between the age of 35 and 40 only about 8,000 oogonia remain. Some will have been used during *oogenesis*, the female equivalent of spermatogenesis.

In the first stage of ovum maturation, the primary *oocytes* develop from *oogonia* which are surrounded by a protective sac of cells known as the *follicle*. Like the male primary spermatocytes they contain 23 pairs of chromosomes and will divide by meiosis. A band of dark material forms between the cell membrane of the oocyte and the surrounding cells, thickening to become an almost transparent membrane

Above: Diagram of a section of a whole testis, the male sex organ in which the sperm, the germ cells, are formed and from which sex hormones are distributed into the bloodstream. The testes are housed in a loose bag of skin called the scrotum so that they can be carried outside the body to be maintained at a lower temperature—otherwise spermatogenesis (sperm production) cannot take place. Inside the testis is a mass of finely coiled tubes, the seminiferous tubules, in which the sperm are produced from the cells lining their interior. Spermatogenesis takes several weeks and the spermatogonia remain in the seminiferous tubules until they are almost mature with heads, mid-pieces and tails. They are then (cross-section below) moved to the *epididymis*, a convoluted tube lying outside the testis in which the sperm may be stored for up to a month until they are used or re-absorbed by the body.

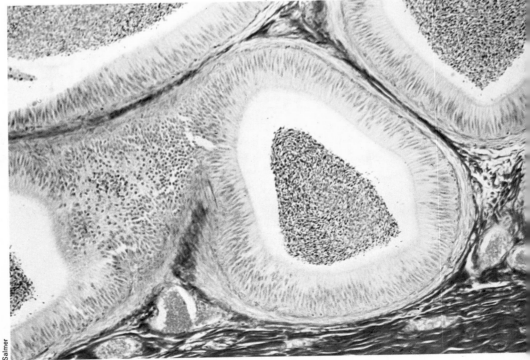

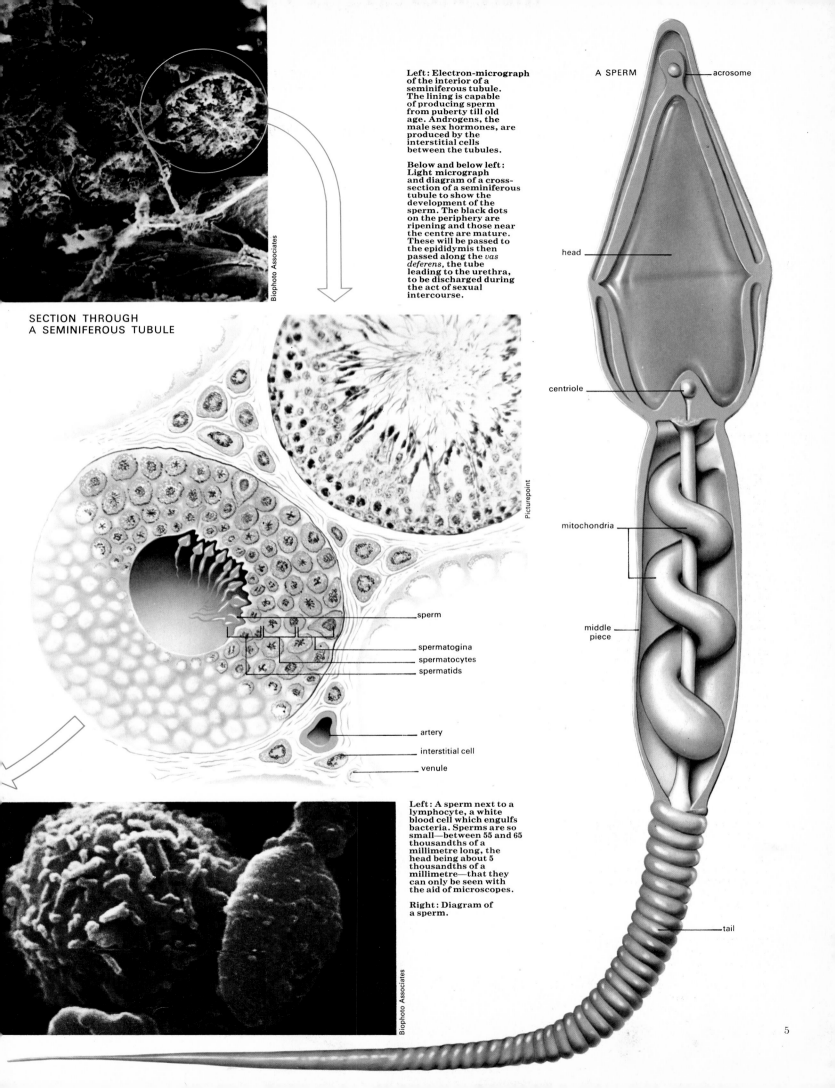

Left: Electron-micrograph
of the interior of a
seminiferous tubule.
The lining is capable
of producing sperm
from puberty till old
age. Androgens, the
male sex hormones, are
produced by the
interstitial cells
between the tubules.

Below and below left:
Light micrograph
and diagram of a cross-
section of a seminiferous
tubule to show the
development of the
sperm. The black dots
on the periphery are
ripening and those near
the centre are mature.
These will be passed to
the epididymis then
passed along the *vas
deferens*, the tube
leading to the urethra,
to be discharged during
the act of sexual
intercourse.

A SPERM

acrosome

head

centriole

mitochondria

middle
piece

tail

SECTION THROUGH
A SEMINIFEROUS TUBULE

sperm

spermatogina

spermatocytes

spermatids

artery

interstitial cell

venule

Left: A sperm next to a
lymphocyte, a white
blood cell which engulfs
bacteria. Sperms are so
small—between 55 and 65
thousandths of a
millimetre long, the
head being about 5
thousandths of a
millimetre—that they
can only be seen with
the aid of microscopes.

Right: Diagram of
a sperm.

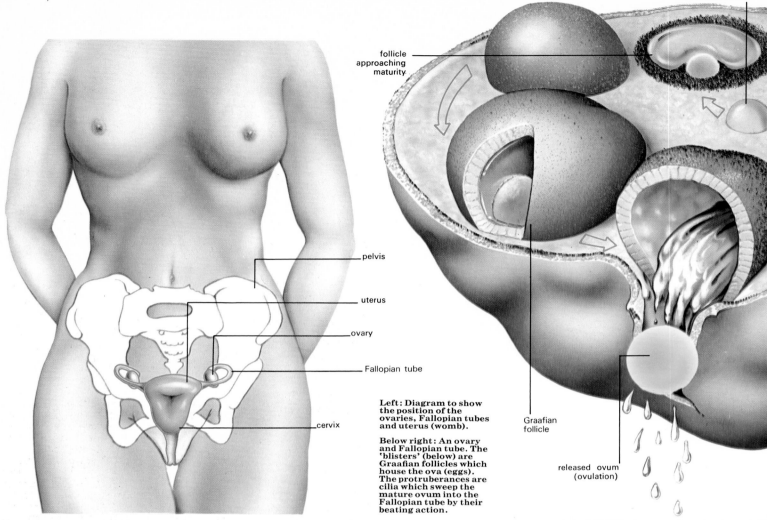

ripening follicle

follicle approaching maturity

pelvis

uterus

ovary

Fallopian tube

cervix

Graafian follicle

released ovum (ovulation)

Left: Diagram to show the position of the ovaries, Fallopian tubes and uterus (womb).

Below right: An ovary and Fallopian tube. The 'blisters' (below) are Graafian follicles which house the ova (eggs). The protruberances are cilia which sweep the mature ovum into the Fallopian tube by their beating action.

—this is called the *zona pellucida*.

The surrounding cells increase rapidly in number to form the *Graafian follicle*, a cavity filled with fluid forming between the follicle and the developing egg it contains. Some follicular cells remain around the zona pellucida. They are attached by a gelatinous substance and are known collectively as the *corona radiata*.

Once a month, ovulation occurs, when a single follicle is ruptured to release a developing egg cell. About two days before this the primary oocyte undergoes its first meiotic division to reduce its chromosome number by half. The outcome of this meiosis is different from division in the corresponding male cell in that two separate secondary oocytes are not formed. One of the two bodies formed during the division is larger than the other and remains in the egg as the secondary oocyte containing 23 chromosomes. The smaller one is known as the first polar body and moves out into the zona pellucida where it normally degenerates.

The maturing egg is now much larger than the sperm or a normal body cell. It is spherical, with a diameter of about 110-160 μ including the zona pellucida which is 10-20 μ thick. The egg does not begin its second meiotic division until ovulation, when it journeys down the Fallopian tube to the uterus.

The egg cannot move by itself but is collected by the *fimbria*, finger-like projections from the open end of the Fallopian tube. A current formed by the beating of tiny hair-like structures on the fimbria, together with contractions of the tube itself, carries the egg downwards. The egg can survive for about 24 hours before degenerating. During this time it must be reached by the sperm if fertilization is to take place.

The union of the sex cells

During intercourse the sperm travel from the epididymis through the *vas deferens*, and finally the urethra, a tube in the male organ which transmits them to the vagina. They are suspended in fluid known as *seminal plasma* and deposited around the cervix of the uterus. On average about 250 million sperm will be emitted and will normally survive for up to 72 hours, when they must reach the egg.

Ovulation

In all mammals except humans the female is only receptive to the male for a short period before ovulation, so that the sperm arrive in the female tract at exactly the right time to fertilize the egg. But the human female is potentially receptive at all times of her monthly cycle. Consequently the likelihood that both sperm and egg will be in the right state for fertilization is very much reduced. For fertilization to occur while both egg and sperm are in optimum condition intercourse must occur just a few hours before ovulation: when the egg begins to age, or if the sperm have been present for a considerable time before ovulation, the possibility of truly healthy children decreases.

One cause of male infertility is known to be a low sperm count—too few sperm per millilitre of semen. Although this may be accompanied by slow-moving sperm, or an abnormally high number of poorly-formed sperm which are incapable of fertilization, quantity is still important. Comparison of the dimensions of the

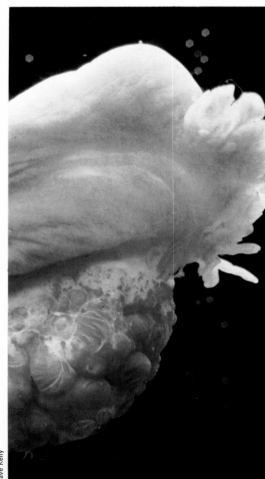

Dave Kelly

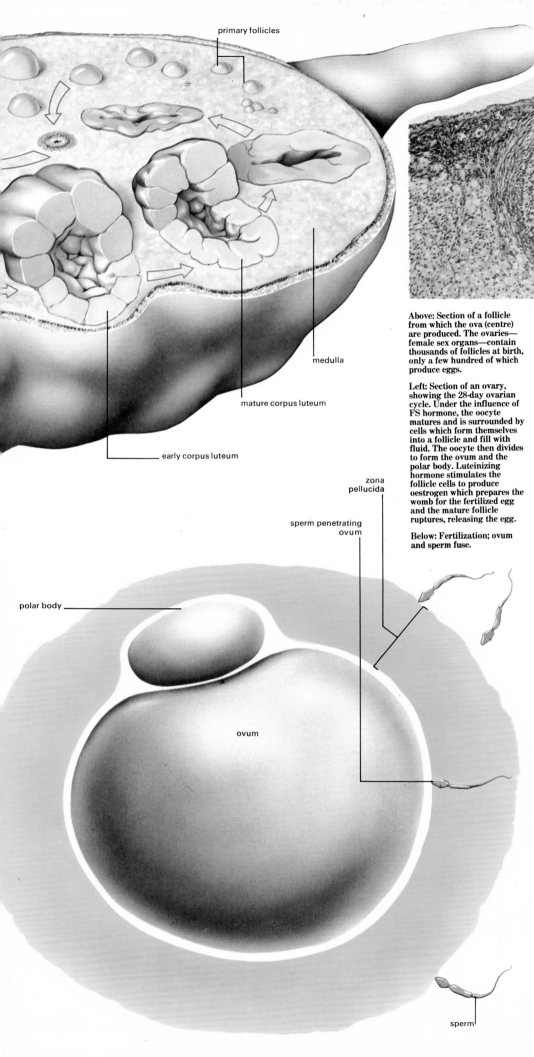

primary follicles

medulla

mature corpus luteum

early corpus luteum

zona pellucida

sperm penetrating ovum

polar body

ovum

sperm

Salmer

Above: Section of a follicle from which the ova (centre) are produced. The ovaries—female sex organs—contain thousands of follicles at birth, only a few hundred of which produce eggs.

Left: Section of an ovary, showing the 28-day ovarian cycle. Under the influence of FS hormone, the oocyte matures and is surrounded by cells which form themselves into a follicle and fill with fluid. The oocyte then divides to form the ovum and the polar body. Luteinizing hormone stimulates the follicle cells to produce oestrogen which prepares the womb for the fertilized egg and the mature follicle ruptures, releasing the egg.

Below: Fertilization; ovum and sperm fuse.

female organs and the sperm shows that a formidable journey awaits them; propelled partly by movements of their tail and by contractions of the female organs the sperm pass through the cervix and uterus and only a few thousand ever reach the Fallopian tubes. Hence there must be an allowance for this great loss.

Capacitation
It was discovered during the 1950s that the sperm must spend a certain time in the female system to become capable of fertilizing the egg. The process they undergo there is known as *capacitation*.

In humans it takes about seven hours, and involves activation of the acrosome reaction by substances in the female organs. The *acrosome*, or tip, of the sperm contains *hyaluronidase*, an enzyme capable of dissolving the gel of the corona radiata which is held together by hyaluronic acid. This allows the sperm to move through the corona and to penetrate the zona pellucida. The acrosome reaction must occur in many sperm around the egg, since the enzyme produced by a single sperm is insufficient to break down the barrier, but only one sperm will actually penetrate the egg.

The fertilized egg
Once penetrated by a sperm the egg becomes resistant to any other. Its surface layer moves out to engulf the sperm, the cell membranes surrounding sperm and egg fuse so that they constitute a single cell. The sperm has now fertilized the egg.

The entry of the sperm activates the egg which only now completes its second meiotic division. This is similar to the second division in the male, but, again in the female, two new cells do not form. The strands of chromosome which will eventually unite with those of the sperm remain in the egg to complete themselves.

The chromosomes of both the sperm and egg then form two separate units known as the male and female *pronucleus*. These enlarge and move towards each other, meeting in the centre of the egg. The membranes surrounding them finally fuse so that their respective groups of chromosomes come together. The maternal and paternal contributions of hereditary material are at last united into a single cell called the *zygote*. This cell with its full complement of 46 chromosomes (half of each pair from each parent) now contains all of the information necessary to guide the development of a new individual who will share the characteristics of both parents.

7

Pregnancy is divided into three periods known as *trimesters*. The first is from the beginning of the last menstrual period to the 14th week, the second from the 15th to the 28th week, and the third from the 29th to the 40th week, around which time the baby is delivered.

The Developing Being

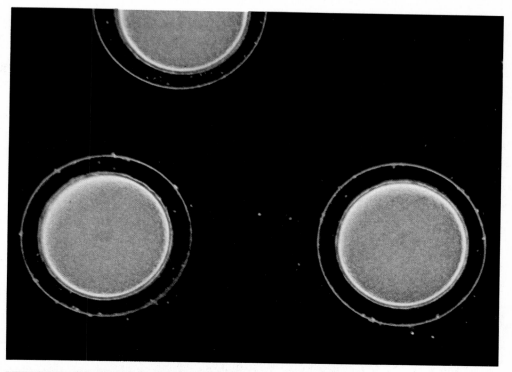

The *zygote*, which is formed by the union of the male and female sex cells, the ovum and sperm, is one of the biggest cells in the body. There is about twice as much cytoplasm as nucleus, which is much higher proportionally than in a normal cell.

Almost immediately after it is formed, the zygote begins to divide by *mitosis*, or splitting, and in less than 30 hours has become two cells, called *blastomeres*. Repeated mitotic divisions, known as cleavage, rapidly increase the number of blastomeres. This occurs without increasing the total size of the zygote—it remains within its zona pellucida, the thick jelly-like layer beneath the outer layer of cells—and results in further reduction and equal distribution of the nucleus throughout the group of cells.

While undergoing cleavage the zygote is passed along the Fallopian tube partly by currents created by the beating of the *cilia* the hair-like structures lining the tube, and partly by muscular contractions of the tube itself. By the time it reaches the uterine cavity, or womb, some three to five days after ovulation, it consists of 20 to 50 blastomeres enclosed within the zona pellucida, and is known as a *morula* or mulberry. The zygote's nutritional requirements for this journey along the Fallopian tube are slight. Its needs are chiefly met by secretions from the tube permeating through the zona pellucida, although some nutrition is provided by the yolk granules of the egg.

At about four to six days the morula takes in uterine fluid and develops into what is known as the hollow *blastocyst*. It consists of a *trophoblast*, a circle of peripheral cells and an inner cell mass, a cluster of centrally placed cells at one pole. The change from morula to blastocyst doubles the size of the conceptus—the embryo—and causes the zona pellucida to become thin and eventually disappear.

The trophoblast is now exposed and attaches itself to the *endometrium*, or lining, of the uterus, usually implanting itself high up and toward the back of the uterus. It is not yet known what factors are involved in choosing any one particular place in the uterus rather than another. But the relationship between the blastocyst and the endometrium is influenced by the hormone secreted to prepare the lining for implantation.

The blastocyst becomes completely buried in the endometrium in about 10 days. Its point of entry is marked by a slight swelling and, for a time, a small plug of fibrin—fibrous protein which forms the scars during blood clotting. This later disappears and the endometrium heals over completely.

At this stage nutrition is supplied to the embryo by diffusion through the outer trophoblast layer. During the process of invasion of the endometrium by the blastocyst, the trophoblast puts out finger-like projections or villi, which can absorb dissolved substances such as nutrients from maternal blood as soon as they make contact with it. At first, villi

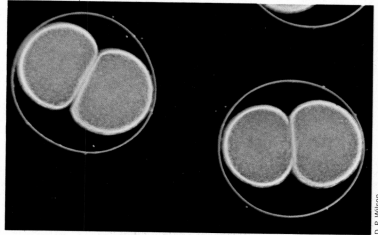

Above, left and below: Three stages of the fertilization process in the sea urchin. The thin lines surrounding the ova (above) are the membranes, reinforced to prevent the surrounding sperm from entering. This indicates that the eggs have already been fertilized. Some two hours later the ova have begun mitotic division (left) into two blastomeres, which continue to split into eight, 16 and 32 (below). This process, known as *cleavage*, continues until there are 128 cells within the ovum. By this stage, some three hours after fertilization, the membrane splits and the blastocyst—a ball of cells with a hollow interior filled with fluid —emerges.

D. P. Wilson

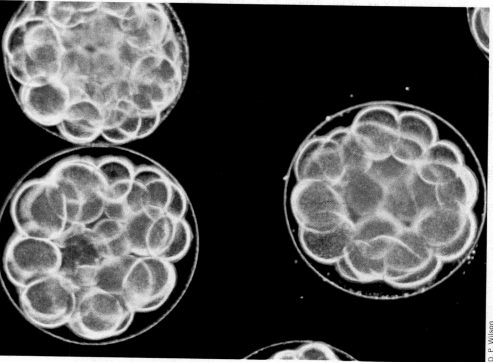

D. P. Wilson

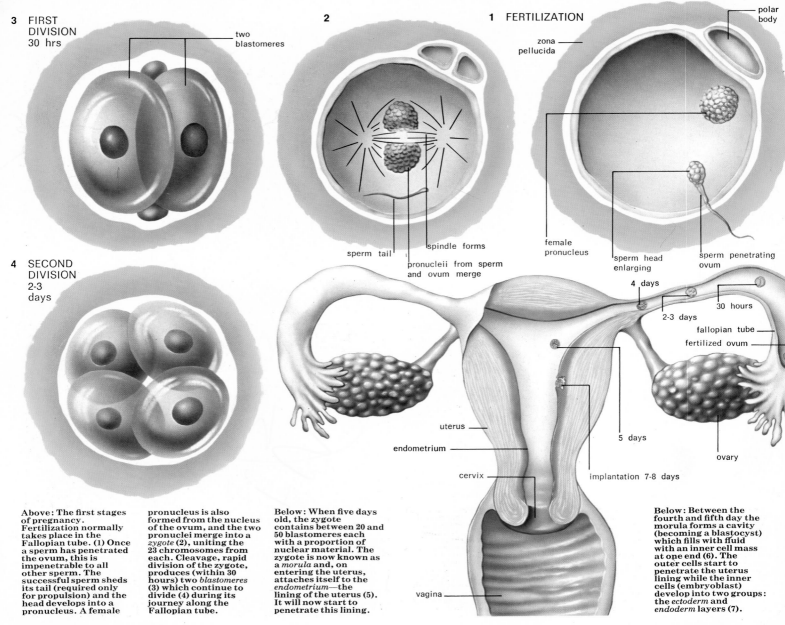

3 FIRST DIVISION 30 hrs

two blastomeres

2

sperm tail

spindle forms

pronuclei from sperm and ovum merge

1 FERTILIZATION

polar body

zona pellucida

female pronucleus

sperm head enlarging

sperm penetrating ovum

4 SECOND DIVISION 2-3 days

4 days

30 hours

2-3 days

fallopian tube

fertilized ovum

uterus

endometrium

5 days

cervix

implantation 7-8 days

ovary

vagina

Above: The first stages of pregnancy. Fertilization normally takes place in the Fallopian tube. (1) Once a sperm has penetrated the ovum, this is impenetrable to all other sperm. The successful sperm sheds its tail (required only for propulsion) and the head develops into a pronucleus. A female pronucleus is also formed from the nucleus of the ovum, and the two pronuclei merge into a *zygote* (2), uniting the 23 chromosomes from each. Cleavage, rapid division of the zygote, produces (within 30 hours) two *blastomeres* (3) which continue to divide (4) during its journey along the Fallopian tube.

Below: When five days old, the zygote contains between 20 and 50 blastomeres each with a proportion of nuclear material. The zygote is now known as a *morula* and, on entering the uterus, attaches itself to the *endometrium*—the lining of the uterus (5). It will now start to penetrate this lining.

Below: Between the fourth and fifth day the morula forms a cavity (becoming a blastocyst) which fills with fluid with an inner cell mass at one end (6). The outer cells start to penetrate the uterus lining while the inner cells (embryoblast) develop into two groups: the *ectoderm* and *endoderm* layers (7).

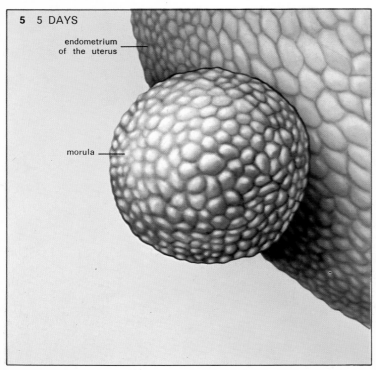

5 5 DAYS

endometrium of the uterus

morula

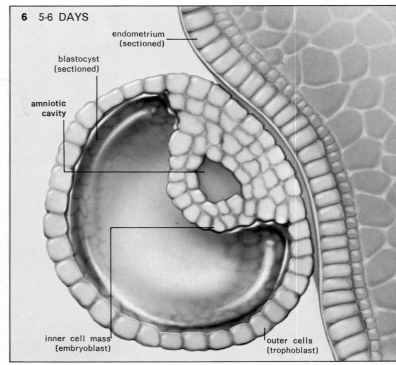

6 5-6 DAYS

endometrium (sectioned)

blastocyst (sectioned)

amniotic cavity

inner cell mass (embryoblast)

outer cells (trophoblast)

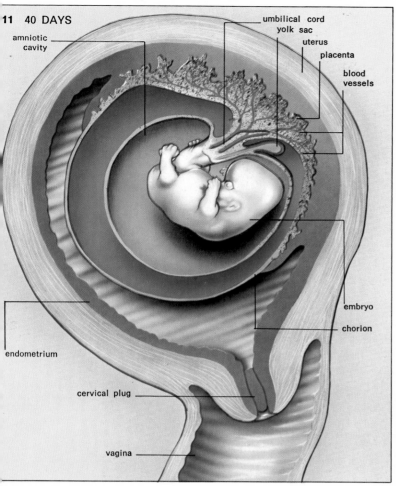

11 40 DAYS

- amniotic cavity
- umbilical cord
- yolk sac
- uterus
- placenta
- blood vessels
- embryo
- chorion
- endometrium
- cervical plug
- vagina

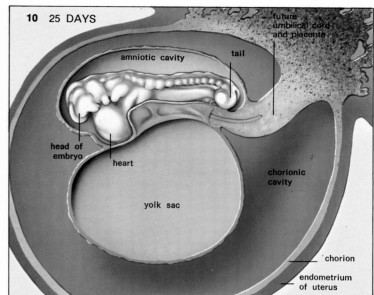

10 25 DAYS

- amniotic cavity
- tail
- future umbilical cord and placenta
- head of embryo
- heart
- chorionic cavity
- yolk sac
- chorion
- endometrium of uterus

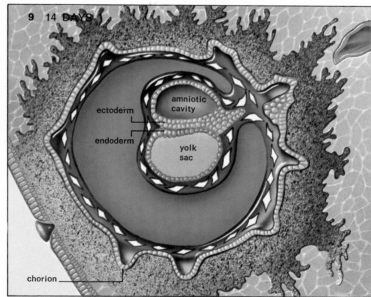

9 14 DAYS

- ectoderm
- amniotic cavity
- endoderm
- yolk sac
- chorion

Below and below right: By the seventh day a cavity appears between the ectoderm and the trophoblast—the *amniotic cavity* (7). Endoderm cells form a layer around the other cavity creating the *secondary yolk sac*. The trophoblast splits into two layers with a cavity in between called the *chorionic cavity*. (8).

Right: By the 13th day the embryoblast's only connection to the trophoblast is the *connecting stalk* (future umbilical cord). The two layers between the amniotic and secondary yolk sac flatten out into the *bilaminar germ disc* (9) from which the embryo will develop. The ectoderm layer develops into the skin

and nervous system. The endoderm becomes the digestive organs and lungs. Between these two layers the *mesoderm* forms from which bones, blood and muscles form. The *umbilical cord* and *placenta* develop (10). The ectoderm folds in on itself, squeezing off most of the yolk sac, and becomes surrounded by the amniotic sac (11).

7 7 DAYS

- implantation in the uterus beginning
- amniotic cavity
- endodermal cells
- ectoderm
- chorionic cavity developing
- chorion

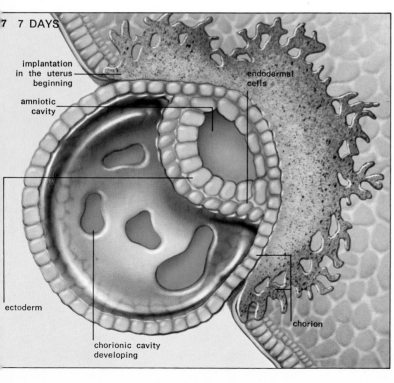

8 12 DAYS

- spaces in the uterus filling with blood
- connecting stalk
- yolk sac
- chorionic cavity
- plug
- embryonic disc
  - mesoderm)
  - endoderm)
  - ectoderm)

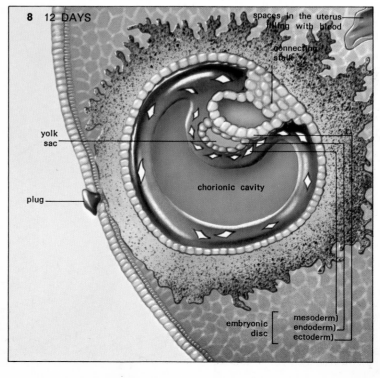

sprout into the endometrium all around the blastocyst but quite quickly most of them die so that only those lying deep in the lining of the uterus continue to grow. The rest of the trophoblast forms itself into a tough, protecting membrane around the embryo, the *chorion*.

Development of the placenta

About two weeks after implantation, blood vessels are formed within the villi. These link up with the embryonic circulatory system which develops at the same time. The villi come together to form the *placenta* (literally 'flat cake'), an extraordinary and elaborate organ with many highly sophisticated functions, mainly anchoring the conceptus firmly to the uterine wall, but also able to detach itself at birth without injury to mother or baby. It allows food and respiratory gases to reach the embryo and transport embryonic waste back to the mother. In this way it acts as lungs, liver and kidneys for the embryo.

The placenta can store certain substances such as glycogen—a carbohydrate formed from large glucose molecules. In conjunction with the embryo, it manufactures various hormones which prevent the uterus from expelling its contents too soon and which prepare the mother's breasts for milk production. The placenta also serves as a barrier between embryo and mother, keeping out a variety of toxins, hormones and metabolites (chemical substances involved in metabolism) present in the maternal circulation which could harm the embryo. The blood of the foetus and the mother do not come into direct contact. The maternal blood forms pools in the spaces around the placenta villi.

The formation of the embryo

Soon after implantation has begun—about one week after ovulation—the cells comprising the inner cell mass of the blastocyst begin to differentiate, that is, to become specialized to carry out different tasks. This process eventually results in the formation of the embryo.

A cavity forms between the cells of the inner cell mass close to the trophoblast lying immediately next to it. It is within this cavity, lined with the *amnion* (membrane) and filled with fluid, that the embryo actually develops. The tissues of the inner cell mass now form a disc with the *amniotic cavity* on one side and the blastocyst cavity on the other. At the same time a layer of cells lines the base of the disc and the whole inner surface of the trophoblastic shell. This lining then separates from the trophoblast to form the 'yolk-sac' cavity. In common with other mammalian eggs—and unlike a bird's egg—this sac does not contain yolk. Unlike the amnion, it does not persist and grow with the embryo, but disappears by mid-pregnancy.

By the twelfth day after fertilization the embryo has developed into a flattened two-layered disc bounded by two fluid-filled spaces. It is joined to the inner surface of the trophoblast by a connecting stalk which later contains the umbilical cord. Facing the amniotic cavity is the embryonic ectoderm (outer layer), while the embryonic endoderm (inner layer) faces the yolk-sac cavity. About three days later, the embryonic mesoderm, a third or middle layer, appears.

Although the division of the early em-

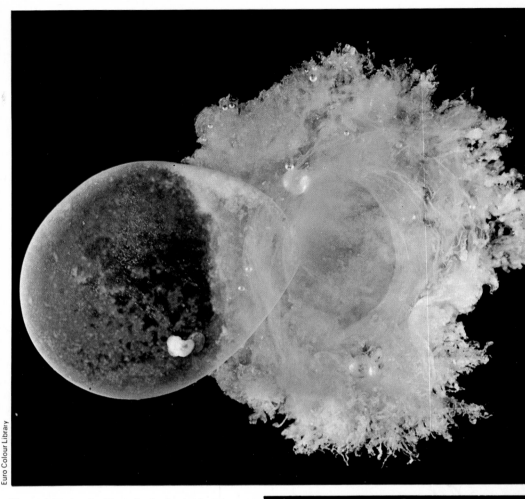

Above: A two-week-old embryo surrounded by the amnion, or amniotic sac, a liquid-filled balloon which protects the growing child and which expands with it.

Right and below: The embryo between its fourth and fifth weeks. Still only the size of a pea, it is already beginning to show quite dramatic changes. During this time the arches which will become the upper and lower jaws become visible. The regions where the eyes and ears will eventually develop are also differentiating and becoming distinct. Somites indicate where muscles will develop.

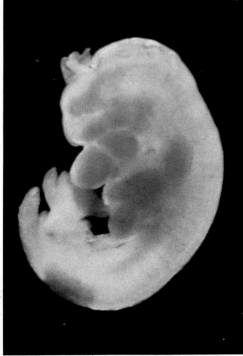

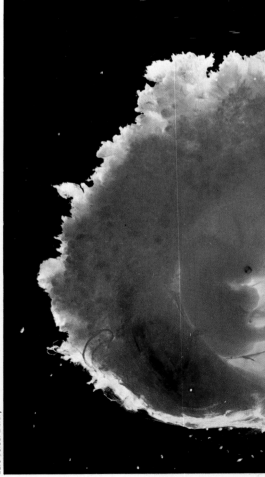

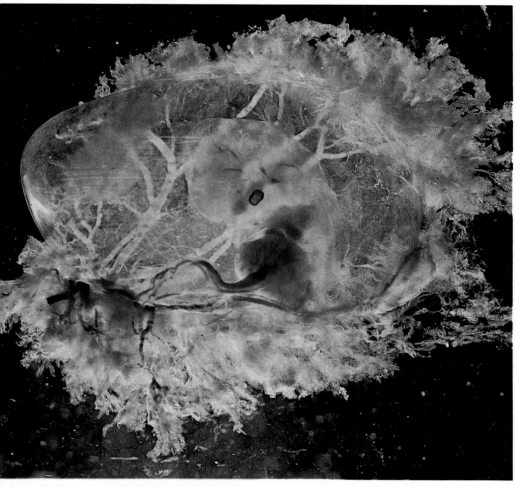

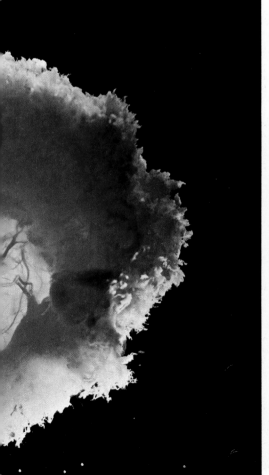

bryo into these three primary germ (cell) layers is mainly for descriptive convenience, it does seem that the endoderm produces the lining of many different organs, including the lungs and the alimentary canal; the mesoderm is responsible for the formation of muscles, connective tissues and blood; while from the ectoderm develop the skin, the lens of the eye and the nervous system.

At about the time the embryonic mesoderm is formed—roughly two weeks after fertilization—the ectodermal cells heap together into what is called the primitive streak. Along this line develops the neural groove. Its edges then fold over, forming the neural tube. Ultimately this gives rise to the brain, spinal cord and entire nervous system.

Some 20 days after fertilization, and two weeks after implantation, a circulatory system begins to develop in the mesoderm of the embryo. At first the embryonic heart is no more than a straight tube. The chambers and valves do not develop until much later. But even an organ as rudimentary as this is capable of function and heart beats may be recorded from a six-week old embryo.

The emerging human

At the end of the third week, the cells of the mesoderm, already heaped up on either side of the neural groove, begin to group themselves into a series of paired mesodermal *somites* (little bodies) which are a prominent feature during the fourth and fifth weeks after fertilization. Most of the skeleton and muscles eventually develops from these somites.

Arm buds appear at the beginning of the second month, and leg buds a little later. At first the hands and feet are paddle-shaped. Later they take on a webbed appearance and, finally, the fingers and the toes separate from each other. By the seventh week, the ends of the digits are flattened and thumb and fingerprints can be seen. During the third month these flat-ended pads grow smaller and disappear, so that the hands, then the feet, become truly human.

The second month also sees the development of several structures of the head and face. The neck becomes more visible making the head distinct from the body. The ears develop from two folds of tissue very low down along the sides of the head. The eyes, located on either side of the head (as are the nostrils at this stage), are visible by the sixth week but are lidless at first. The mouth at six weeks is merely a broad gash.

At this time the embryo appears grotesque, a monstrous caricature of a human. But within about two more weeks, by the end of the second month, the humanity of the embryo is beyond question. The eyes are in place and sealed by the eyelids; the nostrils have moved closer together and the nose is almost completed; the ears have developed tiny lobes, and the mouth has acquired lips.

By the eighth week of development, therefore, the ground plan of physical individuality has been established. All the human features are present, although not in proportion. The head, for example, takes up half the total length of the embryo, which from this stage onwards becomes known as the *foetus*. Incredible though it seems, it is still barely 2.5 cm (1 in) long and weighs about one gramme. Its major task now is to grow.

Above: By the sixth week most of the basic systems have appeared in a primitive form and its heart has begun beating. Tiny limb buds—first hands then feet—also emerge.

Below: At seven weeks the embryo is beginning to look more human. The swelling of the nose and the shape of the jaw are well established, the brain continues to develop and the eyes are forming. Although it is still only about 3 cm long, the limb buds are well defined. Paddle-shaped at first, they later become web-like, finally flattening out and separating so that the thumb- and finger-prints can be seen.

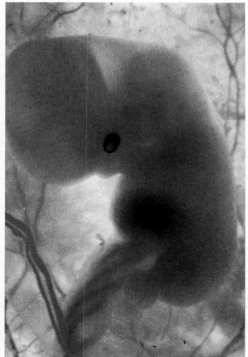

Euro Colour Library

John Hillelson Agency

13

The Foetus

By the end of the embryonic stage, about eight weeks after fertilization, the embryo takes on a recognizably human form although it is still barely an inch (2.5 cm) long. The main external features (limbs, eyes, ears, mouth, nose and sexual organs) can be clearly seen and internal organs such as the heart, lungs, liver, kidneys, digestive tract and brain have formed but are not yet fully developed. The embryo is now called a foetus and for the remainder of its time in the womb the changes it will experience concern size and sophistication.

The cardiovascular system
A primitive cardiovascular system (CVS) has already been established by the end of the embryonic period, but during the next stage of development it becomes much more elaborate. The foetal CVS has adapted to cope with the fact that the placenta functions as the organ of respiration rather than the lungs. It must also, however, be capable of carrying out the changeover at birth from placenta to lungs with minimal delay and no loss of efficiency. The key factors in this special circulation system are three 'short circuits' whereby blood can bypass specific organs.

The placenta and the foetus are joined through the umbilical cord by three great blood vessels—two arteries carrying blood from the foetus and one vein carrying blood from the placenta. Blood

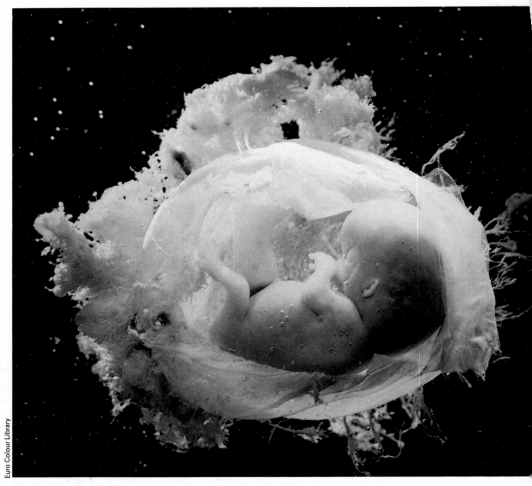

Euro Colour Library

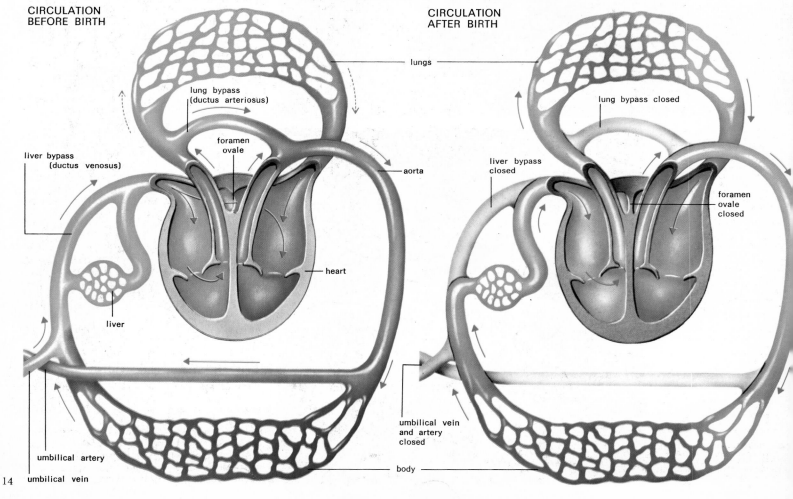

CIRCULATION BEFORE BIRTH

lungs

lung bypass (ductus arteriosus)

foramen ovale

liver bypass (ductus venosus)

aorta

liver

heart

umbilical artery

umbilical vein

CIRCULATION AFTER BIRTH

lungs

lung bypass closed

liver bypass closed

foramen ovale closed

umbilical vein and artery closed

body

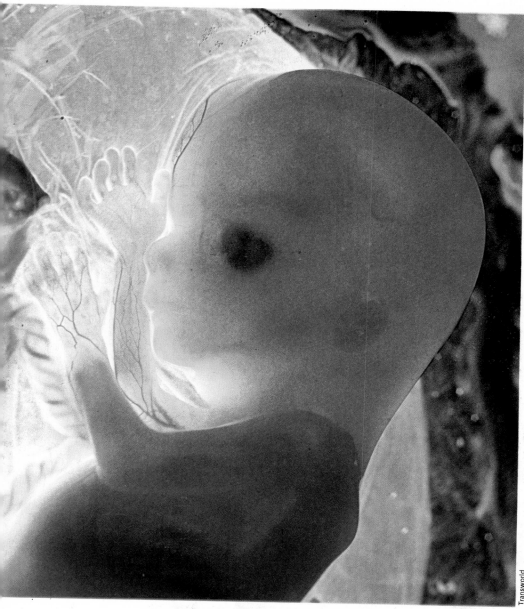

returning from the placenta through the umbilical vein flows towards the liver. Some of it passes through the liver and into the inferior *vena cava* (large vein) while much of it bypasses the liver through the first short circuit, the *ductus venosus*. The blood now moves toward the heart. Entering the right side of the heart, most of the blood is sent through the second short circuit, the *foramen ovale*, which is a flap valve in the tissues dividing the right and left sides of the heart.

Having entered the left side of the heart, this highly oxygenated blood is pumped into the systemic circulation, whose first branches go to the head and upper limbs. The blood which does not pass through the foramen ovale remains in the right side of the heart and mingles with blood returning from the head and upper limbs. Now partially deoxygenated, this mixture of blood leaves the heart and travels towards the lungs. But, instead of entering the lungs, nearly all of it enters the third short circuit, the *ductus arteriosus*, and thereby enters the lower half of the body, returning to the placenta through the two umbilical arteries. Thus, foetal liver and lungs receive very little blood while the placenta performs their future functions.

The Head

The three short circuits in the foetal circulation mean that arterial and venous blood are not completely separated. The most fully oxygenated blood passes to the upper body first, ensuring adequate nutrition for the brain. The consequences of this preferential supply of blood to the upper half of the body are easily seen in its much more advanced development at birth. The arms are longer than the legs, and the circumference of the head is a little greater than that of the chest. This latter feature is a result of the size of the cranium (the bony casing around the brain), the facial features being in fact quite small, especially the jaws which are particularly underdeveloped at birth. The skull bones are soft, with gaps between them called *fontanelles*. This allows for considerable moulding of the head to occur during birth without getting crushed by the birth canal.

Formation of the brain begins early, even before the neural tube is fully sealed which is during the fourth week. By the time closure is complete, the three main subdivisions of the brain are recognizable. The forebrain shows the greatest degree of subsequent differentiation, forming as it does the complex folds of the cerebral cortex. The midbrain and hindbrain undergo much less differentiation, and the cerebellum, which is concerned with the unconscious control of willed movements, does not begin to develop until late in foetal life.

The head and face, so large and apparently misshapen during the first few weeks, soon become obviously human. The eyes, which begin to form by the third week and are clearly visible by the sixth week, start as cup-shaped growths emerging from the forebrain. This growth closes in on itself to form the optic stalk (within which the optic nerve fibres will develop) and the optic cup. The overlying ectoderm layer (the layer of cells in the embryo from which the skin and nervous system develop) follows the contours of these forebrain outgrowths. It bulges

Top left: The foetus at nine weeks enclosed in its amniotic sac. At this age the foetus is about 3½ cm long and weighs approximately one gram. Yet even at this age and size it has all the external human features and the rudiments of all the internal organs.

Above: When the foetus is 11 weeks old it is 6¼ cm in length. Notice that the eyelids are fused together—they will remain so until the sixth month. The mother can at last feel her uterus enlarging. Individual facial expressions appear and the sex of the foetus can be identified.

Left: The foetal circulation includes three short circuits which bypass the liver, heart and lungs. The lungs are not functional until birth and receive only 10% of the blood. Oxygen comes from the placenta which also acts as a liver. At birth, during the transition from water to air, these bypasses close.

Right: Foetus at 14 weeks (length 13 cm). During the fourth month the blood system develops and simple reflexes start.

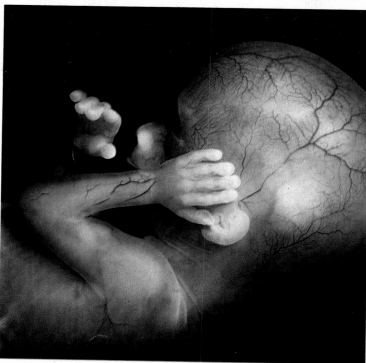

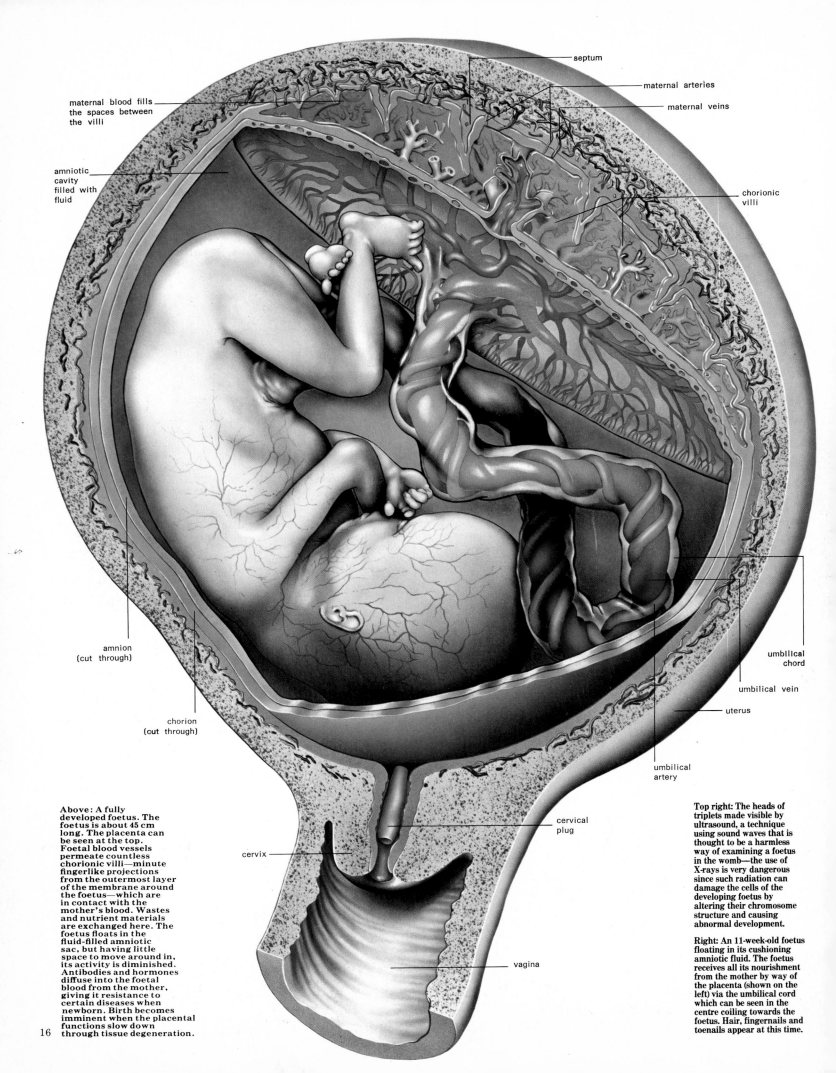

septum

maternal arteries

maternal veins

maternal blood fills
the spaces between
the villi

chorionic
villi

amniotic
cavity
filled with
fluid

amnion
(cut through)

umbilical
chord

umbilical vein

chorion
(cut through)

uterus

umbilical
artery

Above: A fully
developed foetus. The
foetus is about 45 cm
long. The placenta can
be seen at the top.
Foetal blood vessels
permeate countless
chorionic villi—minute
fingerlike projections
from the outermost layer
of the membrane around
the foetus—which are
in contact with the
mother's blood. Wastes
and nutrient materials
are exchanged here. The
foetus floats in the
fluid-filled amniotic
sac, but having little
space to move around in,
its activity is diminished.
Antibodies and hormones
diffuse into the foetal
blood from the mother,
giving it resistance to
certain diseases when
newborn. Birth becomes
imminent when the placental
functions slow down
16 through tissue degeneration.

cervical
plug

cervix

vagina

Top right: The heads of
triplets made visible by
ultrasound, a technique
using sound waves that is
thought to be a harmless
way of examining a foetus
in the womb—the use of
X-rays is very dangerous
since such radiation can
damage the cells of the
developing foetus by
altering their chromosome
structure and causing
abnormal development.

Right: An 11-week-old foetus
floating in its cushioning
amniotic fluid. The
foetus receives all its nourishment
from the mother by way of
the placenta (shown on the
left) via the umbilical cord
which can be seen in the
centre coiling towards the
foetus. Hair, fingernails and
toenails appear at this time.

into each optic cup until a pocket of cells is formed which breaks from the surface ectoderm. These pockets will eventually become the lenses.

Between the lens and the surface a cavity appears. The tissue forming the outer wall of this cavity becomes the transparent cornea and the inner wall becomes the *pupillary membrane* hiding the pupil. By the beginning of the foetal stage, the surface ectoderm is forming folds which will become the eyelids, by the ninth week the optic stalk has transformed into the optic nerve and by the 25th week the various layers of the retina (formed on the inside of the optic cup) can be distinguished. The eyelids separate at about six months, but the pupillary membrane does not disappear until the seventh month.

Growth

During embryogenesis, organ development and differentiation is the keynote, but during the foetal period rapid growth is the major factor. The foetus grows at about 1.5 mm (1/20 inch) each day, doubling its length during the third month—9 to 18 cm (3½ to 7 inches)—and reaching almost half its full term length by the end of the fifth month (25 cm,

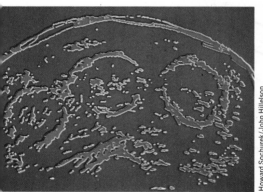

Howard Sochurek/John Hillelson

10 inches). Weight gain as distinct from length increase begins in the seventh month when ordinary white fat is deposited under the skin all over the body. In addition during the last few weeks of life in the womb, a peculiar form of fat called brown fat is deposited across the shoulders and at other sites on the upper body. By the end of pregnancy, the foetus will probably weigh somewhere between 3 and 4 kg (6—9 lbs) and be about 50 cm (20 inches) long.

The late appearance of fat means that up to about seven months the foetus has a decidedly scrawny look. At four months it is pitifully thin, a huge head dominating its appearance and the blood vessels glowing brightly through the fatless, transparent skin. A few weeks later the skin, although very wrinkled, is less translucent because it is covered with a fine downy hair called *lanugo*. This drops out by the end of pregnancy except perhaps across the shoulders. During the seventh month the skin, a little less wrinkled as fat develops, becomes covered in a creamy waxy substance, *vernix caseosa*, which is manufactured by glands under the skin. This is thought to 'waterproof' the skin.

Life in the womb

As the foetus grows, so do the membranes which surround it. The external trophoblast has become the tough chorion, the amniotic sac containing the foetus has expanded inside the chorion and the remnant of the yolk sac usually gets flattened between them. Frequently the chorion and amnion fuse. Secure within the double membrane the foetus floats in amniotic fluid. It can move about freely (at least while still relatively small) and is cushioned from mechanical pressure of the uterine walls or sudden injury should the mother have an accident.

As early as the third month, the foetus begins to swallow some of the amniotic

fluid and excrete drops of urine into it. By late pregnancy it may swallow almost a pint a day. Although most foetal waste enters the placental circulation and is excreted by the mother, a small amount of amniotic fluid is made up of foetal urine. It is uncertain what role, if any, amniotic fluid plays in foetal nutrition.

The rate of growth of the placenta is very different from that of the embryo and foetus. At the end of the third month, it weighs about six times as much as the foetus. Placental growth then diminishes so that by the end of the fourth month it weighs as much as the foetus, and at birth it is only a fifth as heavy.

As well as functioning by itself as the organ of transfer between mother and baby, the placenta should also be considered as part of an endocrine (that is, hormone secreting) structure. The hormones produced by this unit have profound effects on the mother. Her heart rate and output are increased, her kidneys step up production, and her entire metabolism is changed so that digestion is slower and absorption of nutrients more thorough. Progesterone in particular is responsible for softening all tissues and muscles, especially uterus and cervix, which aids implantation, prevents the uterus from expelling its contents too soon by reducing its irritability, and prepares the cervix for the stretching it will undergo during the baby's birth. Foetoplacental hormones are also responsible for preparing the mother's breasts for lactation.

By contrast, maternal hormones cannot normally pass the placenta into the foetus. Any that do are usually neutralized by specific placental enzymes. During late pregnancy, however, the placenta allows a number of antibodies to pass from the mother to the baby so that the newborn child has a degree of immunity to many of the diseases to which its mother has previously built an immunity.

Foetal activity

It has been suggested that the foetus swallows fluid because it needs to practice swallowing. There is increasing evidence to show that the foetus does practice all kinds of complex behaviour patterns such as breathing, swallowing and sucking. Sensory functioning in the uterus may of necessity be limited but it occurs.

There seem to be three distinct states of activity shown by the foetus. During 'deep sleep' it makes few and feeble spontaneous movements and does not react to stimuli. During the 'waking state' its eyes may open and it moves frequently and spontaneously. Foetal movement actually begins as soon as the limbs develop but the mother is rarely aware of the movements until about the fourth month. During waking it responds to stimuli—such as a very loud noise, a sudden flash of light, or a rapid change in the mother's position, and these may evoke a quick and vigorous reaction from the foetus.

The third state is rapid eye movement or REM sleep. During this time, the foetus shows rapid horizontal movements of the (closed) eyes and twitching movements of the limbs, trunk and face and he may practice quite strong rhythmic breathing movements of the chest. We know that in children and adults, REM sleep is associated with dreaming, and it is possible that the foetus also dreams in this state.

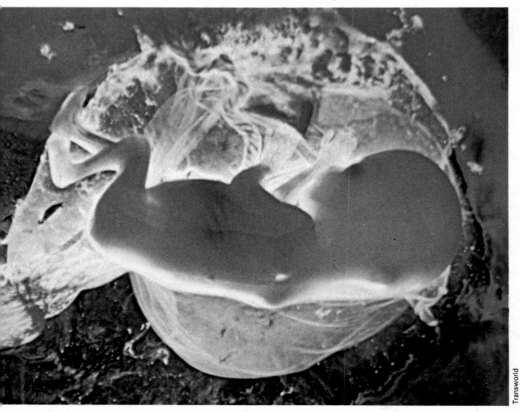

Transworld

Progesterone crystals. This hormone softens up muscles and ligaments – especially the pelvis, uterus and cervix – to make them more elastic for the birth. Levels of progesterone in the blood rise steadily during pregnancy.

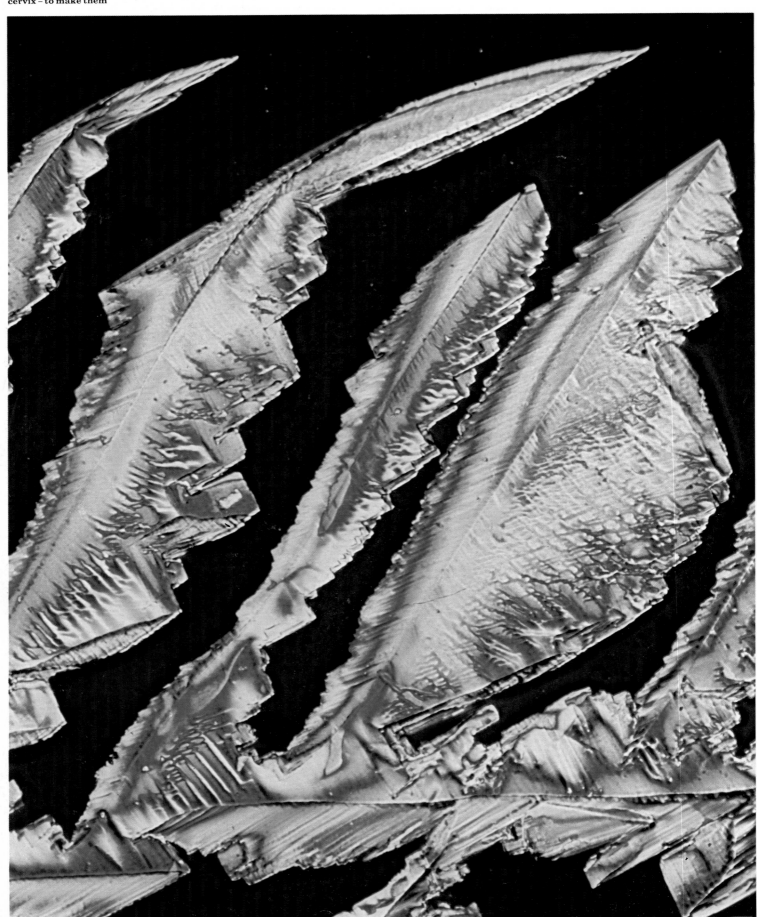

Birth

The mature foetus spends several weeks preparing for the hazardous journey from his mother's womb to the world outside. Most of the preparations are caused by hormones from the adrenal glands.

In a child or adult the adrenal glands, situated just above the kidneys, consist of a *medulla* (core) and a *cortex* (shell). But in a foetus an extra layer of cortex lies between them, making the foetal adrenal relatively huge. After birth the foetal cortex shrinks until at three months the adrenal weighs only half what it did at birth.

Corticosteroids, hormones released by the adrenal cortex, cause large amounts of glycogen to be stored in various parts of the foetus' body, particularly the liver and the heart. The glycogen store in the cardiac muscles is of special importance as it enables the heart to continue beating in the absence of oxygen—thus helping the baby later through the potentially dangerous changeover from placenta to lungs.

During the last two months of pregnancy, the lungs, again due to stimulation by corticosteroids, gradually become ready for the moment that the newborn baby will draw breath. A surface-active compound or *surfactant* is formed within the *alveoli* of the lungs (the minute grape-like air sacs where exchange between air and blood will take place). This surfactant has the distinctive property of exerting a high surface tension when it is stretched, but a low one when its surface is compressed. As a result small alveoli will tend to expand, thus preventing lung collapse following the initial inflation just after birth. Babies born very prematurely, before surfactant has formed, cannot breathe independently for long.

Positions in the womb

The baby's position in the uterus also shows his readiness for birth. Until about six weeks before delivery he may change his position fairly often so that sometimes his head is at the top of the womb, and sometimes at the bottom. As he gets bigger he comes to fill the available space until

British Museum

Above: A medieval caesarean section. The use of such operations has been recorded since Roman times although the survival rate of both mother and child was low because of infection and haemorrhage. The operation, which involves removal of the foetus via an incision of the abdomen and uterus, is widely used today.

Below: Position of the foetus before the onset of labour. This position is known as a *cephalic presentation*—the baby's head will be born first. The baby has already dropped down and its head is in the pelvic cavity—a process known as 'lightening' because it removes the pressure on the mother's lungs caused by the uterus.

POSITION OF THE FOETUS JUST BEFORE BIRTH

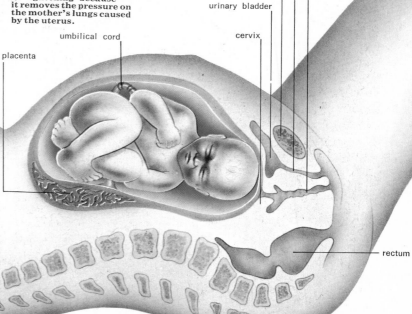

placenta

umbilical cord

vagina

urethra

coxal bone

urinary bladder

cervix

rectum

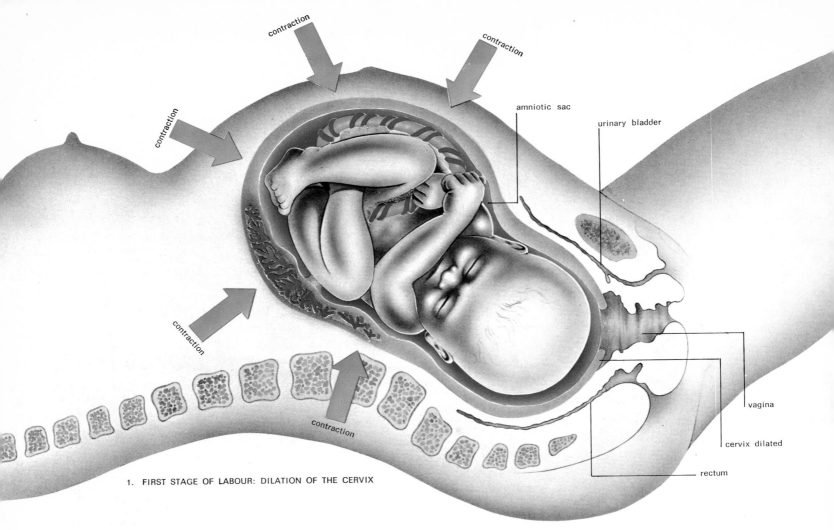

1. FIRST STAGE OF LABOUR: DILATION OF THE CERVIX

no more manoeuvring is possible, and he must settle into one position. In the vast majority of cases this is head downwards, called a *cephalic presentation*. Occasionally a baby settles head upwards, so that his bottom is born first. This is called a *breech presentation*. Later on he may 'drop' into the mother's pelvic cavity. The top of the uterus then also drops and no longer causes pressure on the mother's lungs. Because of this, the process is called 'lightening'; it usually only occurs in white women having first children.

The descent of the foetal head into the pelvic cavity is called the *engagement* of the head. It tends to occur about a month before birth among firstborn children, but not until much nearer delivery, or actually during labour, in second and subsequent deliveries. Its occurrence is a good indication that the mother's pelvic size and shape are adequate for birth.

The onset of labour

Throughout pregnancy the uterus contracts regularly. These practice contractions are mild and rarely detectable by the mother. At some point they begin to increase in strength and duration, and the intervals between them get shorter. It used to be thought that this was caused by a drop in maternal circulatory progesterones. But during recent years evidence has begun to pile up that this change in the nature of uterine contractions, which marks the onset of true labour, is somehow initiated by the foetus itself. A chain of hormonal reactions seems a probable cause, and the foetal hypothalamus is thought to be one of the earliest links in the chain. If the theory is correct, hypothalamic stimula-

Above: The first stage of labour. Contractions increase in intensity and frequency. The amniotic sac (which is incompressible) is forced down against the cervix.

Below: The cervix dilates, the amniotic sac breaks and its contents gush out. At this, the second stage of labour, uterus, cervix and vagina form a continuous *birth canal*.

2. BREAKING OF THE WATERS

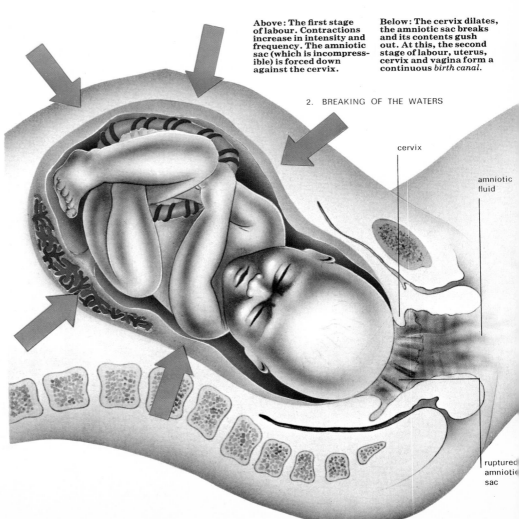

20

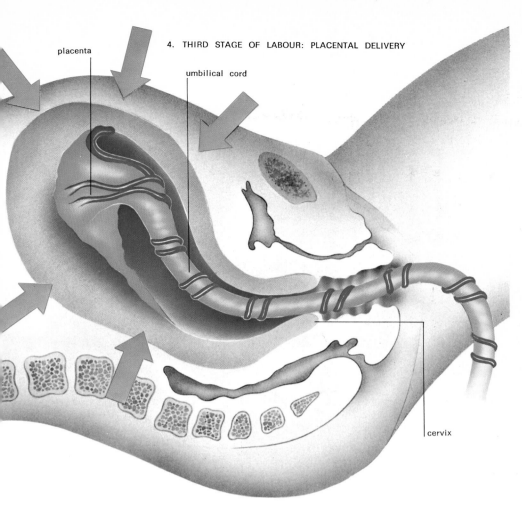

placenta

umbilical cord

cervix

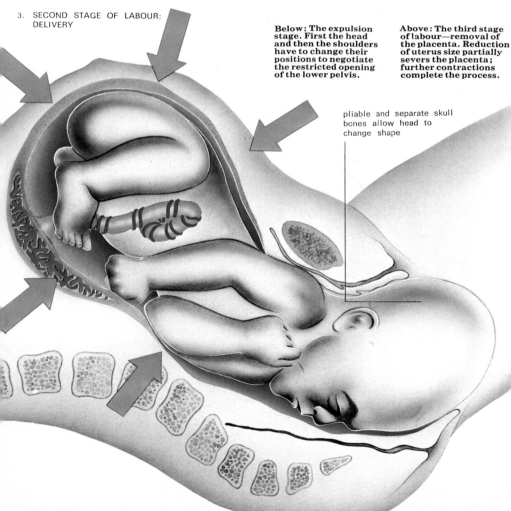

3. SECOND STAGE OF LABOUR: DELIVERY

Below: The expulsion stage. First the head and then the shoulders have to change their positions to negotiate the restricted opening of the lower pelvis.

Above: The third stage of labour—removal of the placenta. Reduction of uterus size partially severs the placenta; further contractions complete the process.

pliable and separate skull bones allow head to change shape

tion causes the pituitary to release ACTH (adrenal corticotrophic hormone) which in its turn stimulates the adrenal cortex to secrete corticosteroids. These steroids cause a change in the hormone balance of the mother and stimulate her tissues to synthesize *prostaglandin*. Minute quantities of prostaglandin cause strong uterine contractions.

The process of childbirth is aptly named labour, for it is a time of extraordinarily hard work. During the first stage most of the efforts of the uterus are directed at opening the neck of the womb, or cervix. The baby flexes his head so that his chin rests on his chest, well tucked in, and the top of his head settles more deeply into his mother's pelvic cavity. As the cervix continues to widen the baby slips down even further so that his head causes pressure on the mother's bladder above and rectum below. When the cervix is fully dilated, the uterus, cervix and vagina form a continuous curved passage —the birth canal—from the baby into the world. At the very end of first stage of labour, although it can occur much earlier, the amniotic sac usually breaks and the amniotic fluid gushes out of the vagina. This is termed the 'breaking of the waters'.

Birth and afterbirth
The second stage of labour begins when the cervix is completely (or almost completely) dilated, and is triggered by the release of another hormone, *oxytocin*, from the maternal pituitary gland. This stage mainly involves the *fundus muscles* which form the top of the uterus. These powerful muscles begin to contract and push downwards on to the baby's bottom, propelling him along the birth canal.

Because of the shape of the muscles across the mother's pelvis, the baby's head is slightly turned so he faces toward her rectum. Evolution has made this, and a complex sequence of other movements, necessary; when man expanded his brain and developed a round skull he made childbirth more difficult. The widest diameter at the entrance to the mother's bony pelvis is the one stretching across it between the hip bones, and the baby adjusts so that the length of his head from the forehead backwards rather than its width, fits into this. In the lower part of the pelvis, the longest diameter stretches backwards from the pubic bone in the front and, having descended this far, the baby must rotate his head to fit the new shape.

Each contraction of the uterus pushes the baby's head nearer the vulval cleft and the outside world until, at last, the top of the back of the head is just visible from the outside at the peak of a contraction. Finally, the head stretches the vaginal entrance and all the tissues around it, and begins to emerge. This is called *crowning*. At this point the baby's shoulders also begin to turn to negotiate their journey through the birth canal. The next contraction pushes the baby down further, his head sweeps over the vulval tissues and emerges into the world: forehead, eyes, nose, mouth and chin appearing successively. Once the head is born the baby turns on to his side, facing his mother's hip. This means that his shoulders and the rest of his body can slip out of the birth canal quite easily, which they usually do with the next contraction. The baby is born.

21

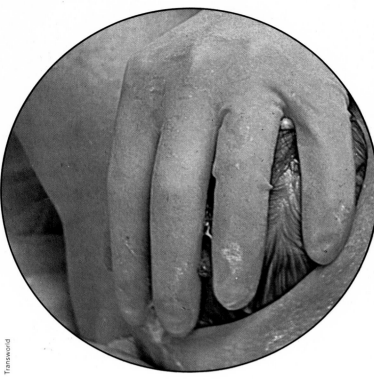

The third stage of labour is the delivery of the *placenta*, also called the afterbirth for obvious reasons. The placenta separates from the uterus during birth, and is usually delivered by uterine contractions within 20 minutes of the baby.

The first few weeks of life

At birth the baby may not be an altogether prepossessing sight. He is greasy and whitish with his covering of *vernix caseosa*, and beneath this he may look grey because his blood circulation has not been fully established. But with the first few breaths his skin turns a healthy pink, although he may still look greasy and wrinkled. The umbilical cord continues to beat for a few minutes after birth to ensure that the baby has time to begin breathing before oxygen supplies from the placenta are completely cut off. The thick muscular walls of the umbilical vessels then contract and pulsation within the cord can no longer be detected. Some obstetricians and midwives prefer not to cut the cord until it has ceased to beat. But usually the cord is tied, which stops the blood flow through it, and cut as soon as the baby is born and has begun to breathe. Because the cord contains no nerves, this cutting does not hurt either mother or baby.

When the baby is properly born, breathing independently and separated from his mother, he is given, sometimes wrapped in a blanket, to his proud parent for a few minutes. Then he is weighed and examined. Birth weights vary, the usual range being 3 to 4 kg (6 to 9 lb), and boys usually weigh a few ounces more than girls. The medical attendant will wipe off most of the vernix caseosa but not remove it entirely as it protects against skin infections during the first week or so.

The newborn's skull is sometimes lopsided or elongated through pressures from the birth canal on the soft skull bones, but it expands measureably during the first week of life, and gradually returns to a normal shape. The eyes, too, may show the effects of pressure during delivery by

Above: The baby's head, emerging from the vulvo-vaginal orifice, being guided by the obstetrician's hand. The head must be held and turned to match the internal rotation of its shoulders as they negotiate the lower pelvis. Within a few minutes the baby will be born.

Right: Amazement—or exhaustion? A mother's reaction, after hours of extremely hard work, as the baby's head emerges. Labour, the process of childbirth, is usually much easier with the second and later births because the muscles surrounding the uterus have been stretched and the birth canal tissues never completely return to their pre-pregnancy size.

being puffy, swollen or bloodshot. They are usually slate blue, and may not attain their individual colour for some months.

So that the lungs can function correctly in supplying oxygen, the newborn's cardiovascular system must re-route its blood supplies to receive it. Before birth, the foetus' circulation system contains three shunts or 'short circuits' which by-pass the liver, the heart and the lungs. These are the *ductus venosus*, the *foramen ovale* and the *ductus arteriosus* respectively. When the newborn begins to breathe, the ductus venosus and the ductus arteriosus close down, partly through muscular contraction of their walls.

As the lungs expand the blood vessels inside them open up. The amount of blood returning to the left side of the heart thus suddenly increases, which pushes a membrane against the foramen ovale, thus sealing it shut and irrevocably separating the two sides of the heart. The closing down of the three 'short circuits' is normally rapid and seems to depend on a number of factors. Most of these are not yet fully understood, although the amount of oxygen in the baby's system is important. Blood may still be shunted through the ductus venosus for hours, or

even days, after birth, however, and since this means that it is not passing through the liver, this incomplete closure of the 'shunt' may contribute to the mild and transient jaundice many newborns show. Occasionally, too, blood may pass through the ductus arteriosus for up to two weeks after birth.

The baby's cardiovascular system must also make other adjustments before it can work properly. During the first few weeks it is common for the baby's extremities (hands and feet) to turn blue. Occasionally the side on which the baby is lying becomes a bright red, while his upper half remains pale with a definite line right down his body marking the junction of red and pale areas. This so-called 'harlequin colour change' is thought to be due to gravity causing the blood to pool, before the circulation has fully learnt to adjust to such things.

Unlike most mammals, the human mother does not produce mature milk immediately after delivery. For the first few days she produces *colostrum*, a clear yellowish fluid rich in protein and in antibodies. The baby's needs are met partly through colostrum and partly through the glycogen stored for this purpose in his liver and white subcu-

22

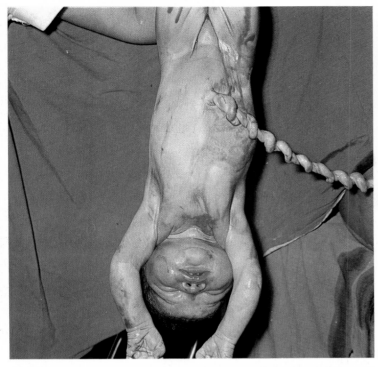

Left: The newly born baby is held upside down to help remove any fluids that may still be in the lungs. If it does not start breathing, the mucus in its mouth and nose may be sucked out.

Below: Its umbilical cord cut, the child begins an independent existence. It is then measured and tagged.

Above: Some obstetricians believe that conventional deliveries, with their bright lights, rough blankets and cold scales, overload the baby with extreme sensations which terrify it. Instead, they believe that babies should be eased gradually into life. This baby is being held in a bath of warm water—for comfort, not cleansing.

Below: This baby has been born into a world of soft lights and soft blankets. It is claimed that babies delivered in this way do not show the usual newborn behaviour of clenched, raised fists, screwed up eyes and loud piercing wails. This one certainly looks as if he is enjoying his first few hours outside the womb that has been his 'home'.

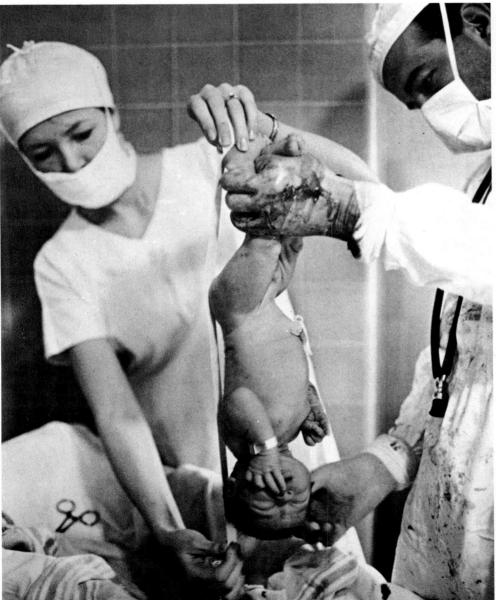

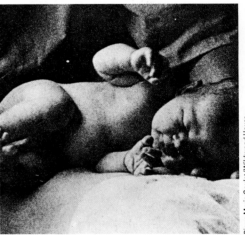

taneous fat. All babies, bottle- and breast-fed, lose weight during the first few days after birth. The baby's suckling encourages milk production, which usually begins within five days, and by ten days of age most babies have regained their birth weight.

Changes in environment

Views about prenatal existence and the meaning of birth have changed radically in recent years. Older research tended to consider the foetus as living in a kind of void, oblivious of his surroundings and wholly unprepared for the experiences and activities awaiting him. Now it is known that development is remarkably complete before birth, both in form and function, and that birth represents a transition from one stage of existence to another, rather than a sudden leap from 'nothingness' to 'being'.

Birth remains in all societies a highly significant event in the lives of the parents and the whole network of friends and relatives into which the child is born. It is as well for the survival of the species that successful reproduction evokes such a profound response; but the reverence is no less genuine because it is functional for this remarkable biological event.

23

Heredity

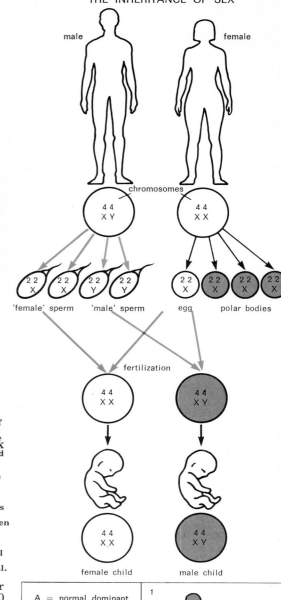

Over 3,000 million people inhabit the earth and, although we all exhibit the same basic features, no two people are exactly alike. The consistency and diversity which can be seen within the human race, and within other forms of life, is a result of the way that information about our form and content is stored within our bodies.

The nucleus of each cell in our body contains a 'blue-print' of ourselves—consisting of a series of instructions, like a string of sentences. Each 'sentence' is called a *gene* and specifies one piece of information. These genes are grouped together in bundles called *chromosomes* and in each cell there is an estimated 100,000 genes which are grouped into precisely 46 chromosomes (except for the specific sex cells which have only 23 chromosomes).

Although we are all different, we do share characteristics in common with our parents and ancestors; the colour of our hair, the shape of the nose, or sometimes unfortunate characteristics such as haemophilia—the bleeding disease. The process of acquiring characteristics from our ancestors and passing them on from one generation to another is known as *heredity* and the study of this is *genetics*.

Chromosomes and sex

To begin to understand genetics we must go back into the microscopic world of the cell and look at those dark-staining threads in the nucleus—the chromosomes. The 46 chromosomes are arranged in pairs (given numbers from one to 23 for convenience), one member of each pair coming from the mother during fertilization, and the other from the father. In males one pair (the sex chromosomes) can be easily distinguished from the rest—they are dissimilar—one is small, hook-shaped and known as the *Y* chromosome, the other is larger, cross-shaped and known as the *X* chromosome. Females, on the other hand, have two *X* sex chromosomes and no *Y* chromosome. The combination *XY* therefore makes a male, and the combination *XX* a female. These *sex chromosomes* are ultimately responsible for the vast range of physical and emotional differences between a man and a woman.

During the production of egg cells or sperm, the cells undergo a special type of division called *meiosis* where exactly half of the original 46 chromosomes are distributed to each egg or sperm. Of these 23 chromosomes one will be a sex chromosome. In a male, therefore, half the sperm will receive 22 plus an *X* chromosome, the other half will have 22 chromosomes plus a *Y* chromosome. During fertilization the 23 chromosomes from the sperm join together with the 23 chromosomes from the egg to form 23 pairs known as *homologous pairs*. The *X* bearing sperm will make an *XX* pair (female), and the *Y* bearing sperm an *XY* pair (male).

Albinism

The two chromosomes in each homologous pair (one from the mother and one from the father) contain genes which

Above: Gregor Johann Mendel, the Augustinian monk who is known as the 'father of genetics.' In 1865 he outlined the principles of inheritance in successive generations of pea plants. At the time his work was ignored as a meaningless obsession. But although he knew nothing about the existence or function of genes or chromosomes, Mendel's laws are still taught because they are fundamental to the science of genetics. The precise structure of the DNA 'code' was not discovered until 1953.

Right: Of the 23 chromosomes paired off during meiosis, one will determine the sex of the child. Males have both X and Y chromosomes and females have two X chromosomes.
Below: Albinism, or the inability to produce melanin (skin pigment) results in a completely white skin. If both genes responsible for skin colour are defective, then albinism will result. But if one of them is normal it will be dominant—melanin will be produced—and skin colouring will be normal.

control the same characteristics. If, for example, a chromosome carries 5,000 genes along its length and the tenth gene is concerned with hair colour, then the tenth gene on the homologous chromosome will also be concerned with hair colour.

These two sets of homologous genes work together to produce the complete internal and external appearance of each individual. To see how they do this we can examine the inheritance of *albinism*—the inability to synthesize the skin pigment *melanin*.

Melanin is a dark yellow pigment formed in special skin cells from the amino acid tyrosine. The conversion of tyrosine to melanin is undertaken by certain enzymes, each of which is coded for by a particular gene. If one of these genes is defective, a defective enzyme will be produced and the synthesis of melanin will not take place. The person will therefore be an *albino* and have completely white skin. There are two genes which code for the enzyme, one on each of the chromosomes making up the homologous pair; and only if both genes are defective albinism will result. The combination of one defective and one normal gene will mean that melanin will be produced—the normal gene masks the effect of the defective gene, and is said to be *dominant* over the *recessive* abnormal gene.

Albinism is an extreme example of the

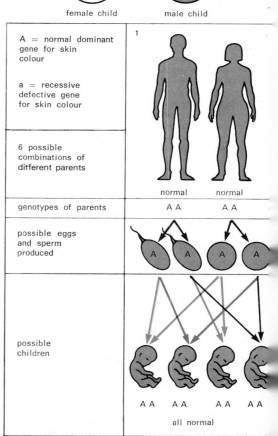

	1
A = normal dominant gene for skin colour	
a = recessive defective gene for skin colour	
6 possible combinations of different parents	normal normal
genotypes of parents	A A A A
possible eggs and sperm produced	A A A A
possible children	A A A A A A A A
	all normal

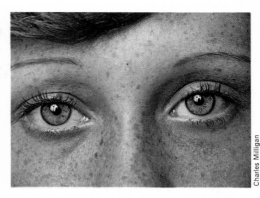

DOMINANT	RECESSIVE
Curly hair	Straight hair
Dark hair	Light hair
Nonred hair	Red hair
Coarse body hair	Normal body hair
Normal skin pigmentation	Albinism
Brown eyes	Blue or grey eyes
Near or farsightedness	Normal vision
Normal hearing	Deafness
Normal colour vision	Colour blindness
Normal blood clotting	Haemophilia
Broad lips	Thin lips
Large eyes	Small eyes
Short stature	Tall stature
Polydactylism	Normal digits
Brachydactylism	Normal digits
Syndactylism	Normal digits
Normal muscle tone	Muscular dystrophy
Hypertension	Normal blood pressure
Diabetes insipidus	Normal excretion
Huntington's chorea	Normal nervous system
Normal mentality	Schizophrenia
Nervous temperament	Calm temperament
Average intellect	Genius or idiocy
Migraine headaches	Normal
Resistance to disease	Susceptibility to disease
Enlarged spleen	Normal spleen
Enlarged colon	Normal colon
A or B blood group	O blood group
Rh blood group	No Rh blood group

Above and below: Example of the mechanism of inheritance: all our characteristics are received through the genetic code. The gene that codes for brown eyes is dominant over that for blue or grey eyes (top right) and the gene responsible for curly hair dominates over that for straight hair (far right).

Below centre: The giant chromosomes of the fruit fly *Drosophila*. Staining reveals light and dark bands along the length of the chromosome. The bands are thought to represent genes arranged along the length of the chromosome, which in turn contains the double-stranded molecule DNA—the blueprint for the new individual.

Left: The current list of hereditary traits as determined by the universal genetic code. It is quite likely that the list will be added to or modified as more research is done in this field—the science of genetics is relatively new. The fatal bleeding disease, haemophilia, for example, which afflicted Queen Victoria's male offspring is now understood to have been due to the passing on of a recessive gene through a line of female carriers, who did not themselves suffer from it. Schizophrenia is also blamed on defective genes and some controversial studies are taking place to determine the role of genetic disturbance among violent criminals.

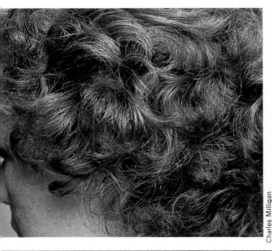

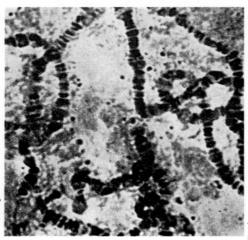

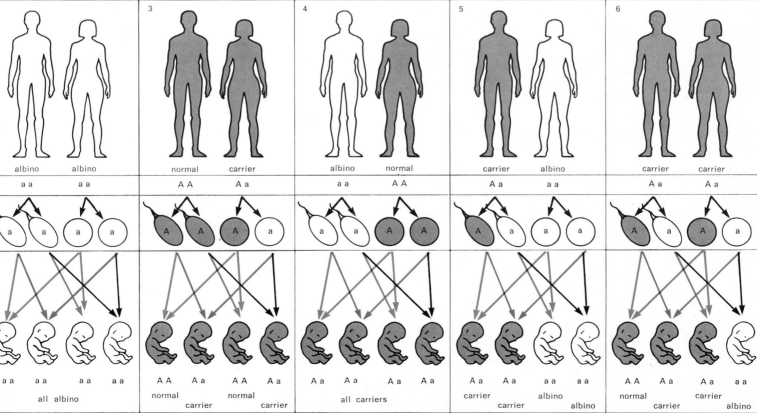

THE INHERITANCE OF ALBINISM

Kunsthistoriches Museum, Vienna

Above: The ill-fated royal house of Hapsburg. The Emperor Maximilian I and his family suffered from massive genetic mutation. The disease known as *acrocephaly* is an endocrine disorder producing distinctive physical and mental abnormalities. The lower jaw protrudes so that its teeth lie in front of the upper ones and the mouth often hangs open. Carlos 'The Bewitched' (below) inherited mental defects, too. Epilepsy, sexual fear and other abnormalities, ascribed at the time to witchcraft, are now seen as a direct result of genetic malformation—due, in turn, to chronic inbreeding which was rife in European royal families until very recent times.

Right: Colour blindness —the inability to distinguish between red and green—is due to a gene found only in the X chromosome. Normal colour vision is actually a dominant characteristic, but a recessive gene can replace the normal colour vision gene. Males, having one X chromosome, need just one recessive gene.

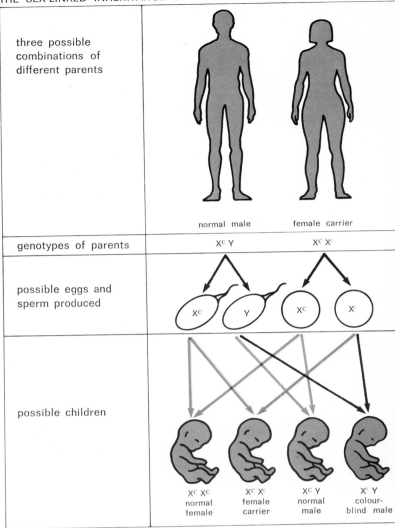

three possible combinations of different parents	normal male	female carrier
genotypes of parents	$X^C Y$	$X^C X^c$
possible eggs and sperm produced	X^C Y	X^C X^c
possible children	$X^C X^C$ normal female $X^C X^c$ female carrier	$X^C Y$ normal male $X^c Y$ colour-blind male

X^C female sex chromosome with dominant normal colour vision gene

X^c female sex chromosome with recessive colour-blindness gene

Kunsthistoriches Museum, Vienna

26

Above: The sex-linked inheritance of colour blindness. Colour blindness among women is extremely rare because they need two recessive genes to be colour blind. If they possess one normal and one recessive colour-distinguishing gene the normal gene will predominate, giving accurate colour vision.

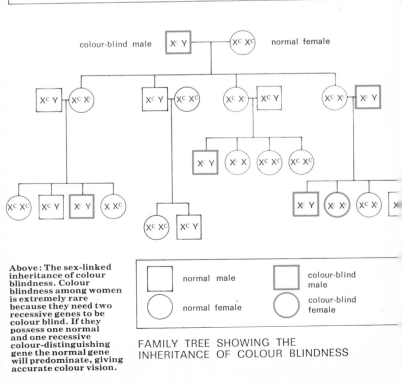

☐ normal male	☐ colour-blind male
◯ normal female	◯ colour-blind female

FAMILY TREE SHOWING THE INHERITANCE OF COLOUR BLINDNESS

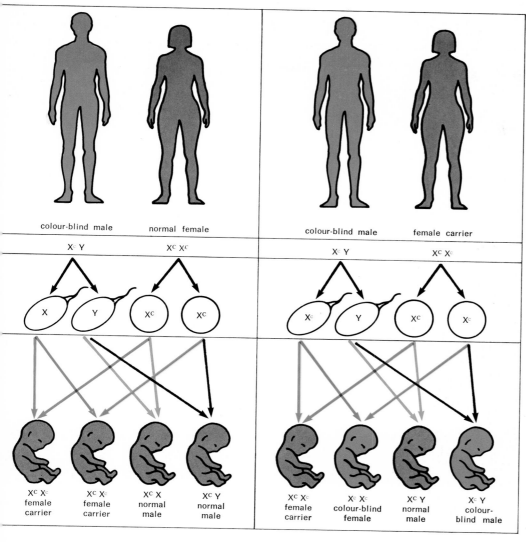

colour-blind male — normal female

X Y — X^c X^c

X — Y — X^c — X^c

X^c X^c female carrier — X^c X^c female carrier — X^c X normal male — X^c Y normal male

colour-blind male — female carrier

X^c Y — X^c X^c

X^c — Y — X^c — X^c

X^c X^c female carrier — X^c X^c colour-blind female — X^c Y normal male — X^c Y colour-blind male

mechanisms of inheritance. All our internal organs are the result of the interactions of the gene combinations received from our parents. The gene for curly hair, for example, is dominant over that for straight hair, whereas the gene for red hair is recessive to that for non-red hair.

There are many more known recessive and dominant genes, and one interesting fact which emerges is that normal characteristics are not always dominant over abnormal ones. However, people who inherit severe disorders often do not live long enough to reproduce and pass the gene onto the next generation. Damaging inherited characteristics are in this way gradually weeded out of the population while advantageous ones (like dark skin in tropical countries) slowly increase.

Sex linked inheritance

The X and Y chromosomes, as we have already said, determine the sex of the child. They also contain certain genes which are not concerned with sexual characteristics. These are known as *sex linked* genes since they are inherited along with the sex chromosomes. Unlike other chromosomes the X and Y chromosomes have no genes in common. The X chromosome in particular contains many genes for which there are no homologous genes on the Y chromosome, one of which is the gene for colour vision.

The ability to discriminate between the colours red and green is completely dependent on a gene located only on the X chromosome. Normal colour vision is a dominant characteristic but there is also a recessive gene which causes colour blindness, and can replace the normal colour vision gene on the X chromosome. As male sex chromosomes have only one X chromosome, if this contains the recessive colour vision gene the male is colour blind. With a female, however, having two X chromosomes, both must have recessive colour vision genes for colour blindness to occur because if one gene is the dominant normal vision type, this will mask the recessive gene.

Recessive sex linked genes like colour blindness are always masked in females who have the dominant gene. Whereas in males they are always expressed when they appear. Men, therefore, are much more likely to be colour blind than women.

Haemophilia is another sex linked recessive characteristic found only on the X chromosome. It is a very rare disease in which the person's blood fails to clot or clots very slowly. The most famous sufferers from haemophilia were the royal family of Queen Victoria in which certain male offspring inherited the disease. The Queen herself was a carrier, and everytime the defective gene was passed on to a male the disease appeared. A female, however, needs a double dose of the gene to inherit haemophilia—the gene itself is very rare, and a double dose almost unknown.

Chromosome abnormalities

Haemophilia and Queen Victoria poses another interesting problem in genetics because none of her ancestors suffered from the disease. Where, then, did the gene come from?

During the early stages in producing a sex cell (by the process of *meiosis*) the chromosomes are carefully copied—this is a complex chemical process. Chromosomes have a 'spiral staircase' structure consisting of a long double-helix DNA molecule with 'rungs' of certain chemicals in between. These rungs are the 'words' which make up the 'sentence instructions' or *genes*. Thus, in copying the genes faithfully (and there maybe 5000 of these in a single chromosome) it is necessary to copy every chemical rung correctly.

It is inevitable, therefore, that out of the millions of times that this process occurs, and the millions of chemicals to be copied each time, that mistakes will occur and even a simple change in the order of the chemicals will change the message coded in that gene. If this change is then passed on during fertilization it will be reproduced over and over again in all the cells of the offspring. It is thought that this chance occurrence (called a *gene mutation*) happened in one of the sex cells of one of Queen Victoria's parents, or in one of her own embryonic cells.

The natural rate of gene mutation is very slow. It can, however, be increased dramatically by the effect of certain chemicals and radiation. X-rays and nuclear fallout are the two main culprits and, for this reason, X-ray photographs are rarely taken of developing foetuses, the ovaries and testes and strict precautions are taken to shield people from nuclear radiation. We cannot, however, shield ourselves from cosmic rays striking the earth, and other sources of natural radiation (like radioactive elements found in the food and soil), all of which contribute to the slow, but highly significant, natural rate of mutation.

It must be stressed that mutations are chance occurrences and, like all chance occurrences, they can be good or bad. Unfortunately, chance changes in such a complex, delicately balanced system as life are usually for the worse. Yet the advantageous ones are the wheels which propel evolution forward. Genes arise by duplication of genes already in existence, and without the element of change introduced by mutation, evolution would come to a complete standstill. Life would not have progressed from the most primitive, single-celled organisms floating around in the primordial soup. The human race is the result of millions of such advantageous mutations.

Although mutation is the only means available to produce new genes, nature has developed an ingenious method for reshuffling the genes on homologous chromosome pairs. This reshuffling, which greatly increases the number of gene combinations and hence the variety of new individuals is accomplished during meiosis when homologous chromosomes can be seen to curl round each other. They, in fact, exchange genes during this evolutionary dance, which is known as *crossing over*.

There are other types of chromosome abnormalities: crossing over may go wrong, for instance, adding extra pieces onto some chromosomes, or one sex cell 27

HOW DOWN'S SYNDROME IS INHERITED

parent with
normal
chromosomes

Left: The genetic origin of *Down's syndrome* **or** *mongolism.* **Children with this disease are usually born to older mothers: it seems that the defect arises when the homologous chromosomes curl around each other, sometimes breaking up and sometimes accumulating extra pieces. The normal pairing off of the 46 chromosomes is disrupted and Down's syndrome results.**

Right: Down's syndrome children can be easily distinguished by their unusually flattened faces, slight squints and broad hands. Many such children, given correct care and training, live fairly normal lives; without this, they will remain severely handicapped.

National Society for Mentally Handicapped Children

oocyte receives
2 pairs of
chromosome
no 21 instead
of one pair

1st polar body does
not receive
chromosome
no 21

egg has
2 chromosomes
no 21

2nd polar body
has 2 chromosomes
no 21

fertilization

normal sperm
with one chromosome
no 21

fertilized egg

child has 3 pairs of
chromosome no 21
instead of two, causing
Down's syndrome

Dr. S. M. Lewis

Below: Three 21s in the chromosome pattern always results in Down's syndrome. The loss of 21 is fatal but an extra one, making a total of 24 chromosomes, survives well (even though it results in a genetic mutation). One in six hundred live births is likely to by affected by this or a similar malformation.

Above: Sickle-cell anaemia together with some 1,500 other human disorders, is based on a genetic mutation. In this case a change in a single DNA molecule results in the inability of the red blood cells to transport oxygen, changes their shape and produces many distressing, or even fatal, symptoms.

might receive extra chromosomes due to faulty separation of the chromosomes during meiosis. The latter case is fairly common (1 in 600 live births), happening generally in older mothers, and usually involving chromosome 21. One of the egg cells receives an extra chromosome 21, giving it a total of 24 chromosomes, while the other egg cell receives only 22 chromosomes. The loss of chromosome 21 is fatal, but the egg receiving an extra chromosome survives well, producing an embryo with totally 47 chromosomes. The child, however, is severely mentally retarded, has mongolian eyelids, broad hands, a flattened face and other serious defects. This condition is known as Down's syndrome. With proper care and training, many of these children lead relatively normal lives, attending school and fitting in with the community.

Polygenes

The inheritance of characteristics like albinism or haemophilia depend solely on the behaviour of a single pair of genes. The individual will be either albino, for example, or have pigmented skin. When we come to consider characteristics like height or intelligence we find such a wide range that it seems that these characteristics cannot be controlled by such highly specific units as genes. These variable characteristics are, in fact, controlled by a number of genes acting together—called *polygenes*—each one contributing a small part to the total effect.

Many of the characteristics controlled by polygenes (height, weight and skin colour for example) can be strongly modified by the environment. The amount and type of food we eat contributes to our height and weight; exposure to the sun darkens the skin. Even so, it is possible for one abnormal gene to alter completely the effect of polygenes. Genes and the environment can, and do, work together to produce a species—the human race—capable of adapting itself to environments as radically different as the frozen north and the scorching Sahara.

THE CHROMOSOME COMPLEMENT OF A PERSON WITH DOWN'S SYNDROME

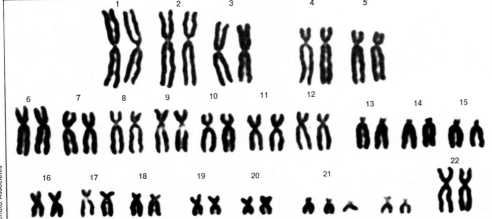

1 2 3 4 5

6 7 8 9 10 11 12 13 14 15

16 17 18 19 20 21 22

Biophoto Associates

Roughly one in every 80 deliveries is a twin birth. Identical, or *monozygotic* twins come from one egg which splits after fertilisation.

Non-identical (*dizygotic*) twins are the result of two eggs being released at the same time, each fertilised by a different sperm.

The Growing Child

Between the ages of five and eleven
the child develops the capacity for
operational thought – the ability to
count, to classify objects, and to order
them into a series, such as size.

Development of the Senses

Information from the senses tells us about the characteristic form, colour, feel, smell and taste of every object around us. This information, along with our experience of time and space, our own bodies and our interactions with other people, is integrated into a complex series of actions and reactions which we call human behaviour.

We know that people are capable of voluntary action but that physical objects are passive and readily subject to our action upon them. However, unlike adult humans, the newborn baby seems passive and helpless. He appears to be incapable of moving, feeding, protecting himself or influencing the world without adult assistance.

For centuries most people believed that the newborn had no basic capacities with which to understand even the simplest aspects of his world. William James, the 19th Century psychologist, claimed that the infant must experience his new environment outside the womb as 'one great blooming, buzzing confusion'.

Developments in psychology since the 1950s, however, involving simple but ingenious techniques of controlled observation and experimentation, show that the newborn is certainly neither passive nor as confused as James believed. At birth he possesses highly organized processes which aid attachment to an adult caretaker. This enables him both to survive and to develop more complex forms of social interaction. His sensory organization also enables him to discover the nature of the world and the consequences of his action upon it.

Brain development

The brain, which is involved in perception, thought and action, is reaching the peak of its growth curve at birth. The head seems abnormally large for the body: the brain constitutes about 12 per cent of the baby's total weight. By the end of the first year the brain will weigh twice as much and by the age of two years will have grown to 80 per cent of its adult size.

At birth many neural (nerve) pathways are partly surrounded by a myelin sheath (the fatty substance making rapid and efficient conduction of neural messages possible) and during the first year, myelination will be completed. More significantly, the growth of the brain involves the formation of many connections between neurons (nerve cells) present at birth. These connections are the basic equipment of learning. The cortex, the highest level of the brain in which complex learning process take place, is only half its adult thickness at birth but becomes thicker as the neural connections develop.

Sensory development

The senses develop more rapidly than motor skills such as sitting, reaching or walking. Vision is of particular importance since it provides most of the information about the world. The eyes are well developed at birth. Both *rods*,

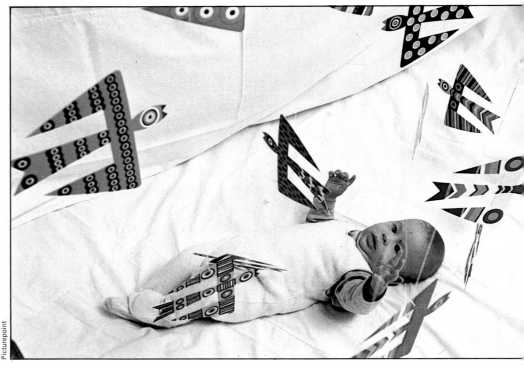

Picturepoint

Left and below: The 'visual cliff', a means of testing depth perception in infants. The baby responds to his mother's calls by crawling towards her until he comes to the 'edge' of the cliff. Although he can feel the glass surface for himself, he refuses to cross what appears to be a sudden drop.

Above: The newborn baby is able to detect colour and brightness changes, follow moving objects and make small exploratory eye movements, but he is unable to perceive detail clearly until about four months old. This five-month old baby is being tested to ensure that his development is normal.

NERVOUS CONNECTIONS AT:
BIRTH   15 MONTHS

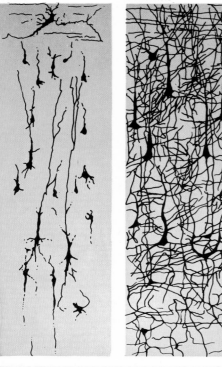

Left: Diagrams showing brain development from birth to 15 months. The cortex, where learning takes place, is made up of inter-connected nerve cells. These connections can form only if the infant is adequately stimulated into exploring and understanding his environment or mental retardation may result.

Camera Press

Above: The glazed look in the baby's eyes denotes 'habituation', the stage at which an object becomes familiar and he stops looking.

Left: This baby, a few hours old, was 'eased into life' with soft lights and voices. The school of thought which proposes gentler methods of delivery claims that the babies do not show the usual newborn behaviour—clenched fists and piercing wails—but are contented and smiling. Babies born conventionally rarely smile until six weeks old.

Below: Results of an experiment to demonstrate that infants prefer patterns to colour or brightness.

Pierre-Marie Goulet/Wildwood House

INFANTS AND PATTERN RECOGNITION

under 3 months
over 3 months

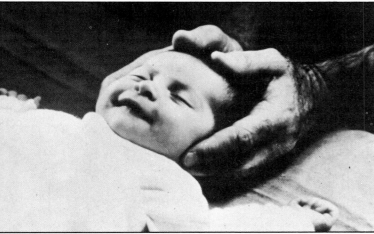

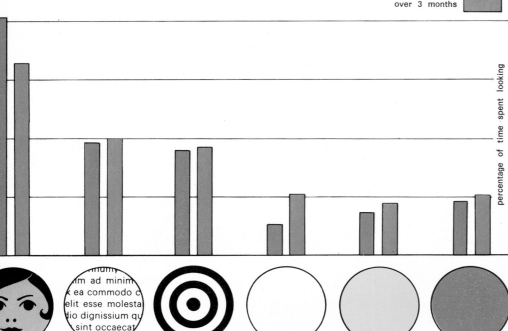

percentage of time spent looking

which detect brightness changes, and *cones*, which detect colours, are functioning. But the *fovea*, the area which makes perception of fine detail possible, is only partially developed at birth. Its growth is completed by about four months.

This highly developed apparatus would be expected to enable the newborn to see quite well, even if he does not understand what he sees. However, a certain lack of response was noted during early vision experiments with many young infants which may be explained by two recent findings. Firstly, the infant's ability to control the lens and muscles of his eyes is limited. His focal length is fixed at about 17—19 cm. for the early months, hence objects must be quite close for him to see them clearly. Secondly, infants tend to be in a drowsy state when flat on their backs, even when awake, whereas they are far more alert when propped up. Even in the first few days of life an infant supported in this way will follow moving objects and may show a highly developed ability to change the direction of his gaze and to make small exploratory eye movements over objects presented to him. This raises the obvious question: does what the infant sees have any meaning for him, or is it received as a coded message which must yet be deciphered?

Depth perception

There is sufficient evidence that the infant has an innate understanding of certain dimensions such as depth. A test known as the *visual cliff* has been devised which consists of a plate-glass table divided into two parts, one of which has a highly textured check fabric fixed directly below it. There is similar fabric several feet below the second half. The infant is placed upon a central board between the two parts and his response noted as his mother calls him from each side of the cliff in turn. One side looks at the same level as the central board, the other appears to be a drop, but the glass ensures that the infant is in no danger of falling. Once a baby can crawl, he will go to his mother only if she is on the 'shallow' side of the cliff. At the 'deep' side he remains firmly on the board, looking apprehensively down at the floor.

To discover whether this response is the result of falling experiences while crawling, much younger infants, not yet able to crawl, can be placed on the cliff and their heart-rate monitored. It has been found that heart-rate changes only when the young infant looks over the 'deep' side of the cliff and experiences anxiety. This type of depth perception is simpler and less accurate than stereoscopic vision, which involves fusion of images from both eyes. The infant's response is probably to the angle presented by the check pattern and by movements of the head from side to side making closer objects appear to move farther than more distant ones. This is confirmed by findings that even infants with vision only in one eye perform competently on the cliff. Also, as the texture of the pattern is reduced more and more, crawling infants will cross the 'deep' side.

If a three week-old baby is propped up and a large object brought increasingly closer to him he shows a very interesting reaction. Besides looking at it he will raise his arms before his face, try to pull back, and may grimace. As with the 'cliff'

33

it implies an understanding of depth but is also important for other reasons. Since the response occurs only if the object is on a collision course it implies that the infant understands when the object is coming towards him. In other words, he can differentiate between an external world and objects within it. Perhaps more surprisingly it suggests that he understands that the object will hit him. He seems to know that visual objects have tactile characteristics long before he has been able to link touch and vision through learning.

It is now known, therefore, that very young infants do not just detect unrelated sensations but solid objects in three-dimensional space, despite their two-dimensional retinal image of the world. But how aware is the infant of the detailed form of these objects? A technique known as 'visual preference' has shed some light on this question.

The infant lies in a crib fitted with a roof, into which two different stimulus objects or pictures can be slotted, one to either side of him. By looking through a central peephole the researcher can observe the reflection of the stimuli in the infant's eyes. This shows which one he is looking at and the time spent looking at each is recorded. The stimulus which receives most attention, as measured by the length of time the infant looks at it, is said to be 'preferred'; it is of greatest interest to the infant.

The effects of patterns
Many studies show that infants find pattern the most interesting aspect of objects. An important, though controversial, finding is that the most 'preferred' stimulus is a diagram of a human face. Certain researchers have found that during the earliest months an infant will look just as long at a face in which the features are scrambled as he will at a normal arrangement. This would suggest that it is not the 'facedness' as such which attracts attention. Nevertheless, very soon the human face is of great interest to infants. This reveals that it is not only the adult who is stimulated into responding to a young infant but that both infant and adult possess innate and complementary behaviour patterns to ensure the formation of a bond between them. The infant is not passive but can influence others as much as they influence him.

The meshing of complementary patterns of behaviour is a fascinating example of evolutionary adaptation. The infant who cannot cling or seek food directly will cry. This cry is unnerving to most adults, who respond by picking him up. Usually this makes access to food possible for the infant. The physical contact invariably quietens the infant, who may begin to explore the adult's face which is now within close range. In one study 249 out of 252 newborns ceased to cry when picked up for the first time. Since this occurred before the first feed the behaviour could not have been learned. Needless to say, the adult feels satisfaction when he or she successfully pacifies the infant.

Even very young babies will turn to look at the source of a sound: their hearing is well developed. By about six weeks they smile regularly and most often at the sight of an adult or the sound of a voice. Other sights or sounds are not as effective in producing this smile.

John Hillelson

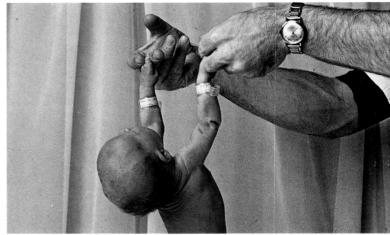

Above: Recent studies have shown the importance of communication between parents and children. Parents who constantly talk to their babies not only stimulate the development of the baby's sensory apparatus (neural network) but may be inadvertently teaching them how to carry out certain actions and physical movements. Some experiments have shown that babies learn certain movements from the actual rhythm and patterns of speech as well as from watching the speaker's body movements. This process is thought to begin as early as a few hours after birth, long before the neural networks are fully formed.

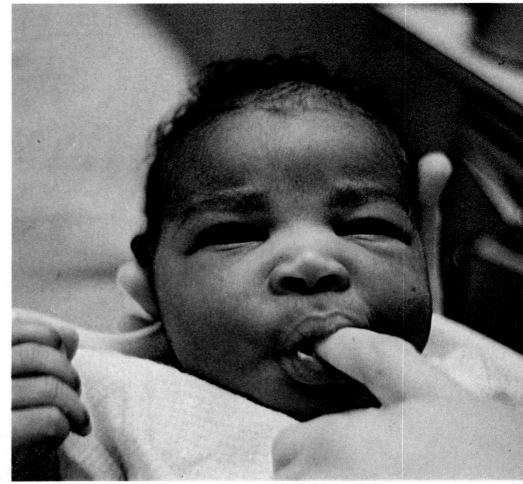

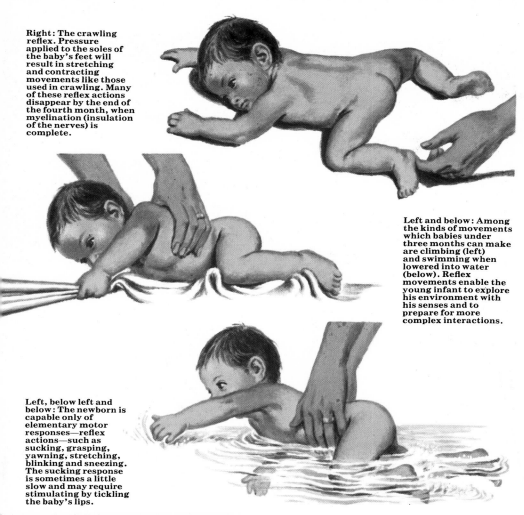

Right: The crawling reflex. Pressure applied to the soles of the baby's feet will result in stretching and contracting movements like those used in crawling. Many of these reflex actions disappear by the end of the fourth month, when myelination (insulation of the nerves) is complete.

Left and below: Among the kinds of movements which babies under three months can make are climbing (left) and swimming when lowered into water (below). Reflex movements enable the young infant to explore his environment with his senses and to prepare for more complex interactions.

Left, below left and below: The newborn is capable only of elementary motor responses—reflex actions—such as sucking, grasping, yawning, stretching, blinking and sneezing. The sucking response is sometimes a little slow and may require stimulating by tickling the baby's lips.

Bill Carter

uninteresting. This is clear because if given a choice he will now look at a new object, but not at the old one. Hence he must remember the old object, otherwise he would not distinguish between the two.

This form of learning is called *habituation*. It does not occur in infants born without a cortex or in an animal whose cortex has been surgically removed. As the infant's model develops he will become increasingly interested in objects and events which do not fit the predictions he is able to make. This is the basis of exploration and curiosity, processes essential for continued learning. If the newborn is not reared in a stimulating environment he will be unable to learn and his motivation to explore further will not develop.

In a normal stimulating environment an infant is mentally very active. He seeks out novel information and shows great pleasure in being able to understand and predict what goes on about him. Researchers have found that a baby of six weeks will learn to suck on a dummy to bring a picture into focus—he wants to see clearly what is going on. Infants exposed to flashing lights learned very quickly to turn their heads in that direction and began to smile each time they appeared.

The critical period
Learning and the development of the brain during this period proceed at a rapid pace. The first two years are a critical period for brain development. If the right experiences are not provided at this stage development of mental processes may be grossly retarded. This is one of the reasons why infants in institutions may show subnormal performance on mental tests even though they are neurologically normal at birth. They may be left for long periods confined to a cot with little stimulation, physical or social. In recent years research findings have led to a great improvement of conditions for such infants.

For the baby reared in a normal family it is important that tests of vision and hearing are carried out regularly to ensure that the infant is able to make normal sensory contact with the world. Defects such as squint or 'lazy eye' can be detected in the early months and surgically corrected. If left for too long the child can become blind in the eye which was not being used. This would make fine manipulations of objects, for which binocular vision is needed, difficult in later life.

Even if the senses are normal care is still necessary. Each infant is an individual at birth, some are more active than others and in some, certain sense organs are more sensitive than others. It is important that the mother is able to adjust to these variations. If a baby is very inactive he will need encouragement from her to explore his environment; it is unlikely that a very passive baby will show the mental development of which he is capable if left to his own devices.

Fortunately many mothers are able to tune in to the personality of their baby and to provide him with experiences to maintain his curiosity and stimulate learning. Infant research has only recently begun to understand what good mothers have been doing for centuries with no specialized knowledge whatsoever.

Smiling at this stage was thought to be caused by wind after a feed, but it has been found that the infant's face and body are relaxed before it occurs, whereas before 'windy smiles' the face may be reddened and facial and bodily muscles contorted.

The smiling response cements the adult-infant bond. Many mothers report that their baby first seems like a real person when he makes eye contact with them and smiles.

The infant's preoccupation with pattern extends beyond the human face. The responses to basic characteristics of the environment are relatively simple. There appears to be an ability at birth to pick out certain features of objects and space and to give a precise response, such as avoidance, to them.

The complexity and variety of human societies—particularly technological societies—means that the human blueprint must be flexible. The infant cannot 'know' everything about his particular society at birth. His interest in pattern predisposes him to learn the characteristics of the many complex objects he will encounter and need to deal with in everyday life.

Responding to objects
When a newborn infant is presented with an object the intensity of his attention may be very amusing. Body movements cease, the pupils dilate and the eyes take on a glazed appearance. He seems unable to move and is sometimes described as 'stuck' on the object. Eventually he stops looking, but he is not just tired, he has built a 'model' or representation of the object and it is now predictable and

The Growing Child

The period of transition from infancy to adulthood, called 'growing up' does not only involve a change in the child's size, but in his basic anatomy and physiology, which alters the structure of both brain and body. As the cells of the brain and body specialize, their overall shape changes enabling them to perform different functions. This process is known as maturation and it is determined by the genetic blueprint laid down at conception.

Maturation and experience interact at all stages of physical and psychological development. Maturation provides a state of 'readiness' in which experience, information acquired by the child in his repeated interactions with the environment through his sensory apparatus, may play their part in fulfilling the potential outlined by heredity. These experiences produce further changes in physical structure and in behaviour. Defects of either maturation or experience prevent a human being from reaching his or her full potential. Height, for example, is genetically determined but without adequate nutrition a child will grow into a shorter adult than he might have been. In the psychological realm, maturation provides the basis for motor and sensory skills, through which understanding of the world becomes possible.

The importance of feeding

Feeding and sleeping are two activities crucial for normal development. Food must provide material for activity, growth and repair of bones and tissues and normal functioning of the endocrine glands—which produce the hormones directing growth.

Protein is the most crucial foodstuff for growth and repair. Certain vitamins and minerals are also needed for formation of healthy bone and tissue. During the First World War and the years up to the Second World War, children were smaller as the quantity and quality of their food was not adequate to enable them to grow to their full height. In underdeveloped countries this is still a problem.

If a mother has a diet rich in necessary nutrients her infant will invariably receive all that he requires from her milk. This will also provide certain antibodies to help build his immunity to disease. Immediately after birth the infant needs food every three to four hours, consuming about 600 ml (one pint) of milk a day. By about 6 weeks his hunger cycle will have lengthened and he may pass a night without needing to be fed.

Many mothers now bottle feed their infants, mixing specially adapted formulas with water. These can be a valuable substitute for breast milk, but there are hazards involved. Unless the formula is weighed precisely the feed may be too concentrated.

Some mothers believe that a stronger mix helps the infant to sleep and grow better, but this is faulty reasoning. An overstrong feed will contain too much sodium and the infant's kidneys must work furiously to eliminate it. This can produce dehydration, a dangerous condition if maintained for any length of time. A further hazard is that the infant may appear to be growing quickly but in fact he will not be building extra bone and muscle, he will accumulate excess fat. The number of fat cells is determined during the first year of life, consequently a fat baby will probably grow into a fat adult. Obese people have more cardiac and respiratory problems than normal and a shorter life-span. A fat child cannot join fully in games with other children. He may suffer emotionally from isolation and feelings of unattractiveness.

During the second part of the first year the infant is weaned, he progresses from milk to solid food. It is important that a balanced diet is maintained and that sugar is not used, as it is fattening and bad for the teeth. Low-fat milk should be drunk to avoid later artery disease.

The importance of sleep

Sleep provides a time for growth and restoration of the brain and body. Two-thirds of a newborn's day is spent asleep. Half of this time is in *REM* (rapid eye-movement) sleep, when body, face and eyes are active. The other half is spent in *NREM* (non-REM) or quiet sleep when body, face and eyes are relaxed. During

Above: From birth through the first year or so, many major developments in a child's life, such as walking, take place. They depend on *maturation*, the process by which the cells of the brain and body become specialized into different types of tissue—for example, bone to form the skeleton (below).

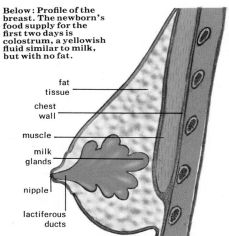

Below: Profile of the breast. The newborn's food supply for the first two days is colostrum, a yellowish fluid similar to milk, but with no fat.

fat tissue

chest wall

muscle

milk glands

nipple

lactiferous ducts

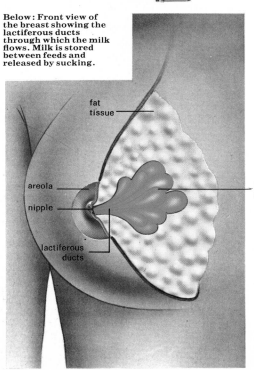

Below: Front view of the breast showing the lactiferous ducts through which the milk flows. Milk is stored between feeds and released by sucking.

fat tissue

areola

nipple

lactiferous ducts

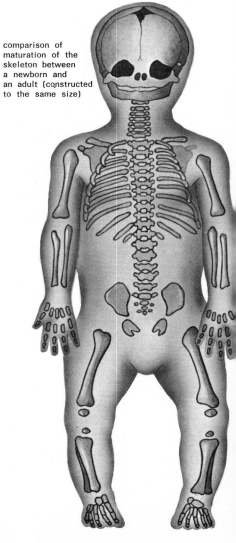

comparison of maturation of the skeleton between a newborn and an adult (constructed to the same size)

milk glands

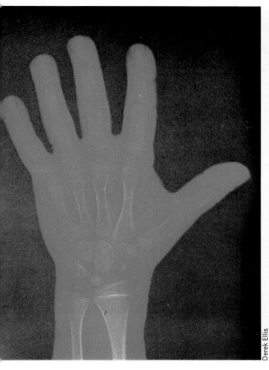

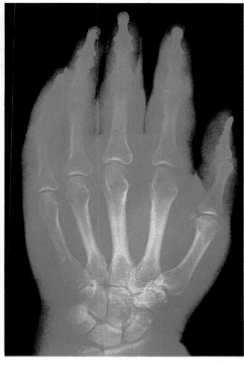

Below left and below: Diagrams to illustrate the beginning and end of maturation in the skeleton. The process takes about 20 years to complete.

Cartilage—the first stage of ossification—is quite soft, and it is several months before the skeleton can fully support the baby's limbs.

Above left and above: X-rays showing the difference between bone development in a child's and an adult's hands. The X-ray process is the only means by which it can be accurately assessed if the child's growth is proceeding at a normal pace. Frequent X-rays are dangerous, however, since they can

damage certain organs. Weight and height, therefore, are the usual means of predicting the child's potential adult size.

Below and bottom: X-rays of a child's and of an adult's skull. The main difference is in the chin, which is the last part of the child's skull to mature.

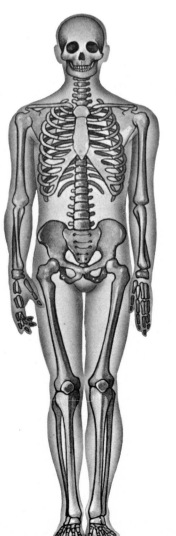

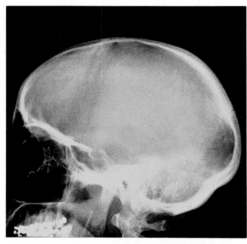

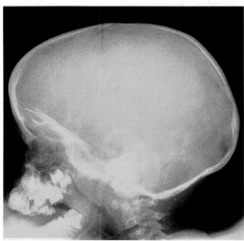

development the total amount of sleep and the proportion of REM sleep decrease. Between three and five years, 11 hours are spent asleep, 20 per cent of this time being REM sleep.

No one knows why we need to sleep. Once it was thought that NREM sleep was needed for growth but, according to a number of recent studies, this no longer appears to be true. There are differing theories about the function of REM sleep due to its association with dreaming in adults. Several recent theories, however, suggest that the brain needs constant stimulation to develop and function efficiently. REM sleep may be a result of the brain activating itself, particularly in the area of the cortex, during periods of low external stimulation. People who are kept awake but deprived of all sensory input eventually have hallucinations. This may be the brain attempting to stimulate itself, as in REM sleep. Severely mentally retarded people show less REM sleep than normal people, which may be related to the inefficiency of their brains. REM sleep may also be involved in protein synthesis in the brain for its maturation and formation of new neural connections. Even an unborn foetus shows large amounts of REM sleep as do people going through periods of rapid change and learning.

The rapid growth phase
At birth the average full-term infant is about 51cm (20 inches) long and weighs 3-4.5 kg (6-10 lb). During the first year he increases in length by almost 50 per cent, to about 72.4 cm (28½ inches) and the baby becomes three times as heavy. During the second year, a further 11.4 cm (4½ inches) or so will be added to height, (no longer regarded as length since the infant is now able to stand), and the baby will be four times heavier than at birth. This extremely rapid growth now settles to a slower pace. During each successive year height will increase by just over 5 cm (2 inches) and weight by 2.3-3 kg (5-6 lbs). This rate of increase continues until the adolescent growth spurt at puberty.

At birth neither weight nor height can predict adult size since they have already been influenced by conditions inside the womb. A premature baby, or a twin or triplet may be smaller than normal but will grow more rapidly during the early months until he makes up the deficit and returns to his genetically determined growth curve. By the time he is two years old his adult size will be predictable.

During periods of severe malnutrition or illness growth may be restricted. Following such periods the child shows a growth spurt until he regains the size he should have reached by that time with normal development. This process is known as *homeorhesis*.

Physical maturity
Since each individual's size is destined to be unique, measures of height and weight at a particular time are poor indicators of how well growth is proceeding. If a child is shorter than others of his age he may be growing too slowly or he may merely be genetically programmed to become a smaller adult. (He may be gaining weight but this could be due to development of bone and muscle or fat.)

The best index of physical maturity is skeletal age. At birth many bones are formed in cartilage which gradually

37

becomes true bone. X-rays allow the shape of formed bone to be seen and an assessment of the skeleton's maturity to be made.

In young infants, the ankle and knee are generally examined and so is the hand in older children. Since everyone eventually achieves the same skeletal pattern, skeletal maturity provides an absolute guide to the amount of growth completed. This method of prediction has one severe disadvantage, however. Radiation from the X-ray itself is potentially harmful in that it may retard growth of certain parts of the body, particularly the sex glands.

Major developments in the infant

As brain and body mature two major developments of infancy become possible —reaching for objects and walking. These enable a fuller exploration and understanding of the world. Newborns show automatic or reflexive reaching and walking movements. With maturation the cortex of the brain develops inhibitory control of lower motor areas making voluntary control of these behaviours possible.

A two-month-old-infant will swipe at an object with his hand closed but by four months he can open his hand as he reaches. At this age he glances continuously between the object and his hand as if checking the relationship between them. By five or six months he can grasp the object even if he cannot see his hand before he begins to reach. Initially the infant grasps crudely with his palm. As the shape of the hand develops and control improves, however, he will be able

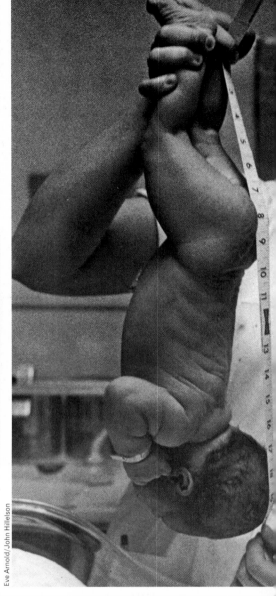

Eve Arnold/John Hillelson

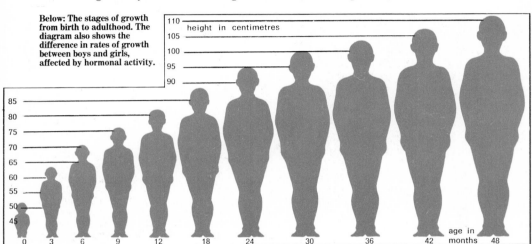

Below: The stages of growth from birth to adulthood. The diagram also shows the difference in rates of growth between boys and girls, affected by hormonal activity.

height in centimetres

age in months

Bruce Coleman

Left and below: Malnutrition is still a problem in under-developed countries. Poor soil and unpredictable rainfall severely limit the amount and types of fruit and vegetables produced. As well as obvious symptoms of malnutrition, like the West African child's bloated belly, the growth of all these children is probably stunted, preventing them from reaching their full potential. Lack of protein and some minerals also accounts for thin hair, emanciated limbs and poor brain functioning. They also have little resistance to infectious diseases like typhoid and cholera.

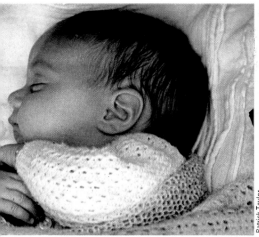

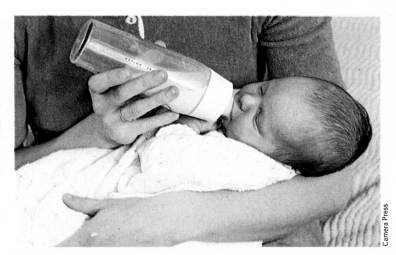

Far left: Babies are weighed and measured at birth to check that development is normal. The average full-term infant is about 51 cm (20 inches) long and weighs 3-4.5 kg (6-10 lb).

Left: Babies vary greatly in the amount of sleep they need. Some will sleep for 20 hours a day, but others seem to need hardly any sleep. It is now known that a baby does not need sleep to grow.

Right: The period of weaning from breast-feeding to bottle-feeding is slightly hazardous for the mother of the newborn. She must ensure that her baby receives an adequate amount of nutrition without over-feeding.

Patrick Taylor

Camera Press

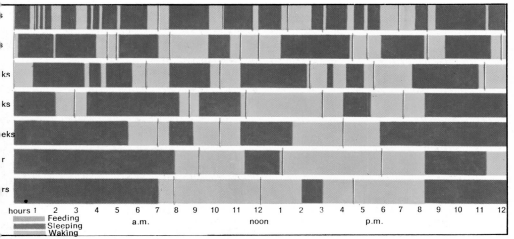

hours 1 2 3 4 5 6 7 8 9 10 11 12 1 2 3 4 5 6 7 8 9 10 11 12
              a.m.   noon   p.m.

Feeding
Sleeping
Waking

Below: Indian babies, like this young Apache infant, spend a large proportion of their day strapped to boards on their mothers' backs, except for short periods of play. But there is no evidence that their development is in any way retarded since they learn to crawl and walk at about the same age as babies in other societies, who have more freedom of movement.

Above: Diagram of a baby's pattern of activity—sleeping, walking and feeding—from birth to four years. As daytime waking increases, the nocturnal pattern of behaviour becomes established.

Unicef

Reaching or walking consumes all of the infant's concentration at first. He must continually concentrate on what he is trying to do. As his actions become more skilled, however, they can be controlled by lower areas of the brain permitting attention to be freed for further activities. This is similar to an adult learning a new skill such as driving a car. At first there seem to be too many things to do simultaneously but it soon becomes more automatic.

The relative importance of maturation and learning is difficult to assess. In activities such as toilet training, learning seems to play no part. In a study carried out with twins, one of them was toilet-trained throughout the first year until completely in control. The untrained twin achieved control at almost precisely the same time. This result suggests that learning is unimportant compared with the normal course of neuromuscular development.

Hopi Indian infants are confined to a cradle board during the first year of life, yet they walk at the same time as infants free to crawl around. Even infants reared in institutions, with free movement and toys to play with, develop reaching and walking normally without adult help. The conditions of a normal home probably provide the experience necessary for motor development.

As the infant begins to explore his world through manipulation and movement his understanding of it becomes increasingly complex. At six months an infant will not reach for a toy if it is covered with a cloth. He acts as if 'out of sight is out of mind'. By nine months he will overcome this and search beneath the cloth. If he finds an object in this way several times he will show an interesting error if it is now hidden in a new place. Even though he sees it hidden he will return to the first hiding-place to search for it. This is because his understanding of space is still limited. He is not very mobile so he remembers the positions of things with reference to his own body and actions.

When the infant begins to crawl and walk this type of memory code is no longer useful since his own position is no longer constant. Consequently, he must develop an understanding of space in terms of the relations between objects themselves. One result of this is that he will now understand his own position in space better. He must realize that he is one more object in a common space, not the key reference point. In this way the infant becomes less egocentric.

to make use of the opposition of the finger and thumb in complementary movements giving him more sophisticated manual control. When the child is able to guide his reaching movements with his eyes, he is able to expand his repertoire of experiences because of the feedback with which he is provided. This feedback consists of the signals the infant's brain receives from his own body and from changes in external sensory input as he moves. He must learn to 'fit' his body to the world and know where parts of his body are in relation to each other. Feedback information tells him where his hand is without him having to look for it.

Development of the limbs
Most infants can crawl on four limbs and pull themselves to a standing position with the help of furniture by the age of nine months. At birth the lower limbs are poorly developed: they make up only one-third of the length of the body as compared with half the height of an adult. This means that the infant's centre of gravity is very high because he is top-heavy.

In his first attempts at standing he must keep his legs far apart to prevent toppling over. By 10 months the infant may walk with help and by 12-15 months he can walk unaided. He will be bow-legged at first but as the proportions of the limbs alter the centre of gravity moves downwards and posture becomes more stable.

By the age of two years, most children can stand on one foot and run without toppling over. The same kind of feedback is needed to develop walking in just the same way as in reaching, in the form of nerve impulses to the brain informing it of changes in the position of the limbs.

39

A child's early speech consists of words uttered one at a time, each of which is intended to convey the meaning of a whole adult sentence. Early language, known as *telegraphic*, omits all small words and word endings which change meaning, such as tense s and plural forms.

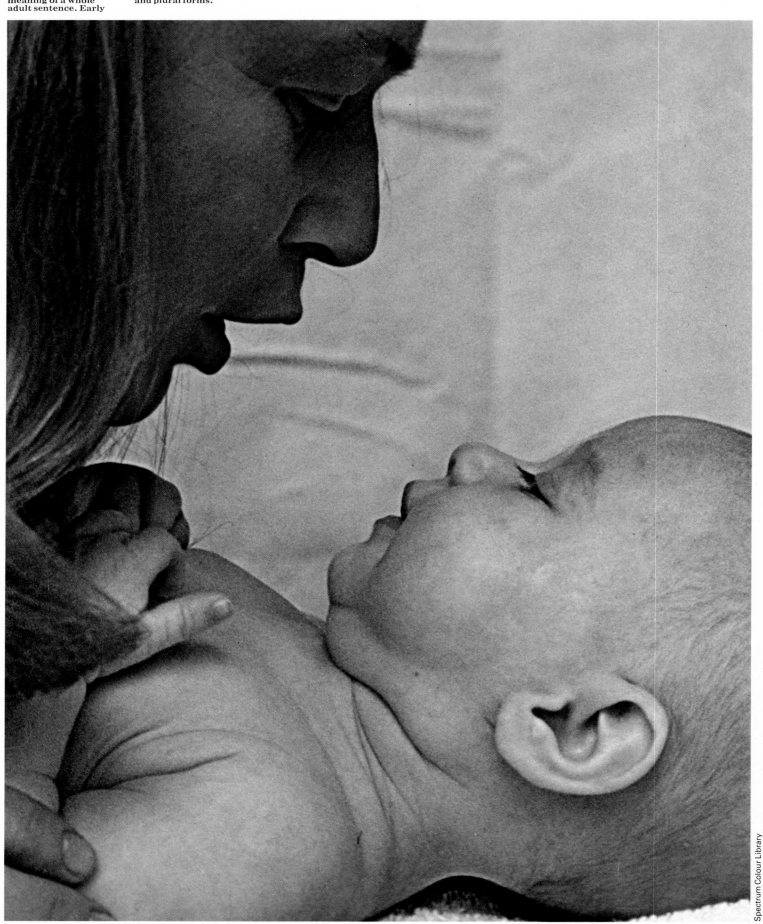

Learning to Speak

Animals show many varied ways of communicating with others of their own kind. Ants send messages to each other in chemical form, certain fishes use electrical discharges. Higher animals, including man, rely mainly on sound and on gestures of the face and body. Those gestures which convey information about inner emotional states or feelings are surprisingly similar in man and his closest evolutionary relative, the chimpanzee. However, the chimpanzee's use of sound to send messages is much more limited than that of man.

The basis of language

Man, unlike animals, is able to form symbols which stand for things he knows about even when they are not actually present. Language is a major kind of symbolism; speech is its spoken form. There are two main parts to every language. The first is a set of symbols which stand for things we know about or understand; these symbols, whether in spoken or written language, are *words*.

The second part of a language is its grammar. This is a set of rules by which words can be combined to express precise relationships between objects and events and to convey new, more complex meanings. The simple sentence, 'John hit Jim' has a different meaning, for example, from, 'Jim hit John'. Although the words are identical the difference in grammatical order changes the way they are understood.

The first sound message

Crying, the baby's first sound message, is much more like animal communication than human speech. Mothers quickly come to distinguish between cries indicating hunger, anger and pain, but they do this largely by considering the conditions surrounding the baby at the time. When a crying baby is hidden behind a screen, mothers and nurses find it hard to determine the 'meaning' of the cry unless they are given clues—such as the time of the baby's last feed, or when his nappy was last changed.

Recent studies have shown that if a mother is sensitive to her baby by responding quickly and regularly to his early cries, he will cry less by the end of the first year than the baby of a mother who is not sensitive in this way. Besides crying less, such babies appear to be better at communicating with gestures and sounds.

By the age of four or five months most babies are making speech-like sounds which are rhythmically repeated in a form of vocal play called babbling. It was once thought that babies, who all over the world initially make the same sounds, continued to use only those which their mothers recognized from their own language and responded to most favourably. This is now thought to be an unlikely basis for speech development.

It seems that babies continue babbling not because they are 'rewarded' but because they enjoy the sounds that they make. Even deaf babies begin to babble at

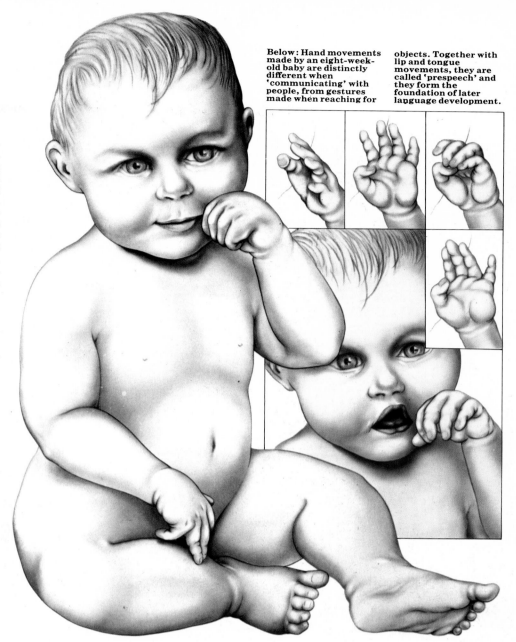

Below: Hand movements made by an eight-week-old baby are distinctly different when 'communicating' with people, from gestures made when reaching for objects. Together with lip and tongue movements, they are called 'prespeech' and they form the foundation of later language development.

the normal age, showing that this is inherited behaviour, although they soon stop unless deafness is diagnosed and a hearing aid provided. Besides enjoyment, babbling gives the baby an opportunity to learn the relationships between the movements of his mouth, tongue and so on and the sounds they produce—experience essential for learning to use speech later.

Very young babies appear to be able to distinguish speech from other types of sound, just as adults do. If a baby of one or two months is taught to suck a dummy to a repeated speech sound—for example, a vowel such as *a*—he will eventually stop sucking as he gets bored with the sound; in other words, when he has built a 'memory model' of it so that it is no longer novel and interesting. When the sound is changed to another vowel, such as *i*, the baby's sucking will increase. He detects the difference and is again interested. But he does not respond in a similar way to, say, musical notes of different pitches.

The way that a baby behaves with physical objects is very different from his behaviour with people. Objects he watches intently, trying to reach for them; but people he tries to 'talk' to from a very early age. In face-to-face contact with his mother a baby will make many facial and bodily gestures similar to those of adults in conversation with each other, and he may move his mouth in what have been called prespeech movements. It is as if the baby wants to talk long before he is able to do so. The expressions and gestures of baby and mother are very similar during such 'conversations'. At first the mother imitates the baby, and it is possible that this is the way in which the mother teaches her baby the social meaning of the gestures which he produces automatically.

Since the 1950s, great advances have been made in understanding the symbolic and grammatical nature of language. These have enabled psychologists and linguists to study children's early speech in great detail and in particular the similarity between children of different countries. Obviously children of different nationalities learn different words. But it is now believed that the meanings expressed by their early words—plus the way the words are placed in an order to convey these meanings, and the way in which sentences gradually become longer and more complex—is the same for every child, regardless of what language he is learning.

At first children use only one word at a time. These words are often nouns referring to people or objects. Studies of the situations in which these words are produced and of the child's accompanying gestures indicate that the child's single word is intended to convey an entire idea which an adult would express in a full sentence. For example, the child may attract his mother's attention while saying 'Milk'; she will understand it in this situation, as 'Give me a drink of milk'.

The number of words a child is able to use in this way increases rapidly, and soon he is using two words together. The child also begins to use words referring to actions (verbs). The role of two-word sentences is the description of relationships between people, objects, actions and events as shown in combinations like 'Daddy hit' and 'Hit ball'. Words are not put together in random order, but in sequences similar to the grammatical order which adults use. While playing a ball game, for example, a child may say, 'Hit ball'; but never, 'Ball hit'. He understands, as an adult does, that this would imply incorrectly that it is the ball rather than himself which is carrying out the action of hitting. He is beginning, in fact, to learn grammar.

The telegraphic period
In this early language, known as 'telegraphic', all small words and word endings which change meaning in subtle ways are missing, as they would be in a telegram. All of the parts of speech which convey number (such as plural forms), time (tenses other than the present) and exact object or place are omitted. Where an adult would say, 'The book is on the table', a small child is likely to describe this relationship by, 'Book table'.

Sentences become longer and more precise in meaning in two ways. Sometimes two thoughts will be put together to form a three-word sentence which expresses them both simultaneously: for example, 'Daddy hit' and, 'Hit ball' may be combined to form, 'Daddy hit ball'. Also, an extra word may be added to describe (more fully) the objects mentioned: for example, 'Sit chair' may now become, 'Sit Mummy chair'. This pattern of development is common to children in all countries so far studied. All extend the length of their sentences in the same way.

Babies do not acquire language just by imitating their parents, for they *say* many things which they have never *heard*. During their first 18 months, it is thought, they gradually learn to 'decode' adult speech. Next they learn the words and ordering rules they can use to express their understanding through speech. The child continues to produce longer sentences as he adds the parts of speech omitted during the 'telegraphic' period and, by the age of four or five, will be able to hold adult-like conversations.

Universal language development
The universal nature of children's language development, and studies of the human brain which show that the left hemisphere is specialized to hear and produce speech, imply that man may be biologically unique in his capacity for language. The vocal systems of other animals are not suited to speech production, but it is possible that the more intelligent might be able to use symbols other than spoken words to express an

42

Right: Though unable to hold a conversation as such, young children will try out their repertoire of words and phrases on strangers without inhibition.

Below: Visual communication through facial expressions is common to many species. Among primates facial expressions are important—for example, when one ape approaches another to show lack of hostility and gain acceptance. There are many similarities between facial expressions used by chimpanzees and by humans—made possible by the similarity in the muscular set-up of the face. But it is dangerous to 'humanize' expressions used by apes, since these visual signals are the result of an inherited pattern of behaviour influenced by environment: it presents challenges different from those encountered by man.

ZEFA

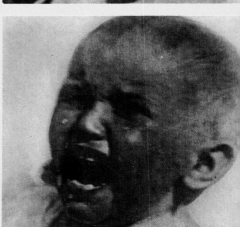

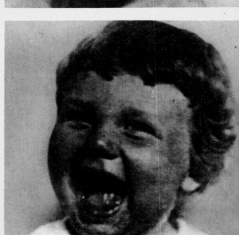

Royal College of Surgeons

Picturepoint

TEACHING LANGUAGE TO A CHIMPANZEE

apple · name of

banana · name of

banana · not · name of

apple · not · name of

Above: By the age of four to five years, most children are able to hold adult-like conversations.

Left and below: Studies conducted with young chimpanzees have yielded surprising information about their skills in using language through symbols and gestures. One chimp called Sarah was taught to use plastic symbols of different shapes and colours, each of which represents a word: noun, adjective or verb—and a concept or condition. These symbols were placed next to the real item (left) and in this way Sarah gradually learned the words for objects. Eventually she was able to use quite complex sentences which required intelligence as well as memory. In other experiments, chimps have been taught American Sign Language (below). However, these experiments with language and chimpanzees have recently been the subject of controversy, since some researchers feel that the apes' 'language' is actually a complicated form of imitation and not like human language.

understanding of the world just as sophisticated as that of man.

Attempts have been made to teach American Sign Language (ASL), used by the deaf, to a chimpanzee called Washoe. In many ways Washoe's progress has been similar to that of a young child learning a first language. When taught the sign for a flower Washoe used that sign for all flowers—not just for the one she was first shown. This means that she understands that the sign 'flower' stands for the characteristics which all flowers have in common. Like human symbols, her signs stand for what she knows about objects.

Washoe has even made up her own signs. The first time she saw a duck, she signed 'water-bird' to her human companion. Washoe soon began to put signs together in short sentences, as a young child would, and the meanings she expressed were the same as those of young children. But here a crucial difference emerged for, unlike a child, Washoe does not use order consistently to make her meanings clear. When she asks someone to tickle her, Washoe is as likely to sign 'Tickle you' as she is to sign 'You tickle'. She names the parts of a situation, but does not use a grammatical order to make their relationship clear. This may be because chimpanzees in the wild are not very interested in relations between physical objects: they are social creatures. They do not have the intense curiosity about the way the world works that a human child has. It is also significant that although Washoe is good at answering questions she rarely asks them, unlike a young child who seems to ask, 'Why?' or, 'How?' on a vast number of occasions.

It is possible that only man has needed to evolve a communications system as complicated and sophisticated as language. But this is a possibility, not a proven fact. Washoe, for instance, did not begin to learn ASL until she was over a year old; this may have hindered her development of language. Although studies of baby chimpanzees reared by humans from birth are continuing, it has been suggested that chimpanzees such as Washoe were actually being told what to do (rather than initiating ideas) by picking up subtle and unconscious signals from their trainers.

Paul Fusco/John Hillelson Agency

Stages of Learning

Physical growth can be studied directly by measuring and observing changes in the size and form of brain and body, but we cannot see the mind. The processes of *learning*, *memory* and *understanding* are not visible like the growth of a limb, so their existence must be inferred from behaviour. A person's behaviour—the way he reacts to situations and other people—can provide valuable information about the mental skills which he has developed for dealing with the world.

As food provides the material for physical growth, experiences in the world produce changes in behaviour. These changes show that *learning* has occurred and for learning to be possible there must be *memory*, a record of past experiences. Both learning and memory are closely related to the mental structures which we have available for organizing or *understanding* our experiences. We can only remember and learn effectively to the extent that we can understand the information or task involved.

The process of adaptation

Adaptation to the world is a continuous and active process. Initially it is possible only to behave efficiently in a situation if a mental structure exists which is adequate to understand it, that is, if we can *assimilate* the situation. However, as our experiences alter, our mental structures must change to *accommodate* them.

At birth the baby has structures which enable him to make contact with the world through actions such as looking and sucking. It is very noticeable that a baby will try to put even the most improbable objects in his mouth and suck them but this is one of his few ways of understanding or assimilating his world. In the early months the baby can come to recognize objects when they reappear but his memory is not yet good enough for him to recall them when they are not present. This ability emerges between six and 12 months. At this stage the baby can remember that his mother exists even when he cannot see her. He may insist loudly that she stays to play with him whereas a few months earlier he would appear to forget her soon after she had left the room and play happily by himself.

During the first 18 months of life the baby's developing understanding is reflected in an increasing capacity to respond to and search for objects in different situations. He now has the ability to treat an object as if it remains the same even when he sees it from different angles, in different positions and at different times.

Understanding and memory

The next stage of development in the young child involves understanding and memory. These enable the child to encode and understand objects and events in their absence at the level of thought as well as action. Whereas the child under 18 months plays by manipulating objects the child over 18 months will pretend or 'make-believe'. When he lays a cloth on the ground saying 'This is my bed, I'm going to sleep' he knows that the cloth is not really a bed and he is not really sleeping. What the child is doing is revealing his new ability to show an understanding of the nature of an object or action in the absence of the object or action.

Speech, which is also developing at this time, reflects the formation of a system of social symbols whose meaning is the same for adult and child. These are unlike the symbols of play. They vary markedly from child to child and may be difficult for adults to understand unless accompanied by speech.

The third stage of development involves images of things seen and their locations in space. A child of three or four years can learn to make his way alone from home to a shop or nursery school but if he is asked how he gets there he describes the route in terms of his actions by saying 'I turn like that', 'I go like this' and gesturing or attempting to make the actions as he describes them. But if the child is provided with a model of his neighbourhood and asked to point out his route he finds this impossible. He has no mental map or 'image' of his route of the kind that an adult or older child has.

During this period the child's understanding gradually frees itself from the need for direct sense impressions or actions. But it is still far from adult. For example, if a five-year-old looks at a model of a landscape with animals on it he is easily able to select from a set of pictures showing different views of it the one which shows it from the position he can see it from. However, if he is asked to select a picture of what someone sitting on the

Katharine Perry

Above, below, right and far right: The drawings of a five-year-old and a nine-year-old demonstrate the child's developing ability to conceptualize. Both children were asked to make two drawings of a scene, one from their own viewpoint and the other from another angle. The five-year-old accurately described the order in which she saw a number of objects on the table in front of her. She drew them without difficulty, but when asked to draw them from the opposite angle she could describe the reverse order but could not hold on to the concept long enough to capture it on paper.

Mary Evans Picture Library

"The Age of Intellect"

Above: From the age of 11 years, the child goes through a period of rapid intellectual growth, absorbing a great deal of information. As the cartoon aptly points out, however, information is of little use without experience, the other essential ingredient of maturity.

Camera Press

Left: Jean Piaget, the Swiss psychologist who is regarded as having made the greatest contribution to the study of children. Trained as a biologist, he became fascinated by the behaviour of his own children and began a systematic chronological study of the stages of their development.

Katharine Perry

Right and far right: Unlike the five-year-old, the nine-year-old child has developed the ability to hold on to abstract concepts. She was asked first to draw her own house from the front. Then, when asked to draw it as if she were looking at it from the back, she did so with meticulous attention to detail.

Keystone

Bruce Coleman

opposite side of the model sees he will again select the same picture. Until the age of about six, the child is still very dependent upon what he sees and is tied to one viewpoint—his own.

The child is unable at this stage to grasp the more abstract characteristics of objects such as number, weight or volume. These concepts involve an understanding which often conflicts strongly with immediate sense impressions. This is evident from the hesitation which even an adult may show when asked the classic riddle: 'Which is heavier, a pound of lead or a pound of feathers?'

At this age the child believes that there is more of something when it goes further. For example, if a row of sweets is placed before him and then spread out he will say 'There are more now'. Similarly, if the child is shown a short, wide beaker full of water and sees it poured into a tall, thin beaker he will also say that there is now more because he believes that the volume changes when the level of the water rises.

However, as the child begins to realize that his intuitive notions are inadequate he will develop mental structures which enable him to co-ordinate several viewpoints. These mental structures or operations develop during the period from six to 11 years. They enable the child to understand that spreading out a row of sweets does not increase their number because not only does the row become longer the sweets are also farther apart and the net result of the two changes is to cancel each other out. Similarly, the child now understands that pouring water into a taller, thinner beaker does not increase its volume because the decrease in width cancels out the increase in height. Before

these faculties develop the child can consider height or width but he cannot relate the two.

In the third period of development the child is able to perform mentally the activities which he can act out with objects—he can count them, classify them and order them in a series such as size.

Classification and seriation

The development of classification can be illustrated by the child's behaviour with a bunch of flowers. If a child is shown six primroses and six daisies and asked if there are more flowers or more primroses he will usually answer that there are just as many flowers as there are primroses. He will then be confused if asked whether the primroses are not also flowers. He knows that both primroses and daisies are flowers but he cannot consider the whole class (primroses plus daisies) and part of it (the primroses) at the same time. But when his ability to classify develops, he also begins to understand seriation.

If a child is presented with a set of sticks he will have little difficulty in putting them in order—from the smallest to the largest. He can understand that if the first stick is larger than the second and the second stick is larger than the third then the first stick must also be larger than the third.

In comparison, the younger child who has not developed this ability—known as operational thought—cannot understand this overall relationship and can only form a series by trial and error, comparing every stick with every other stick.

Operational thought forms the basis for logical thought about the world. It is probably no coincidence that schooling

Above left: Children develop skills in many different types of learning situations. This Mexican nine-year-old is learning to weave.

Above: The understanding of the relationship of objects in space is one of the most important developments in the young child. Up to the age of nine months, when an object is hidden —in a paper bag, for example— he will continue to search in the place he first found it, even though he sees it hidden elsewhere. After this age, he will begin to look elsewhere when he fails to find it in the first hiding-place.

Eve Arnold/John Hillelson Agency

Above and right: For the child between five and 11 years, learning and education are almost synonymous. But the methods by which the basic skills of literacy and numeracy are taught have changed considerably since formal schooling became compulsory in many countries. Children were once forced to learn everything by rote and punished if they failed to do so. Educational and technological research have heralded more enlightened teaching methods in which children are encouraged and stimulated into learning.

Below: Six-year-olds having their ability to think logically—which develops around this age—tested.

usually begins at the age of five or six years when the child is ready to begin thinking in this way. Just as a child cannot be taught to walk until he has reached an adequate level of neuro-muscular maturity he cannot be taught number concepts until he has been through all the usual stages of development up to this point.

The child is like a scientist with an inadequate theory of the world and to accelerate his mental growth he must be provided with experiences which challenge that theory and force him to modify it until it becomes more like the theories of the adults around him. Language is of great importance in this development. It enables adults to tell the child when his theory conflicts with their own. In this way the child can learn about and benefit from the experiences of others without having to undergo them himself.

The development of logical thought

The final period of mental development does not begin until the age of about 11 years. During this period the young adult develops his ability to think about things and events which are possible although not necessarily present in the world of concrete experience. The young adult can do more than think logically about objects, he can think about his thoughts. This is shown by his ability to work out whether or not an argument is logical.

It is important to realize that mental skills do not develop in isolation. Examinations and intelligence tests can measure a child's ability to understand and think but a poor performance does not necessarily indicate low potential. Mental, emotional and physical development are intricately connected in ways which are not yet fully understood and the reasons why a child may fail to develop his full mental potential, at any given stage, are numerous and complex.

Emotions are intimately linked with the reasons why we do things, and with our motives. As we develop, both change as a result of our experiences. When we are successful at learning we feel good and this supports our motivation to learn further, but the opposite occurs if we fail. We feel so anxious that we are unable to learn effectively—there is a 'mental block'. The very young child shows an innate curiosity and desire to learn but these need adult support if they are to continue. Adults who set unrealistically high goals for children will be placing them continually in situations where failure is inevitable. The goals set for a child must take into consideration his current level of ability for if they exceed it greatly he will learn less. Worse, he will lose the desire to learn.

Personality and behaviour

The developing child learns not only about the world around him but about himself. He learns about the type of person he is largely by observing the reactions of other people to his behaviour. Gestural communication develops before speech and children of a very young age are able to tell when an adult is disappointed with them even though the adult may say that he is pleased with their performance. In this way the child may come to see himself as a failure and will believe that he is incapable of learning, an attitude which may shape the rest of his life and his relationships with others.

The Child at Play

Play is one of the most important activities in a child's development. Through it he can gradually experience the skills, attitudes and modes of behaviour appropriate to adult life.

Until only a few decades ago, play was not regarded as a serious subject of study. It was felt in scientific circles that it was not a manageable activity for experimental research. 'Cowboys-and-indians' and other fantasy games—with which children are preoccupied during certain phases of their development—could neither be defined nor kept within certain limits necessary to comply with the sober-minded approach with which psychologists generally scrutinized human behaviour. The respected critic, Harold Schlosberg, of Brown University published a paper advising researchers to steer clear of this field of enquiry since he maintained that 'so antic a phenomenon as play' would provide little data of worth and was unlikely to give any insights into early human development.

However, the subject was not closed. Enquiries into behaviour among other primates provided vital clues which furnished experimental psychologists with a new approach to child behaviour. From observation of young monkeys, early investigators such as the Dutch primatologist J. A. R. A. M. van Hooff, observed that there was a distinct difference between activities in which survival skills were practised and play. They were accompanied by very clear forms of signalling to indicate that when play was intended, aggression was not, so that real fighting only occurred when one monkey did not see the signal sent by another. It was gradually noted by later observers—David Hamburg of Stanford and Jane van Lawick-Goodall—that young chimpanzees spend a great deal of their first five years observing adult forms of behaviour and incorporating them into their play. Eventually the resemblances between child and chimpanzee behaviour were recognized and a pattern of child behaviour became apparent.

The purpose of play

It has been established by experiments done by a number of investigators that the central requirement of play is the opportunity to acquire skill in certain specific activities. In fact it has even been postulated that play is a means of neutralizing the effects of the 'push' or force which drives children to complete an act successfully. And, indeed, it would seem that there is a need for children to

Bowling (1378)

Trap-ball (1381)

Club-ball 14th century

Early form of golf

Mansell

Above: Ball games. Although they probably began as unstructured forms of play requiring only something to kick or hit, most ball games have developed into highly structured games with complex rules. These games (above) popular in the 14th century, are developments of games played by the Romans and the ancient Greeks and may be the precursors of many popular modern games. Games of this nature have a timeless, universal appeal to children. Through them they can develop their judgment and muscular co-ordination and pit themselves against their own last performance as well as against their playmate's.

Michael Holford

Above: A 17th century Chinese scroll painting of *wayeng golek*, or puppetry. Puppets can be made in almost any shape to portray information on almost any subject, and as such, provide a valuable tool for the education of children. Apart from improving dexterity, puppetry gives children the opportunity to be creative and organized in the making of the costumes and in the actual performance.

Right: Like many traditional games the meaning of *Oranges and Lemons* is almost forgotten. The 'oranges' and 'lemons' represent bells which pealed along the 16th century London 'traitors' route' to execution.

Mansell

alleviate pressure.

In an experiment done at Harvard University in the early 1970s, three-, four-, and five-year olds—divided equally into groups of 36—were given the task of fishing an object out of a container which was just out of reach. They were all given a number of sticks which, when properly clamped together, provided an effective fishing rod. The 'training' procedures varied among the groups. One was shown how to clamp the sticks together, another was allowed to practise clamping the sticks together, a third was allowed to watch the experimenter carry out the complete task, while a fourth was left to play with the materials and it was implied to the children in this group that the task was part of the play.

The group to which the complete task was demonstrated and the play group had significantly better results than the other groups; their success rate was twice as high as that of the other groups—in other words, twice as many children in each of those two groups successfully completed the task.

But what is perhaps of greater significance is that the experimenters noticed a different approach to the task between the play group and all the other groups. They were less intense about completing the task because they regarded it as a form of play. Consequently, they gave up less easily on failed attempts and were eventually able to solve the problem.

Above: For children in some societies the boundaries between work and play are indistinct, since the periods spent in learning are not restricted to formal schooling. This young member of the Karaja tribe of Brazil has to learn how to make and use weapons and the art of hunting. Learning to use a bow and arrow may be merely a game at the moment but his life will depend on it when he is an adult.

Below: 'Children's Games' by Pieter Breugel, the 16th century Flemish artist.

The stages of play

At all stages in a child's development play is a means of discovery: the child can be attempting to understand what is happening, how something works or to achieve a new skill. After he has made the discovery he seems to enjoy repeating the action 'just for fun', through which he acquires the skill and which he will go on repeating long after there is any new information to be gained from the action. But it appears to be necessary for children to 'waste' time in this way. It takes them much longer than adults to assimilate a new experience and the younger the child is, the longer it takes.

Children begin to play at a very early age. At four to five months, an infant will enjoy a game of peek-a-boo, and it is common for babies of this age to pull their mother's hair and to chuckle happily when she pretends to be startled.

Playing with sand and water is popular with young children, because the effect of their action upon it is immediately visible. They soon grow out of this, however, as it does not lead to the development of skills and so children eventually become bored with it. Up to the age of ten years, building is a favourite activity with both sexes. Building with bricks offers almost unlimited potential.

The kinds of activities that play involves are many and varied, but they can be roughly divided into *structured* and *unstructured* play. Structured play includes all those types of games which have rules or are organized in a specific way, some of which have been played since the dawn of recorded time—*tug-of-war* and *blind man's buff* are known to be pre-Roman, for example. Unstructured, or 'free', play starts from chance happenings. A child will discover his effect on something—sand, for example—and will follow it up: perhaps making his first sandcastle.

Play and the environment

Play allows the child to explore his environment but it also enables him to experiment with the skills he has acquired in using his own body and in manipulating objects. He needs a certain amount of exercise to promote the development of the co-ordination of his muscles and nervous system. Many traditional games provide this opportunity and also enable him to explore his physical capabilities to his own satisfaction. Games and pastimes such as *follow the leader*, *skating*, *cycling*, and *hopscotch* fall into this category, since they depend on improvement on the child's own last performance as much as the performance of his playmates. Some of his physical limits will also be tested by taunts and dares, and others by direct testing of his strength in fighting.

There is a noticeable difference between the way boys play compared with girls and this difference shows up quite distinctly by the time they are five years old. 'Rough and tumble' play is probably the best illustration of this difference. It involves wrestling, tumbling and jumping up and down. It is much more attractive to boys than to girls, who are inclined to be a little more timid about joining in this kind of boisterous activity. Although 'rough and tumble' play usually only occurs between friends, or in a very

J. Allan Cash

Philippe Ledru/John Hillelson Agency

Left: A young Lebanese soldier. Kicking a football alleviates some of the stress of being forced into an adult role before he is fully equipped for it.

Below: No matter how sophisticated toys have become, children are still fascinated by everyday, mundane materials. Discarded cardboard boxes have great potential for their imaginations to work on.

J. Allan Cash

friendly context, less confident children have difficulty joining in.

Imitation and make-believe

The most important developments in the child's socialization take place through imitation. The child's postures, vocabulary, emotional reactions and mental attitudes have been copied from the behaviour of those around him. He may learn simply by watching an action or game being carried out, or he may insist on acting it out himself. Between the ages of two to eight, for example, he will progress from emulating his parents' activities—making cakes like Mummy does—to imitating generalized social situations like playing 'shop'.

Through this kind of play, both at school and in the home, the child can be taught some basic skills such as counting, understanding weight, quantity and the cost of items. Through games of this nature, the child will also develop his verbal facility. He will become practised in the kinds of interactions he is likely to become involved in later on in life and in this way can store and digest impressions which lessen anxiety and teach him the social rules which govern acceptable behaviour.

A child has his own private world filled with anxieties, aspirations, dreams and fantasies. He has feelings about his environment—that it is safe and friendly or insecure and hostile. Some of the child's outward behaviour reflects his inner feelings, but his inner experience cannot be totally understood using only his behaviour as a basis for interpretation. A child's world of make believe

develops between the ages of 18 months and eight years. It allows the child to bend reality to fit his own intellectual or emotional requirements. For example, children sometimes enact events in the way they would have liked them to happen, rather than the way they actually did happen. They also tend to act out events they have never experienced or are likely to experience just to see what they 'feel' like—being chased by tigers, for example.

The child also learns through the imaginary acting out of various roles what it feels like to be on the receiving end or the giving end of various situations —shopkeeper and customer, doctor and patient, teacher and pupil, employer and employee. Some or all of these he will eventually experience as an adult and through the combination of enacting the fantasy and the reality will gradually make the transition from the child's to the adult world.

But in order to make this transition smoothly, he must be aided by understanding adults. It is easy for adults to forget the contours of the child's world— both inner and outer—and to overlook the fact that play is not merely an activity to while away the time until he is able to take on more responsible adult-like activities. The child who is not allowed to play or to play in a way that is conducive to learning and the development of skills will probably not grow into a responsible adult. Without the opportunity to explore and experiment and to experience what it means to be a child, he will never learn to explore and experience what it really means to be an adult.

Above: A 'glue-in' at a community centre in San Francisco.

Below: Dressing-up. Make-believe is an essential form of play for two- to eight-year olds. It enables them to explore reality by bending it to fit their own requirements.

Right: Nepalese children learning to count and name things through the universally popular game of 'shop', or 'store'.

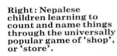

Burt Glinn/John Hillelson Agency

UNICEF/Abigail Heymar

Play is one of the main activities in a child's development. It is a means of acquiring the skills, attitudes, and modes of behaviour in preparation for adult life.

Learning and Intelligence

Everybody knows roughly what intelligence is, but it is hard to define precisely—and even harder to measure. Psychologists themselves cannot agree on it. Over the years, some have called it 'the ability to learn'. Others have called it 'the ability to adapt adequately to the environment'. Still others have thought it 'a general tendency towards achievement'.

One early psychologist, Professor E. L. Thorndike, suggested that intelligence could be broken up into three groups—mechanical, social and abstract. *Mechanical* intelligence meant skill in manipulating tools and gadgets, *social* intelligence covered people's ability to act wisely in human relationships, and *abstract* intelligence was the ability to handle symbols (words and numbers) and scientific principles.

One aspect which Thorndike's classifications certainly undervalued, however, was *creativity*. In the 1950s, J. P. Guildford, dissatisfied with existing methods of testing intelligence, developed his own research along the lines of *divergent* and *convergent* thinking. He defined convergent thinking as a person's ability to produce the 'expected' answer to a problem, and divergent thinking—or creativity—as ability to produce the 'unexpected' answer.

'Unexpected' in this sense does not mean 'wrong'. As one example, in his book *Children Solve Problems* Edward De Bono cites children who were asked to solve the problem of how to build houses more quickly. Most of their drawings showed conventional thinking—more highly mechanized versions of normal building methods. But one highly creative child suggested starting with a huge balloon 'printed on the inside with an attractive wallpaper pattern', inflating it, spraying it with concrete, and then cutting away those areas like doors and windows where concrete was not wanted. This is the exact opposite of normal methods—but a similar system to the child's has in fact been made to work.

R. B. Cattell in 1971 similarly held that there were two types of intelligence, which he called *fluid* and *crystallized*. A child with fluid intelligence, his research showed, could somehow sidestep the learned or expected answer to a problem, producing a creative and unexpected answer. The child with crystallized intelligence, however, would accurately produce an already-formulated answer to a problem, but not attempt to go beyond it.

Intelligence tests

The first, crude attempts to measure people's intelligence were as long ago as the 1890s. Then in 1904 the French Minister for Public Instruction set up a commission to study the problems of 'backward' children. Among its members was a 47-year-old psychologist, Alfred Binet, and his first problem was: who *were* the backward children?

With his assistant, Théophile Simon, Binet set out to devise a series of test

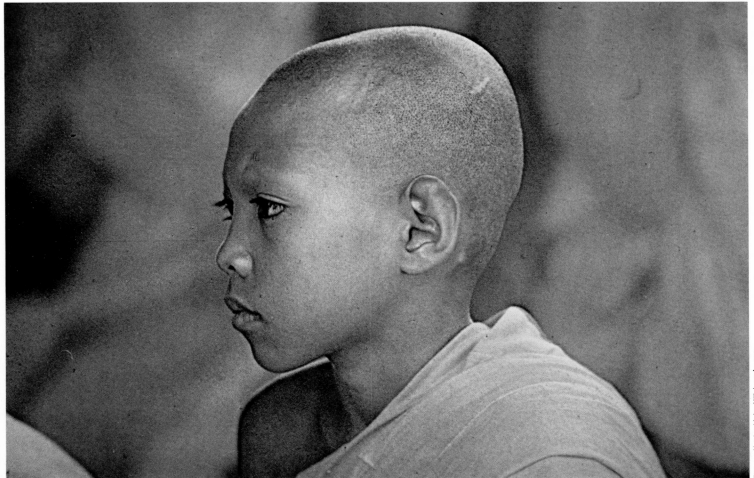

Above and below: Differences in cultural background have an enormous impact on the kind of learning that children acquire, and hence in their performances in traditional IQ tests such as the Stanford-Binet. The young Chinese is learning the philosophy of Chairman Mao—and western algebra—in an attempt to progress in an increasingly industrialized society. The novice Buddhist monk is learning self-denial, meditation and religious belief in an attempt to reach the ultimate purity of the spirit. The Chinese might do better in an IQ test. But is he more intelligent?

Marc Riboud/John Hillelson Agency

Thomas Hopker/John Hillelson Agency

problems—and succeeded, because he had no preconceived ideas of what problems to use. If the average six-year-old could copy a drawing of a square, but the average five-year-old could not, then this test was for Binet a perfectly suitable measure of six-year-old intelligence.

Binet spent the rest of his life revising his tests and, after his death in 1911, the American Lewis Terman carried on the work at Stanford University. Hence tests of this type, still widely used, are called Stanford-Binet tests.

From the results of Binet's work there developed the concept of *mental age*. He supposed that a child's brain increased in intellectual power year by year. So two children shown by the tests to have the same intellectual power had the same mental age—regardless of their actual ages. A 13-year-old whose results matched those of the average 12-year-old was held to be one year retarded, while a 13-year-old whose results matched those of the average 14-year-old was held to be one year advanced.

But one year's 'backwardness' at the age of, say, five, is far more significant than at the age of 13, since it represents a much greater proportion of the child's total development. So it was later suggested that the *ratio* between mental age and true (chronological) age was a better measure than just the *difference* between them. This ratio, when multiplied by 100, is called the *intelligence quotient*, or IQ. (IQ = mental age multiplied by 100, then divided by chronological age). A child whose mental and chronological ages are the same is, by definition, an average child; his IQ is 100 exactly.

However, a person's intellectual capacity does not go on increasing indefinitely; somewhere between the ages of 14 and 18, it begins to level out.

How does IQ vary from person to person? About 50 per cent of people, on a big enough sample, will have an IQ of somewhere between 90 and 110. About 25 per cent are below IQ 90, and another quarter above IQ 110. The numbers with an IQ below 70 (traditionally taken to be 'retarded') or above 130 (the 'brilliant') are small—about 3 per cent in each case.

Testing by this method shows no differences between the IQs of men as a whole and of women as a whole. But tests have shown marked differences between people of different backgrounds—for example, members of an affluent majority and of a deprived minority in the same country.

This is one reason why many psychol-

Above: Imitating his elders is a normal part of a child's learning process, even if what is learned—such as IRA-type 'weapons' training —is out of the ordinary.

Below: Standards of drawing are a measure of 'fluid intelligence' in pre-school children. Circles, for example, are easily visualized —but too hard to draw.

Above and below: Tests with Kaleidoblocs, with which children can make structures of amazing complexity, can tell psychologists much about the intelligence of unusually gifted or retarded children— such as Paul, aged 7, whose IQ is too high to be measured by standard methods. His mental age may be as high as 11.

Right: Modern IQ tests use universally understood symbols, rather than words or numbers, to eliminate 'cultural bias'.

Below right: Chess requires a special kind of intelligence—the ability to analyze in advance the possible outcomes of an infinite number of moves.

ogists today do not regard such traditional tests as adequate. Children from homes where books, toys, records, lively conversation—among themselves, and especially with adults—and other stimuli are present tend to perform better than others in school discussions with both teachers and testers. Since most tests are based on a child's skill with words, it is difficult to measure accurately the intelligence of children whose homes do not provide such advantages. In fact, some children who appear to be slow, or even dim-witted, in the verbal sections of tests can score well in the non-verbal sections.

Conventional tests are also, according to most psychologists, heavily loaded towards 'crystallized intelligence' rather than 'fluid intelligence', and far too concerned with abstract concepts. So they are useful for measuring intelligence of the kind needed by schools in assessing a child's potential for future academic work, but virtually useless in measuring perseverance or creativity—both important aspects of other types of work, and indeed of a well-rounded human being.

Memory

Much easier to define than intelligence, but equally important in the learning

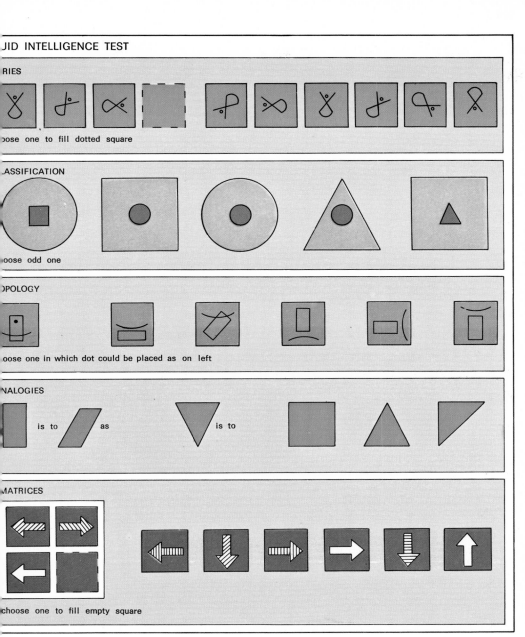

RIES

oose one to fill dotted square

LASSIFICATION

oose odd one

OPOLOGY

oose one in which dot could be placed as on left

NALOGIES

is to [ ] as [ ] is to

MATRICES

choose one to fill empty square

JULIAN HODGSON = HELMUT CARDON

Keystone

process, is memory. It is the ability to learn, retain what we have learned, and retrieve what we have retained when we need it.

Doctors do not know by what process, or even in what part of the brain, memory is developed. They do know, however, that failure to memorize can be caused by deterioration of brain cells which are active in the learning process; by certain types of injuries to, or diseases of, the brain; by activities which intervene between the time we learn something and the time we want to recall it; and last but not least, by repression.

In the learning process, our ability to remember is dependent both on the methods used to convey the information and the circumstances in which the learning takes place. Any schoolchild who has done last-minute 'swotting' for a test knows that what is crammed into the brain today can as easily be forgotten by tomorrow night, or whenever the test is over. What is not so well known is that children who take examinations in a room where they have been taught a particular subject score higher marks than when they are tested in less-familiar surroundings.

In general, forgetting is not caused by the fading out of impressions but rather by the crowding out of old material by a constant inflow of new. Sometimes this new material demands that we unlearn, or reorganize, the original material, causing a 'scrambling' of the original material to the point of confusion—not so much a matter of being unable to remember, but of not knowing *what* to remember.

Repression is another matter. Most people are much more likely to forget a dental appointment than an invitation to a party; the human mind rejects the unpleasant much more readily than the pleasant. The early psycho-analyst Sigmund Freud took this concept a stage further: he built a whole theory of adult behaviour on the belief that we repress certain memories because if we retrieved them they would evoke painful emotions, acute feelings of guilt and a loss of self-esteem.

Some modern psychologists say that the same sort of thing holds true of school-type learning. If teaching methods or the atmosphere in a child's home do not allow for the fact that a child can be hurt or painfully embarrassed, they contend, the child's mind may react by 'blocking out' the material that he is supposed to learn. Similarly, parents who do not help their children to learn, but demand that a child passes examinations in spite of their lack of interest, can make the child forget what he has learned out of unconscious spite.

Tiring during the learning process, or simply losing interest in what is being taught, can also cause memory lapses. In 1932 Van Alstyne discovered that a child's *attention span*—that is, the length of time that he can concentrate on a subject—increases systematically with age. For two-year-olds, he found, the average attention span was seven minutes; for three-year-olds, 8.9 minutes; for four-year-olds, 12.4 minutes; and for five-year-olds, 13.6 minutes. So that, as W. Fowler and O. K. Moore have shown, it is perfectly possible to teach an average child to read by the age of three or four— if they are taught in very short lessons.

Puberty

Puberty is the stage of development when the body makes its great leap forward from childhood into adulthood. This is achieved by several metabolic processes in the physiology of boy and girl, and is accompanied by psychological changes in mood, drive and general behaviour.

The average age of onset of puberty is 13 years—although any age between 11 years and 16 years can be regarded as within the normal limits. Signs of physiological maturing of the body before 11 years is described as 'precocious puberty' and invariably requires medical investigation. In both sexes, there has been a trend over the past century for puberty to arrive earlier, even in the range of normal limits, in children of the affluent and developed countries. This is partly related to improved physical health and better nutrition.

But in poorer countries which have a tropical or sub-tropical climate, there was often evidence of earlier puberty than in temperate climates. The reverse trend in the second half of the twentieth century, with earlier puberty in Western Europe and the North American continent, may be due to increased exposure to artificial light in these societies. This is a theory derived from experimental work on young female rats undertaken by N. Jafarey and co-workers at a Karachi medical school in Pakistan.

The pace of growth

Puberty is another of the phases in life when the pace of body growth changes. Clearly and visibly through childhood, boys and girls make a steady and regular increase in height and in weight. The pace or velocity of these growth changes tends to slow down as puberty nears. Then, just before the effects of puberty become apparent in the human organs and tissues, the pace of growth sharply increases.

This growth spurt is first apparent in the girls who show the height and weight changes around 11 years of age. The spurt appears in the boys around 13 years of age. The actual figures for increase in height vary, due to familiar and inherited characteristics and to nutritional factors. Over a two year period, a rise of around 20 cm and a weight gain of around 18 kilograms is the 'typical pattern' that can emerge.

Other physiological measurements and indications of organ changes also alter at puberty. Blood pressure, as measured in the upper arm is an indication of the force of the output of the human heart and of the resistance in the elastic arteries which carry the blood away from the heart. From infancy and throughout childhood, there is a steady increase in the blood pressure. Again, a spurt in the blood pressure takes place at puberty to accommodate the changes in size and function of other organs. By the age of 15 years, the adolescent blood pressure has reached normal adult levels.

The hormones at work

The physiological maturation process at puberty is organized and set going by hormonal command from the *anterior*

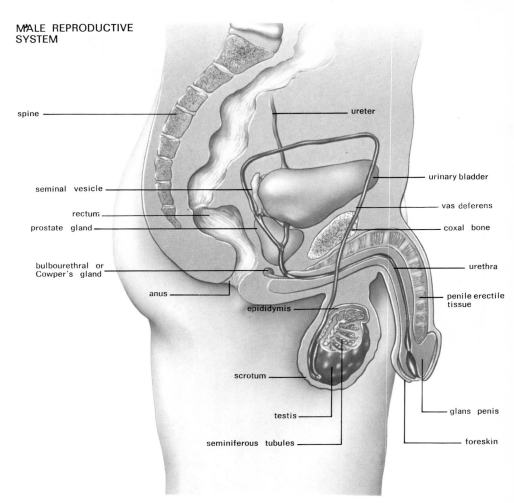

spine — ureter — seminal vesicle — urinary bladder — rectum — vas deferens — prostate gland — coxal bone — bulbourethral or Cowper's gland — urethra — anus — penile erectile tissue — epididymis — scrotum — testis — glans penis — seminiferous tubules — foreskin

Above: Diagram of the male reproductive organs. They consist of the testes—the gonads or sex glands—which produce sperm and various ducts which store or transport the sperm to the exterior. The gonads also contain male hormones responsible for the physical changes which occur during puberty.

Below: A testis, one of the pair of oval-shaped male sex glands. Each testis measures about 5 cm (2 inches) long and is about 2.5 cm (1 inch) in diameter. They lie in the abdominal cavity during foetal development but descend into the outer sac-like scrotum at birth since coolness is essential for sperm manufacture.

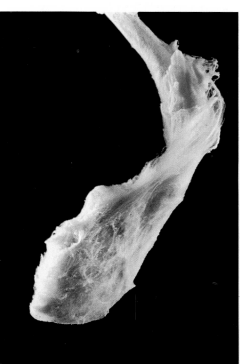

Dave Kelly

A COMPARISON BETWEEN THE MALE AND FEMALE PELVIS

MALE PELVIS

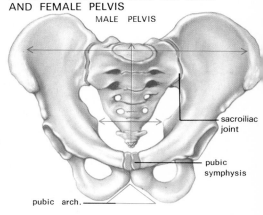

sacroiliac joint — pubic symphysis — pubic arch.

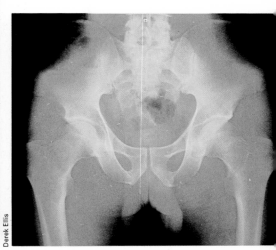

Derek Ellis

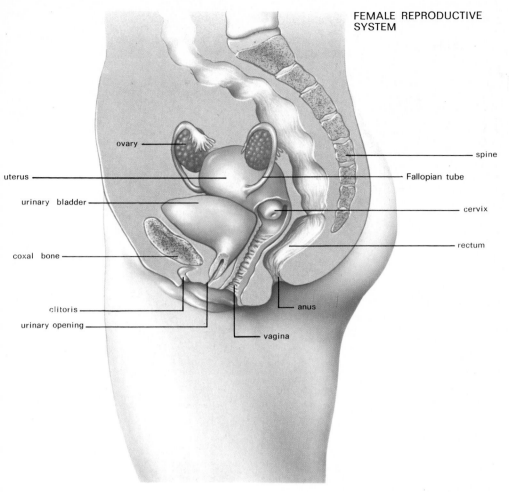

FEMALE REPRODUCTIVE
SYSTEM

ovary

uterus

urinary bladder

coxal bone

clitoris

urinary opening

vagina

spine

Fallopian tube

cervix

rectum

anus

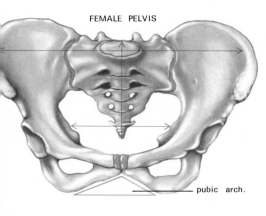

FEMALE PELVIS

pubic arch.

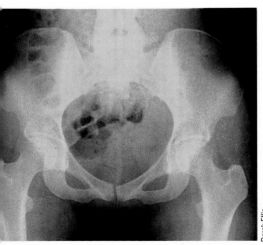

Derek Ellis

Left: The male and female pelvis. The female pelvis enlarges during puberty under the influence of the female hormone oestrogen, in preparation for pregnancy. The pubic bones are also moveable, so that they can be separated to increase the vaginal opening in childbirth.

Above: The female reproductive system. The almond-shaped ovaries release ova (eggs) once a month which are drawn down the Fallopian tubes to the uterus (womb) to await fertilization.

Below left: X-rays of the male and female pelvis in normal adulthod.

pituitary gland of the human brain. The anterior pituitary itself is triggered off by a nerve message supply from the *hypothalamus* which appears to have a built-in genetic regulator that is set to turn on at just the right age in the individual. (Presumably the artificial light effects suggested in some way excite the hypothalamus to a premature turning on.)

The anterior pituitary produces growth hormone, and it is the flow of this chemical which accounts for the increase in height and weight just before the other features of puberty appear. Growth hormone enlarges the bones of the skeleton, increases muscle mass, enlarges individual organs like the heart, and helps build up protein in the human tissue cells. Again, the girls gain from these effects before the boys but after the age of 15, the growth hormone effects on the male body overtake those on the female body.

Puberty announces the arrival of physical sexual maturation. This is achieved through hormones also produced by the anterior pituitary glands. The main hormones involved are FSH (Follicle Stimulating Hormone) and LH (Luteinising Hormone) in the girls, and ICSH (Interstitial Cell Stimulating Hormone)

in boys. Known as *gonadotrophic hormones*, FSH and LH act on the once dormant ovaries to begin major production of the female sex hormones, *oestrogen* and *progesterone*. ICSH acts on the once dormant testes of the boy to produce the male sex hormone, *testosterone*. At the same time, another hormone from the anterior pituitary, ACTH (Adrenal Corticotrophic Hormone) causes the adrenal glands above the kidneys to increase production of androgens in both sexes.

Secondary sexual characteristics

Androgens from the adrenals in the maturing boy and girl are responsible for the appearance and growth of hair under the arms, axillary hair, and pubic hair, hair above and around the genital area. The pubic hair itself shows a distinctive sexual pattern. In the pubertic girl, the upper border of the hairline is concave upwards. In the pubertic boy, the upper border of the pubic hairline is convex upwards. Because the boy has additional male hormones—testosterone from the testes—the overall hairiness of the body is much greater than in the girl.

Moreover the boy also starts to grow considerable facial hair, in the chin and upper lip areas, from the effect of the male sex hormones. The effect of the androgens on hair growth begins about 11 years of age and is not fully complete until the seventeenth year.

The effects of testosterone and androgen in the pubertic boy are considerable. The voice deepens as the larynx grows, and changes from a high pitch to a lower pitch, when it is said to 'break'. In the genital area, the whole picture changes. Apart from the hair growth, the *penis* enlarges and so do the accessory sexual organs—the *prostate*, the *epididymis* and the *seminal vesicles*—that play a part in full sexual activity. The scrotal skin thickens and inside the testes—the pair of oval-shaped gonads, or sex glands— sperm are manufactured, accompanied by the formation of seminal fluid for their transport.

The development of a masculine physique in terms of build and musculature becomes apparent at this time, as the male sex hormones, like the growth hormone, help to build up protein and muscle. The skin also shows changes— the most obvious (and often troublesome) feature being that it become more oily and greasy. This stems from sebum production by the enlarged sebaceous glands. Too much sebum or too 'rich' a content tends to be associated with the skin complaint of *acne*, which is more common in adolescent boys than in adolescent girls.

With the active production of the male sex hormones, and the maturing of the sexual organs, the hormone and nerve link-up controlling sexual activity is completed in a physical sense. Boys become capable of erection of the penis and subsequently of ejaculation of the sperm in the seminal fluid. The sex drive is established in the maturing boy.

The onset of menstruation

The effects of oestrogen and progesterone in girls are also considerable. There is no real voice change parallel to that of boys, although some girls do have a slight deepening of the voice—presumably due to the androgens produced by the adrenal glands. An adult feminine appear-

HEIGHTS OF MATURING BOYS AND GIRLS

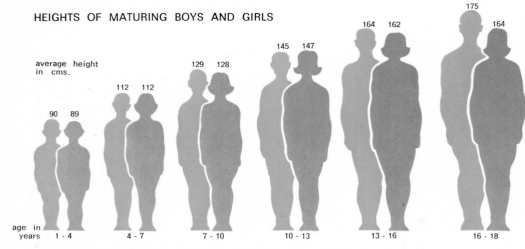

average height in cms.

										175	
						164	162				164
				145	147						
		129	128								
112	112										
90	89										

age in years   1 - 4   4 - 7   7 - 10   10 - 13   13 - 16   16 - 18

Above: Diagram showing the comparative rates of growth between males and females. Girls gain a few inches at the onset of puberty with which the boys catch up and surpass by late adolescence.

Left and below: Circumcision ceremonies. Circumcision, which removes all, or part, of the foreskin of the penis takes place in childhood in some societies—in Morocco, for example (below)—and at puberty—as in the Tanzanian group (left). The underlying motive is the same, however, in as much as it is an initiation ceremony. Circumcision may coincide with the biological transition from childhood to adulthood. Many theories have been advanced about its medical efficacy but there is little evidence that it is 'more hygienic' or that it improves the quality of sexual experience in adult life. It must therefore be seen as part of the religious life and rites of the traditional societies where it is still practised, such as in Judaism.

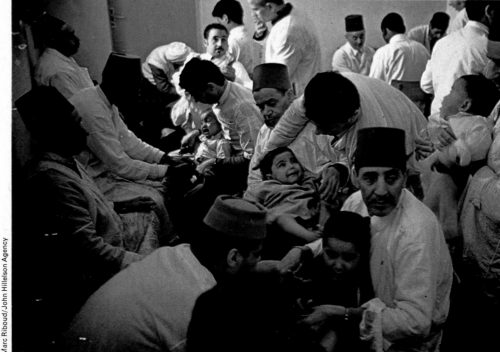

ance begins to take shape. The female shape of the pelvic bones becomes apparent. The breasts begin to grow and develop and the nipples also enlarge. Breast growth is rather uneven at first, giving a slightly assymetrical appearance to the pubertic breast outline, but the growth pattern usually evens out later on in adolescence. The degree of breast enlargement varies a good deal, not only due to the development of new tissue in the interior of each breast but also because of variable quantities of fat deposited in the chest wall.

Increased fat is also laid down in the face, abdomen, thighs and buttocks, helping to create the rounded contours which are seen as distinctively 'feminine' in established medical terms.

The growth of the bones just before puberty is gradually slowed down and usually completed within three years. The rising levels of oestrogen act against the effects of the growth hormone, and the special 'bone ends' or *epiphyses* of the long bones finally close, giving a fixed adult height.

In the genital area, the pubic mound, or *mons veneris*, enlarges beneath the growing pubic hair and the lips of the *vulva* or *labia majora* become much larger. In the inside, the vagina becomes larger and the *uterus*, or womb, also grows in size. The body portion of the uterus becomes functional, being primed by the oestrogen and progesterone hormones in turn. This hormone cycle affecting the quality and lining of the uterus eventually starts off the first *menstruation*, known as the *menarche*. This menarche generally appears in the 13th year, although it can occur as early as the 11th year or as late as the 16th year followed by a normal menstrual pattern. An adolescent who has not yet menstruated after her 16th year should be referred for medical advice. Menstruation is often irregular at the beginning of monthly cycles and no ova may actually be discharged in the early periods.

Oestrogen is responsible for the sheen and bloom of the youthful skin of adolescence and subsequent adulthood. Other hormone-producing glands in the body may be noticeably affected at puberty, although outside the 'sexual gland circle'. The thymus gland starts to wither away, while the thyroid gland in the neck may enlarge.

Once the ovaries start producing ova on a regular basis, and menstruation is properly established, the adolescent is physically mature for human reproduction. For a girl this means that sexual activity with a mature boy and the introduction of semen into the vagina, can result in conception. As with the pubertic boy, the completion of the hormone and nerve link-up to the brain sees the start of the female sex drive and sex interest though this is often more diffuse than in the pubertic boy who has a focal area of sexuality in his new penile function.

Ill-health, for example, anaemia or infection, can sometimes delay the onset of puberty. Disturbances of the endocrine system can also act as delaying factors, and these too may require investigation and treatment. Modern hormone therapy can substitute both male and female hormones where these are absent or insufficient, initiating puberty and helping to ensure subsequent physical and sexual maturation.

The progression from puberty to adolescence is a time of upheaval on many levels, characterised by emotional 'highs' and 'lows'. Society's attitude reflects these confusions – for instance, the British teenager can get a marriage licence before he can get a driving licence.

Roger Scruton

59

When Girl Becomes Woman

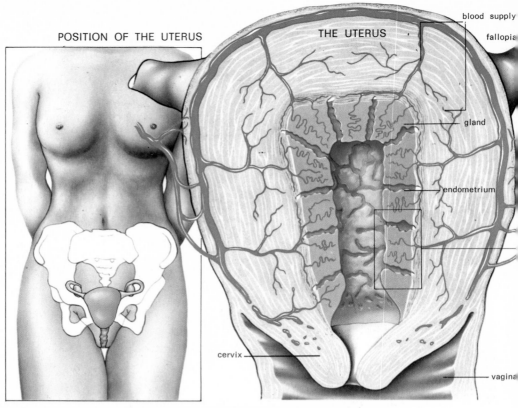

Menstruation generally starts some time after a girl's tenth birthday during the phase of development known as *puberty*. Puberty in the female child is a period of intense hormonal activity during which changes take place in her body, adapting her for the essential biological function of childbearing. By the time she has had her first menstrual period, however, she is not immediately fertile—she is not quite ready to accept and nurture the fertilized *ovum* or egg cell which grows into a new human being.

The first period

The first period is called the *menarche* and a preparatory period of two years follows it without ova being produced. During this time, a monthly cycle is established in which a discharge of mucus, cell fragments and blood is discharged from the *vagina*, the passage from the uterus to the vulva. This discharge is the result of the disintegration of the *endometrium* (endo meaning 'within' and metros, 'mother'), the lining of the *uterus* or womb which has been stimulated by the hormone *progesterone* into forming a thick layer with a special blood supply, ready to receive an embryo if the ovum becomes fertilized. If fertilization does not take place, the *corpus luteum* — the remains of the ovarian follicle which produces progesterone—withers. Deprived of progesterone, the lining is shed, leaving the surface raw. This bleeds for a few days, flushing out the discarded lining.

This monthly loss of blood, known as the *menstrual period*, occurs roughly every 28 days for the next 30 or 40 years of a girl's life. It coincides with the *ovarian cycle*, in which one of the many thousands of immature ova—already present in the ovaries, the sex glands, before a girl is born—is released. The ova are formed from the cells of the *germinal epithelium*, which pass from the surface of the ovary to the interior, where they acquire a primitive membrane or follicle.

The egg producing function of the ovaries is governed by the *pituitary* gland in the brain, which is controlled in turn by the *hypothalamus* lying above it. The pituitary gland releases chemicals called *hormones* into the bloodstream, and these hormones carry out two distinct tasks: they influence the development, or ripening, of an ovum in one of the ovaries, and stimulate that ovary into producing hormones of its own. These ovarian hormones effect the endometrium directly, and the result is that the lining of the womb is prepared to receive the fully developed egg cell in two stages.

The effects of hormone activity

The hormones produced by the ovary when stimulated by the pituitary are *oestrogen* and *progesterone*. The hormone oestrogen brings about the primary preparation of the womb lining, and its partner progesterone later completes this process. Meanwhile, the ovum has reached full maturity within the ovary, and about 14 days after the commencement of menstruation, bursts from its

blood supply

fallopia

gland

endometrium

cervix

vagina

Dave Kelly

Above: Diagram of the female pelvic area. It shows the location of the ovaries, the female sex glands, just above the pubic bone in the middle of the pelvis.

Above right: The uterus or womb showing the arrangement of vessels which supply it with blood. The uterus is a hollow muscle about the size of a duck's egg.

Left: The infundibulum, a group of finger-like projections at the mouth of the Fallopian tubes. They beat the fertilized ovum into the tube along which it travels to the uterus, where it implants itself.

Below: Cervical mucus on the 14th day, the first day of ovulation.

John Watney

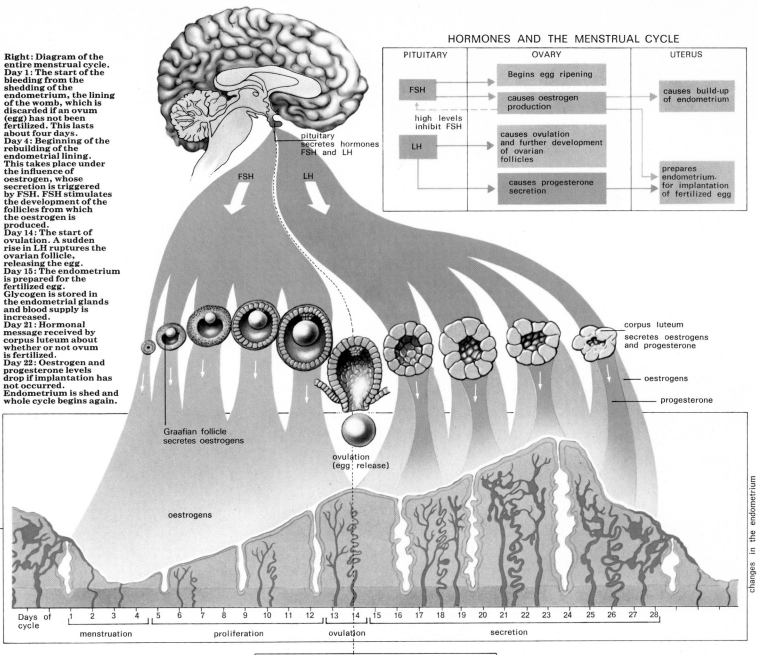

Right: Diagram of the entire menstrual cycle.
Day 1: The start of the bleeding from the shedding of the endometrium, the lining of the womb, which is discarded if an ovum (egg) has not been fertilized. This lasts about four days.
Day 4: Beginning of the rebuilding of the endometrial lining. This takes place under the influence of oestrogen, whose secretion is triggered by FSH. FSH stimulates the development of the follicles from which the oestrogen is produced.
Day 14: The start of ovulation. A sudden rise in LH ruptures the ovarian follicle, releasing the egg.
Day 15: The endometrium is prepared for the fertilized egg. Glycogen is stored in the endometrial glands and blood supply is increased.
Day 21: Hormonal message received by corpus luteum about whether or not ovum is fertilized.
Day 22: Oestrogen and progesterone levels drop if implantation has not occurred. Endometrium is shed and whole cycle begins again.

pituitary secretes hormones FSH and LH

FSH   LH

HORMONES AND THE MENSTRUAL CYCLE

PITUITARY	OVARY	UTERUS
FSH	Begins egg ripening	
	causes oestrogen production	causes build-up of endometrium
high levels inhibit FSH		
LH	causes ovulation and further development of ovarian follicles	
	causes progesterone secretion	prepares endometrium for implantation of fertilized egg

corpus luteum secretes oestrogens and progesterone

oestrogens

progesterone

Graafian follicle secretes oestrogens

ovulation (egg release)

oestrogens

changes in the endometrium

Days of cycle   1 2 3 4 5 6 7 8 9 10 11 12 13 14 15 16 17 18 19 20 21 22 23 24 25 26 27 28

menstruation   proliferation   ovulation   secretion

birthplace and starts out on its journey down the Fallopian tube to the womb. This is the part of the process known as *ovulation*.

The manufacture of the hormone progesterone by the ovary, however, is much more complicated than that of producing oestrogen. It is the ovary itself which must signal to the pituitary gland in the brain that progesterone is required, and the form that this signal, or message, takes is the bursting forth of the fully ripened ovum.

When the pituitary gland receives this signal, it immediately releases a return chemical signal to the ovary, which allows the ovary to manufacture progesterone. All of this is done under the guidance of the hypothalamus. So, as the ovum travels toward the womb, the hormone progesterone is released into the bloodstream, and by the time the ovum reaches it, the womb lining has become a moist bed of *endometrial cells* capable of supporting and nourishing it. However, this bed will be used by the ovum only if it is fertilized by a male sex cell.

The effects of hormone production by the ovary can also be seen during menstruation in the behaviour of the Fallopian tubes, which are connected to the upper

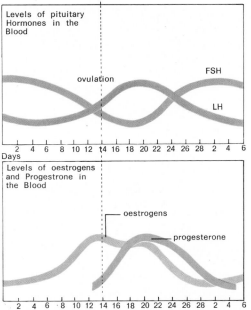

Levels of pituitary Hormones in the Blood

ovulation

FSH

LH

Days   2 4 6 8 10 12 14 16 18 20 22 24 26 28 2 4 6

Levels of oestrogens and Progestrone in the Blood

oestrogens

progesterone

2 4 6 8 10 12 14 16 18 20 22 24 26 28 2 4 6

Above: Graphs showing pattern of hormonal activity throughout a typical 28-day menstrual cycle. The top diagram shows the levels of FSH, which triggers the production of the ovum, and of LH which completes the process. Oestrogen and progesterone (bottom) prepare the endometrium for the fertilized ovum.

part of the uterus at one end and open into the abdominal cavity at the other. When oestrogen production is at maximum, the Fallopian tubes go through a series of contractions which help to transport the ovum, which cannot move on its own, to the uterus.

The linings of the tubes also become active and begin to secrete materials thought to be helpful in the fertilization and nourishment of the journeying egg. The probable fertilization of the egg is also assisted by the fact that during ovulation the cervical mucus at the neck of the womb becomes more fluid, so allowing easier penetration by the approaching spermatazoa. When the ovulation cycle is complete these activities gradually cease due to the domination of progesterone. The first stages of pregnancy are apparent, whether the ovum has been fertilized or not. So that, in effect, a woman becomes 'pregnant' once every month. However, if the egg cell remains unfertilized, it flows out through the neck of the womb along with the endometrial lining and brings the whole process to a stop. But at that very moment yet another egg cell is ripening in one of the ovaries, and the whole process is on the point of starting up all over again.

Left and below: The *menarche*, **the first menstrual period, is celebrated in some societies as** *initiation* **into womanhood, followed by complete acceptance into the rites and traditions of adulthood. Initiation takes many forms, however. For some groups, such as this Nigerian tribe (left) it is a public celebration of feasting with a special initiation dance. Other societies seclude their young women for up to two years, at the end of which they might undergo an initiation ritual. These pubertic Brazilian girls (below) emerge from seclusion with their faces covered by their hair, which is then cut to reveal their transformation into women.**

Bottom: The use of internal tampons, which absorb the flow of menstrual blood, has enabled modern women to lead fuller, less restricted lives.

There is not a day in the life of a woman when she is not subject, in one way or another, to the ebb and flow of hormonal influence directly related to the repetition of the menstrual cycle. During the menstrual period itself, swelling and tenderness of the breasts and abdomen, headaches, irritability and depression, not to mention lack of concentration and poor memory, may sometimes occur. Because many women are ignorant about the changes taking place in their bodies, they are apt to accept the charge—common among men in some societies—that women are over-emotional, or worse, illogical. Research has shown that, since hormones and emotions are strongly linked, this sort of attitude can cause *further* imbalance in hormonal secretion. Most women have experienced, at least once in their lives, a menstrual interruption due to great distress or over-excitement.

Biochemists are attempting to assess the exact amount of hormones circulating in the bloodstream during the menstrual

cycle, for the *dysmenorrhoea* from which between five and eight women out of every 10 suffer has been found to be more than 'merely psychological'.

Basically there are two types of dysmenorrhoea, 'spasmodic' and 'congestive'. On the whole they appear at two different stages of women's lives, although there are always exceptions. Spasmodic dysmenorrhoea is related to the first day of menstruation, and is described as acute colicky pains in the lower abdomen. This kind of pain dulls after a few minutes, then flares up again about twenty minutes later. The spasms may be severe enough to cause fainting or vomiting, and in many ways resemble labour pains.

Spasmodic dysmenorrhoea usually begins a year or two after the onset of menstruation, is most common in teenagers and rarely continues after pregnancy or the age of 25. As it seldom occurs during the first few menstruations at puberty, it is thought to be directly related to the process of ovulation.

Congestive dysmenorrhoea, on the other hand, is composed of pains which erupt prior to menstruation, and constitutes a kind of warning signal. This type of pain is often accompanied by nausea, lack of appetite and constipation, and is closely linked to pre-menstrual syndrome; it is usually found in women over 30. Both types may be caused by release of prostaglandins causing the uterus to contract painfully; antiprostaglandins like aspirin are an effective remedy.

The pre-menstrual syndrome

Pre-menstrual tension, which comes under the blanket title of the *Pre-menstrual Syndrome*, is still not fully understood. From available research, however, it seems that many of the symptoms are characterized by *water retention*—an accumulation of excess cellular fluid.

A good example of this is the marked rise in pressure which can result in the eye due to minute increases of its natural fluid. Such increases in pressure automatically lead to pain in the form of headaches. Similar rises in pressure due to water retention can cause tenderness of the breasts, aching sinuses, pain in the eyeballs, swollen ankles and a host of other annoying (and sometimes disabling) interruptions of daily life. But water retention does not account for all the symptoms which can occur.

The psychological effects of premenstrual tension, such as irritability, depression and lethargy, would seem to be brought about by *sodium retention* and *potassium depletion* in the cells. But the phenomena of fainting, sweating and general weakness which often occur, may very well be due to a drop in the level of blood sugar. The basic reason for this kind of imbalance throughout the system is thought to be the insufficient production of progesterone in the ovary. This insufficiency would cause the same hormone to be drawn from some other source, and as a result, upset the delicate balance of the body's whole metabolism.

Many studies have been carried out in recent years on the biochemical reasons behind pre-menstrual syndrome. One promising avenue of research is the use of low doses of progesterone (or the synthetic progestogen) in the second half of the menstrual cycle which restores the balance of oestrogen and progesterone in the woman's system.

The average age for the arrival of puberty is 13 years, although any age between 11 and 16 is regarded as normal. Improved physical health, better nutrition and greater exposure to artificial light have led to earlier puberty in children from more affluent countries.

Adolescence

Although *puberty* and *adolescence* are commonly regarded as synonymous, they are, in fact, different things. Both mark the transition from childhood to adulthood but each is a different part of the process. Puberty is the biological event which marks the physiological onset of adulthood. It has definite, observable stages—particularly in girls—and takes place within a particular period of time. Adolescence, on the other hand, is the name given to an indefinite period of development in which psychological and sociological changes take place in the maturing boy and girl. It has no observable beginning or end, and some of the problems arising from the adjustments which have to be made during adolescence may take many years to resolve.

In industrialized western countries especially, adolescence is the period which marks the maturing individual's search for identity. He is no longer a child, but he is not yet an adult. So what is he?

The physiological changes

The adolescent is subject to quite violent changes in his body, due to hormonal activity, which require a great deal of mental adjustment. His body image—his ability to understand the relationship of himself to the space around him—is no longer reliable. He is often clumsy and unco-ordinated; his arms and legs seem to be too long, because in a sense they are— he is going through a period of accelerated growth in height and weight.

Sexual maturity and increased awareness of his own and others' sexuality bring special problems for the adolescent. He must decide how to view his sexual impulses: does he see them as a natural part of growing up or is he shocked and upset at their strength? Almost all adolescents masturbate, but many suffer agonizing guilt because they are taught to believe the practice may harm them. Masturbation is a natural and normal activity which cannot cause any harm.

The adolescent boy or girl must also decide what his or her sexual behaviour with others should be. Should they strive for chastity? What rules should govern their sexual conduct? These are questions which may not be resolved even after a lifetime of questioning; but adolescents are so vulnerable to group pressures that many of them feel pushed into courses of action without having a chance to fully think out the consequences. Much of the talk of daring sexual exploits—a major topic of conversation among groups of adolescents—is the equivalent of the fisherman's 'one that got away'. Some members of the group may react with feelings of shame and inadequacy that they cannot match the reported feats of their friends; others may participate unwillingly in sexual activities, afraid of being the 'odd man out'.

This adolescent confusion is reflected in behaviour. As he reaches so impatiently for adulthood and self determination, the teenager can be assailed by doubts and uncertainties of his abilities to cope with the demands of maturity. He has not yet organized his experiences, thoughts and feelings into a consistent

Ian Berry/John Hillelson Agency

Raymond Depardon & Marie-Laure De Decker/John Hillelson Agency

Above: Two English teenagers on holiday in a popular seaside town. The slogan on their hats demonstrates both their new-found sexual awareness and their need to shock their elders into realizing that they are growing up—by being outrageous in their style of dress and in their unpredictable behaviour.

Below: Drum majorettes. A peculiarly American phenomenon approved of by the middle classes, in spite of the fact that, in some ways, it embodies some of the more negative aspects of adolescence—vanity, exhibitionism and extreme competitiveness. However, the drum majorette is also a symbol of patriotism

and order, and as such is upheld as a respectable ideal to which the adolescent should aspire.

Right: A Hell's Angel. Despite the fact that he flaunts society's orthodox codes he will adhere to the laws of his own subculture, which are just as rigid.

Above and right: Every generation of teenagers is fired by some political cause. Since adolescents are only just beginning to exercise their powers of thought and belief, they tend to see things in black and white terms. The Aldermaston marcher (above) was one of thousands protesting against Britain's nuclear defence programme. The fervour of the Red Guards, formed during China's Cultural Revolution, was deliberately employed by Mao to stamp out the traditional values of their parents.

pattern. So his behaviour can fluctuate between childish over-dependence and arrogant rebellion.

He may come to view all adults with the same jaundiced eye as he does the members of his family. He longs for certainty and security and yet is unconvinced of the wisdom of his parents and teachers. Only his peers, those in the same position as himself, offer shelter. Within the group, freed from childhood memories and family pressures, he can find the freedom to become truly himself. But since the other members of the group are likely to be similarly confused as to their status and identity, the group itself becomes all-powerful. It puts on its members even stronger pressures to conform to the group's standards than most family groups do. So to the adult, the adolescent presents a picture of aggressive nonconformity to society's norms of conduct—coupled with rigid adherence to the rules and norms of his own subculture or group.

Examination of these rules may illustrate the relationship of the subgroup to the larger culture within which it occurs. For example, some groups centred around the motorcycle have rituals akin to the marriage ceremony, but in which the bike's handbook takes the place of the Bible. Such a ritual, being a caricature of that of society as a whole, demonstrates the ambivalence of the smaller group toward its parent group. It is not genuinely free-thinking or independent; rather, its rules and rituals are distortions and travesties of those of the parent culture.

The search for autonomy

Along with this search for personal identity and autonomy, the typical western adolescent is striving to understand the nature of the world and of reality. According to the Swiss child-psychologist Jean Piaget, the adolescent is better able to theorize than the child. He is much less restricted by the given data—the concrete reality. He becomes able to suspend judgment and see that many interpretations of data are possible. He becomes aware that his family's way of living, his parent's ideas on morality, his country's policies, are not the only possibilities, and may not even be the best ones in the circumstances. Therefore the adolescent can find himself faced not only with the question 'who am I?' but with the unanswerable questions: 'what is Truth?' and 'what is Reality?' Often he

Above: The Hitler Youth Movement, an organization set up by Hitler to further the cause of the Nazi Party and to outlaw all non-Nazi movements for young people. Through the strict, physical, intellectual and moral training which they received, it was hoped to preserve the spirit of national socialism and Germany's future which rested on the shoulders of its young people.

Below right: Some societies have definite rituals marking off the passage from boyhood to manhood. This Jewish boy is undergoing his *Bar Mitzvah,* after which he will officially be recognized as a man.

Above: The annual Queen Charlotte's Birthday Ball, which, until recent years, marked the opening of London's *debutante* season. Young ladies over the age of 18 were said to have 'come out' at this event, that is, they were presented to aristocratic society as eligible for marriage.

Below: Teenagers travel miles and camp out in uncomfortable conditions to hear their idols play at pop festivals.

Right: Schoolboys from the 'King's College of Our Lady of Eton Beside Windsor' founded by Henry VI in 1440. These teenage boys, seen here during a rowing regatta on the river Thames, are educated as 'future leaders' of the British nation and as such are expected to conform to rigid principles and standards. Individuality is strongly discouraged even among the pupils themselves, who adhere to a hierarchical structure set by hundreds of years of tradition.

sets, with fiery and untempered indignation, the injustices of the world. He burns with untried, hence untarnished, desire to put things right.

Because of this urgent search for ideals and truth, adolescence for most is a time of upheaval on many levels, sometimes making the adolescent vulnerable to extraordinary forces. Some observers even see a connection between adolescents and poltergeists—forces, or 'spirits', which perform mysterious acts such as switching lights on and off, moving furniture or locking and unlocking doors. Poltergeists, they claim, nearly always appear in homes where there is a teenager in the family. Some investigators of the phenomenon think that a spirit, or 'force', is attracted by the upheaval of energy—particularly sexual energy—in the adolescent's body. Others think that the upheaval of energy allows the adolescent to perform a kind of *telekinesis*—to project energy into inanimate objects and make them move—and that it has nothing to do with any kind of external 'force'.

Adolescence can also be a time of religious and political fervour. The mob hysteria and individual devotion of pop fans, in some observers' view, are other aspects of the same type of experience. In many ways the 'worship' of pop idols appears to serve the same functions as religious or political ceremonies. There is the same sense of a common aim, a unity of purpose that transcends individualism and creates feelings of safety and security. In each case the adolescent is trying to find meaning and structure in his life through identification with, and participation in, a group. Star-worship, like gang membership, is usually strongest in early adolescence. Religious and political affiliations tend to become more prominent later on, as the individual exercises his developing powers of thought and belief.

However, a young person's ideas and values may crystallize during adolescence in such a way as to map out the course of his whole future life, or at least a significant portion of it. Decisions now about careers, vocations, political or religious commitments may rapidly propel him into a way of life from which it may be difficult for him to disentangle himself. It is therefore at this period that adequate guidance and support from parents, teachers and other adults can be most valuable.

The attitude of society
Most of the typical adolescent's confusion about himself, his identity and his codes of behaviour may be a direct reflection of western society's confused attitude towards him.

Even the ages at which he is considered to be capable of taking on certain responsibilities can be quite inconsistent. At 16, for example, a British teenager may marry and have children. But he cannot drive a car until he is 17, or even join a public library without someone else's sponsorship until he is 18. He may become a professional soldier, and begin learning the techniques of killing people, before he reaches 18, the age at which he can vote. But if he happens to be homosexual, he may not legally engage in sexual activity with another individual until he is 21.

If most western societies cannot decide at what age an individual becomes an adult, and make apparently random decisions about the ages at which he may assume different kinds of responsibility, then social scientists see it as inevitable that he will be confused. He is undergoing change on all levels: hormonal, physiological, sexual, cognitive and spiritual. If a society does not provide him with clear guidelines about his status, they argue, it is hardly surprising if the end result is a moody, changeable, restless and chronically dissatisfied young person.

Of all the factors which exert pressure on the potential adult, his society's attitudes may well play the biggest part. In many of the world's societies there are distinct events, rituals and tasks which differentiate childhood from adulthood. Before an individual goes through such a ceremony, the person is a child, with the expectations and experiences of childhood. Through the ceremony the individual is initiated into adulthood and accorded the full status, duties and rights of adulthood in that society. Among westernized cultures an equivalent function is performed by, for example, the *Bar Mitzvah* of the Jews. This religious ceremony takes place in a boy's 13th year and celebrates his attainment of manhood.

In cultures where there are clear boundaries between childhood and adulthood, it seems the phenomenon of 'adolescence' is almost unknown. A boy becomes a man and joins the men; a girl becomes a woman and joins the women. The concept of the teenager as part of a separate group exists only in cultures where there are anomalies in the various roles he or she is expected to fulfil. In Western Europe and North America, for example, it is possible for a 17-year-old to wield considerable economic power in terms of earnings but to have no political power because he is not entitled to vote.

So not only does teenaged youth find itself questioning the society's values, but it is also constantly exposed to the changes taking place within society as a whole. Traditional values are being challenged and discarded continuously. Broader and more widespread education and the greater availability of the means to travel (not only within one country but all over the world) have made the twentieth century a time more than any before it marked by instability, change and revolution. Given such a global situation, the adolescent faces a formidable task. He has to decide what kind of person he wishes to become, what kind of life he wishes to lead, and what kind of society he wishes to work towards. This is a lifelong task, and adolescence is just the beginning of the journey towards it.

67

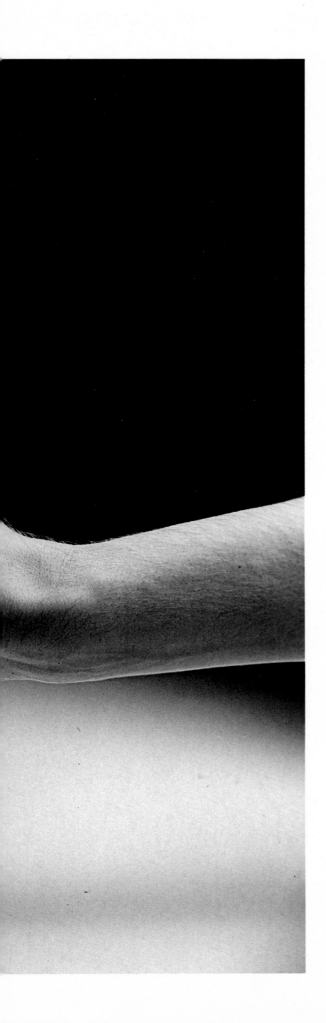

The Adult

Marriage, like other social institutions,
modifies adult behaviour by requiring
partners to maintain a balance
between individuality and the rights
of others.

Adulthood

An adolescent is generally defined as a young person in the process of passing from childhood to adulthood or maturity. But what is this state known as adulthood to which the child is expected to pass? And what guarantee does she or he, or indeed, society as a whole, have that the person will necessarily be mature when they reach it?

The state of adulthood is difficult to define. The man who runs no risks, who keeps himself out of trouble, who is never upset by changes of fortune or by the attitudes of those around him—is he necessarily a more mature person than the artist who feels so strongly about life that despair tempts him to end it?

An example of the dangers of generalizing on what is, and what is not, maturity is the Russian novelist Dostoevsky. He was a compulsive gambler, arrogant and self-pitying—but is still regarded as a genius by literary critics, historians and even some psychiatrists. His novels show a penetrating insight and understanding of human nature. So how, on the evidence of his private life, can he be called emotionally immature? Similarly, should the sustained and forceful ambition necessary, say, to take an American politician through the rigours of campaigning for the Presidency be considered as a product of emotional maturity—or as neurotic drive?

In most societies, a set of rules governing the behaviour of an adult person exists. But the ages at which the individual is allowed to enter fully into the various rights and duties of adulthood can vary, even within one country, so that even when a society sets out laws to which the individual is expected to adhere, these laws—and this is especially true of, for example, English society—may indicate to the individual only what he *cannot* do, rather than what he *can*. Adulthood, therefore, is not a definitive state, but rather a concept or ideal which exists within a particular society. During the 100 or so years which psychology has been in existence, many psychologists have been interested in this problem of whether there is such a state as adulthood, and, if so, how is it actually defined and by whom?

The individual and society

The complications of human life have always presented great challenges. One of the basic problems is how to maintain a balance between behaviour in an individual level and the effect that it has on society. In other words, certain needs and drives which are distinctly human affect not only the individual's life but also the lives of others. Although behaviour may be both natural and human, it may have to be modified or regulated so that its actual effect on the whole society is beneficial, rather than detrimental, to society's other individuals.

Psychologists have observed throughout many years of study that what is considered 'adult' may vary from society to society. Polygamy, an accepted custom in some parts of the world, is forbidden elsewhere. Practices accepted in one period of history may be challenged in later eras. Caning children as a means of

Above and below: Adults in most societies are expected to adhere to a particular code of conduct. The cult of *machismo*—the belief that a man must behave in a certain fashion in order to be a man—predominates in some Mediterranean countries. The *macho* must defend his family's honour and conduct himself with dignity. Although basically the idea of a macho is one who is 'his own man', the importance of masculinity is exaggerated. The transvestites (below) would be regarded by the macho as a travesty of manhood and an insult to women, whose virtue and purity must be protected.

Sunday Times

Constantine Manos/John Hillelson Agency

Mark Godfrey/John Hillelson Agency

Left and below: In most societies adult behaviour is supposed to be self-regulated, but there are generally laws which keep it within certain limits. Those responsible for enforcing the laws may not necessarily have made them. The English judges (left) are part of the formal legal system typical of most

democratically ruled countries, in which power is distributed among different authorities. In societies ruled by dictatorship, on the other hand, absolute power is assumed by the ruler (below). He may not only ignore existing laws and introduce new ones, but may also openly disregard his

own laws while expecting everyone else to obey them. In effect he may be behaving in an 'un-adult' way.

Above: The 1976 American Democratic Convention. Adult members of a democracy have the right to participate in the choosing of their leaders.

discipline was widely accepted in England as normal, adult behaviour until very recent years. Yet today it is increasingly condemned both by teachers and psychologists; and in some countries it has always been considered barbaric.

If adolescents growing up in industrialized Western societies have difficulties in coming to grips with what seem to be conflicting ideals and standards, there are many institutions which can attempt to guide and assist them towards adulthood. They include the family, the education system, the church and the state.

Some of these institutions express directly to the potential adult the ways in which his behaviour will be modified by them; others attempt to redirect it into serving the needs of the group through example.

Criteria of adulthood

An attempt to summarize the observations of the many psychologists who have studied the overlap between an individual's behaviour and the expectations of the social group with which he interacts was made in 1967 by the British psychologist Dr Abraham Sperling. Western society, he found, had eight criteria for adulthood: heterosexuality; independence of family; emotional maturity; social maturity; economic independence; intellectual capability; productive use of leisure; and a coherent view or philosophy of life. Dr Sperling suggested that society expects a mature adult to adhere to these requirements throughout his or her life, and that the outcome will be a balanced and objectively sane individual capable of contributing something of worth and importance to society as well as fulfilling their own personal needs.

However, these eight criteria represent an ideal. Few 'adults' can actually measure up to all of them but none can be considered in isolation. People are unlikely to become emotionally mature unless they develop the coherent *overview*, or philosophy of life, which provides them with a frame of reference to which

John Hillelson Agency

Burk Uzzle/John Hillelson Agency

John Hillelson Agency

Left and above: Modern industrialized societies have become so large and complex that some of its members feel alienated and attempt to provide alternatives. Both the young 'drop-out' (above) and the Ku-Klux-Klan member (left) are attempting to protect certain beliefs or moral values. The KKK member belongs to a secret society which evolved into a political group whose main preoccupation is to prevent the integration of black Americans into a white, mainly middle-class society. The 'drop-out', on the other hand, is part of a movement which feels that individual freedom is being eroded by the 'dehumanizing' effect of technology.

they can relate their behaviour and the behaviour of others. But such a coherent philosophy may not evolve if, for example, the young adult does not become independent of his parents and learn to become financially and emotionally dependable. Again, if his intellectual faculty remains at adolescent level, then it is extremely difficult for him to appreciate the meaning of social maturity or to use his working and leisure time productively and creatively.

The state of adulthood
Many psychologists summarize adulthood as a state of 'good adjustment'. The well-adjusted person, they consider, solves his or her personal problems with the same *objectivity* as that applied to impersonal problems. For example, he will attempt to evaluate an argument with a friend or relative in which he has been emotionally involved as impartially as he would a mathematical problem, in the conclusion of which he has no emotional investment. Then, to ensure that his view of the situation is realistic, he may check it against the opinion of someone who did not participate in the experience. He will then think out the best course of action possible, weigh up the immediate and

long-term results and, finally, act as vigorously and as wholeheartedly as possible.

If, however, his decision proves to be inadequate, he accepts that it was arrived at as honestly as possible from the information available to him at the time and is 'philosophical' about it—that is, he applies an over-view to the situation, accepting it as a lesson from which he can apply knowledge to future encounters of a similar nature.

An individual who is truly adult, therefore, can be said to be one who recognizes that he or she is obliged to conduct themselves in a way that does not hurt anyone else, rob them of human dignity, belittle anyone, or demand participation in actions distasteful to individual conscience. He or she also has the right to expect to be treated similarly by others.

Countless people, in fact, are unable to establish satisfactory relationships with other individuals or with society in general. Many psychologists would consider such people immature; although they never manifest signs of illness, they are unable to fulfil themselves as human beings. To maintain a satisfactory personal relationship in adult life, a person must be able to gratify the needs

of another and to be gratified by the other, to sense the partner's needs and to communicate with him or her. The relationship must include an understanding which is prepared to demand less than perfection and which respects the other's differences. The mature individual, in short, must be able to see another person as a distinct individual—not just as an extension of his own needs and desires, or someone to be exploited in order to fulfill a personal ambition.

'Anti-social' behaviour
Behaviour which varies from what society regards as 'proper conduct', however, may still be regarded as 'adult' by a large number of people. Like all living organisms, a society is made of entities at different stages of growth and development. What one section of a society is only just learning to understand, another has already assimilated and superseded. It has a broader conception, therefore, of the consequences of a given action, event or attitude.

Often, too, extremes of social behaviour, though anti-social in themselves, provide the members of a society with a clearer view of its values and may even provide it with a new sense of direction. Football 'fans' who go on the rampage after a match, beating up rival supporters and wrecking trains and shops, are certainly showing signs of immaturity; but they are also highlighting a weakness, or even illness, in the society which produced them.

An adult person learns how to deal with society's apparently, or actually, conflicting attitudes. He learns how and when to 'toe the line' and behave in a prescribed manner, but he also learns when to 'stick his neck out' and take risks. For a mature person realizes that exploration and discovery are integral ingredients of human nature. They not only require individual expression but also keep society alive and healthy, supplying a mature framework within which its future adults can live a harmonius and productive life.

72

Adolescents coming to maturity in Western societies are confronted by apparently conflicting standards and ideals.

They may wish to 'drop out' of society, at the same time acquiring supposedly 'adult' habits such as drinking alcohol.

Contraception

Contraception is used by couples who wish to engage in sexual intercourse, but wish to prevent pregnancy. The idea of contraception is not new. As early as the nineteenth century BC Egyptian women were mixing honey, natron (sodium carbonate) and crocodile dung to form a vaginal contraceptive paste as a deterrent to conception. Other early references mention the use of various fruit acids, peppermint juice, rock salt and alum. Since such acidic, alkaline or salt solutions are hostile to sperm, these early 'recipes' probably did have some effect in limiting conception, although their reliability must have been highly suspect.

There are now many ways in which pregnancy can be effectively prevented. These can be broadly categorized into five classes: the natural methods; barrier methods; intra-uterine devices (IUDs); oral contraceptives; and sterilization.

Natural methods

The two natural methods of birth control are the rhythm or 'safe period' method and *coitus interruptus*. The biological basis for the rhythm method was not discovered until the 1930s, when two independent research workers showed that ovulation occurs about 14 days after the beginning of the previous menses. For women who have regular 28-day menstrual cycles, abstinence from intercourse three days before and three days after the predicted time of ovulation may prove a successful method of birth control. However, if a woman's cycles do not occur with complete regularity and vary from say, 26 to 31 days, only 12 to 18 days per cycle (including the period of menstruation) would be safe for intercourse.

The second natural method, *coitus interruptus*, involves interrupting sexual intercourse before the man ejaculates. Although this is still widely practised, it is often difficult to predict the correct time of withdrawal, and some sperms can be released before ejaculation proper. It has a high risk factor.

Barrier methods

Barrier contraceptives are those which prevent the viable sperm either from entering the vagina or from reaching the uterus, leaving them unable to 'swim' up the fallopian tubes and fertilize an ovum. They include the male sheath or *condom*, the female *diaphragm* (or 'Dutch cap') and vaginal *chemical contraceptives*.

The earliest condoms were made of animal intestines, silk and other materials and were used mainly as prophylactics against venereal disease. Their production, however, was minimal until the introduction in the mid-nineteenth century of the rubber condom. Strict quality controls on flaws and strength have been enforced in many countries and nowadays the thin rubber condom has become a reliable contraceptive device. The condom is unrolled over the erect penis before intercourse, and disposed of afterwards.

Whereas the condom prevents sperm entering the vagina, the diaphragm prevents the released sperm from reaching the uterus. It is a rubber cap which fits snugly between the pubic bone and the

Left: Casanova, the eighteenth-century Italian lover, is known to have used condoms as contraceptives. His procedure for testing for leaks was something of a party piece.

Above: Family planning posters in Pakistan emphasize the heavy economic burden carried by the man with a large family, in an effort to control the country's population 'explosion'.

Right: Marie Stopes was a pioneer in promoting contraceptive methods, especially the use of diaphragms and caps by women, and she set up an advice clinic in London in 1921. Her ideas on contraception and other sexual matters were highly controversial, but her books helped to change society's views on sex and the need for contraceptives.

Below: The campaign to reduce the numbers of unwanted babies being born in the 1960s and 1970s included posters such as this one in Britain, whose target was the male who takes inadequate contraceptive precautions, or none at all. The Family Planning Association estimates that 200,000 unwanted pregnancies occur every year in Britain. Many of these pregnancies are aborted, and some of the unwanted babies born are adopted.

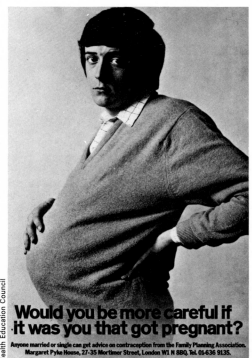

Would you be more careful if it was you that got pregnant?

Anyone married or single can get advice on contraception from the Family Planning Association. Margaret Pyke House, 27-35 Mortimer Street, London W1 N 8BQ. Tel. 01-636 9135.

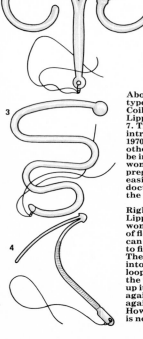

Above and left: Some types of IUD. 1. Saf-T-Coil. 2. Copper T. 3. Lippes loop. 4. Copper 7. The last-named was introduced in the early 1970s and unlike many other IUDs, can be inserted even if a woman has never been pregnant. IUDs can be easily removed by a doctor who merely tugs the attached threads.

Right: Insertion of a Lippes loop into the womb. The loop is made of flexible plastic and can be straightened out to fit into a syringe. The syringe is inserted into the cervix and the loop ejected. Once in the womb, it takes up its natural form again, fitting securely against the womb walls. How IUDs actually work is not precisely known.

74

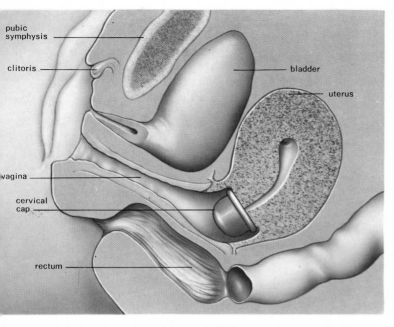

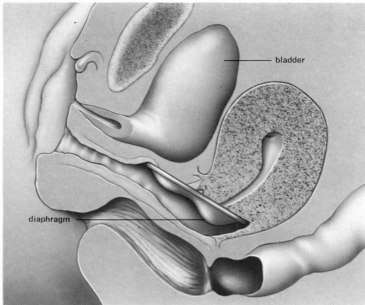

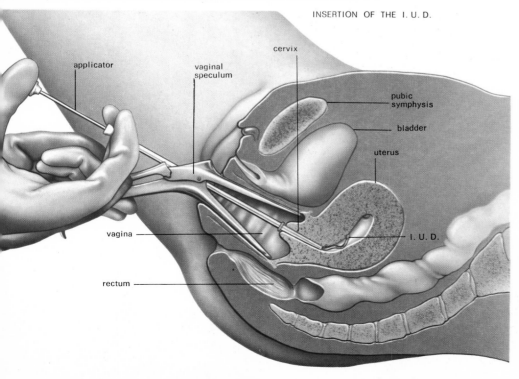

INSERTION OF THE I.U.D.

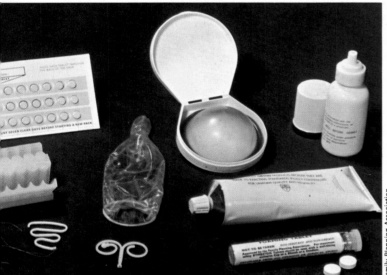

Family Planning Association

Above left: A cervical cap in place. In order to block sperm from entering the womb, the cap must fit the cervix closely and securely. Thus, the cervix must be long, parallel-sided, healthy and readily accessible, if a cervical cap is to be fitted.

Above right: The Dutch cap or diaphragm is the largest of the caps. It can be obtained in sizes between 50 and 100mm in external diameter. It is made of soft rubber and fits across the vaginal vault, shielding the cervix from direct insemination. The Dutch cap should be used only with a spermicide and must be left inside the vagina for at least six hours after intercourse.

Left: An illustration of the relative sizes of some contraceptives. A couple usually choose the device they find the most comfortable and convenient to use.

back of the vagina and covers the cervix (the entrance to the womb).

Before the wide distribution of oral contraceptives and IUDs the diaphragm was the most effective contraceptive for women. Other types of uterine barrier include the *cervical cap* and the *vimule*, although their use is not as widespread.

Vaginal chemical contraceptives or spermicides have been in use for thousands of years. Today's creams, jellies or suppositories are made of a relatively inert base material, which physically blocks sperm, plus an active spermicidal agent which chemically immobilizes or destroys sperm. Their failure rate is relatively high, however, unless they are used in conjunction with either a condom or a diaphragm.

Intra-uterine devices

An almost infinite variety of intra-uterine devices (IUDs) are now available in different parts of the world—rings, loops, spirals, coils, Novagard devices, Copper T's, Copper 7's—all shapes and sizes. These small devices, ranging from just under 1in to 3in (2-7cm) in length or diameter, are inserted into the uterine cavity. Some of these devices can be used both by women who have had previous pregnancies and by those who have never conceived. IUDs have, over the years, proved to be quite reliable contraceptives, though how they work is not precisely known. Some women find menstrual flow to be increased, and IUDs do slightly increase the chance of contracting a pelvic infection. Another problem is that of involuntary expulsion of the device which, if unnoticed, can lead to pregnancy. But cervical threads, or 'tails' (made from synthetics, most often polypropylene or polymer) attached to the IUD can be used to check that the IUD is in place.

Oral contraceptives

Oral contraceptives, commonly known as 'the pill', were first marketed in the 1960s. As early as 1945 the potential of sex steroids in preventing pregnancy had been foreseen but it was not until 1956 that large-scale clinical trials to test their effectiveness and side actions were undertaken in Puerto Rico.

The pill contains the hormones oestro-

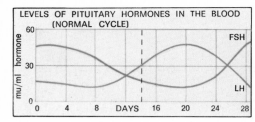

LEVELS OF PITUITARY HORMONES IN THE BLOOD (NORMAL CYCLE)

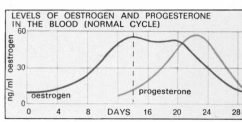

LEVELS OF OESTROGEN AND PROGESTERONE IN THE BLOOD (NORMAL CYCLE)

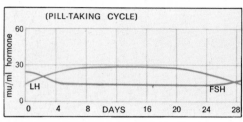

(PILL-TAKING CYCLE)

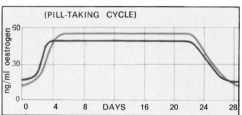

(PILL-TAKING CYCLE)

Syntex Pharmaceutical

Left: Variation in blood hormone levels during normal cycle and pill-taking cycle. Variations during the normal cycle in the levels of oestrogen and progesterone act on the pituitary to change the levels of LH and FSH, and this triggers ovulation. During pill taking, oestrogen and progestogen levels are kept at a constant high level, and this acts on the pituitary to level out the secretion of LH and FSH. Thus ovulation does not occur.

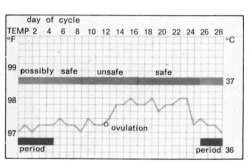

Above: The mexican yam, *Dioscoreus composita*, a steriod extract of which is used as the basis for the synthesis of potent progesterone analogues, used in the pill.

Left: Some women find that ovulation can be detected by changes in body temperature. A drop in temperature occurs at ovulation and is followed by a rise. This can form the basis of the 'rhythm method', in which intercourse is avoided around ovulation.

gen and progesterone. These are also produced naturally by the ovaries, acting on the pituitary gland to produce a surge of the gonadotrophin hormones LH (luteinizing hormone) and FSH (follicle stimulating hormone), which trigger ovulation. When the pill is taken for 21 days of the menstrual cycle, the oestrogen and progesterone are maintained at a constant high level, and as a result the gonadotrophin surge does not take place. Thus ovulation is not triggered, and without an ovum, pregnancy cannot occur.

The first pills to be marketed contained high doses of oestrogen and progestogen (synthetic progesterone), but levels of these have now been reduced to avoid side-effects. Some women taking the pill may suffer such things as nausea, dizziness or headaches, but these often disappear after a couple of months. They may also be alleviated by changing to another brand of pill.

Taking the pill means introducing strong steroids into the body which can have a wide range of effects. These effects can take as long as 20 years to show themselves, and research into them continues on a world-wide basis. It is now thought that the pill is best used by women under the age of 30 who do not smoke (circulatory disease is five times more likely if a pill-taker smokes), and has been shown to provide some protection against cancer of the uterus and ovaries. On the other hand, it has been implicated in increases of cancer of the cervix and breasts and in strokes and heart disease.

Another form of oral contraceptive is the *minipill* which contains only progestogen. It is not as widely used because it is less effective than the combined oral contraceptives and produces a higher incidence of breakthrough bleeding and other menstrual irregularities. However, minipills can be used by women who require oral contraception but who are lactating or who should avoid oestrogens for other reasons.

Sterilization

Sterilization is an extremely effective method of contraception because it is permanent. It can be performed by a surgeon on either men or women. In men, the sperms are prevented from leaving the testes, where they are formed, by cutting and tying the *vas deferens*, along which they must pass from the testes to the penis. The operation, *vasectomy*, is normally irreversible, although in certain cases the vas deferens may be rejoined. In women, the surgeon closes the Fallopian tubes along which the egg cells must pass in order to reach the uterus. This operation usually requires a few days in hospital. It is also normally irreversible.

Neither operation results in any loss of sexual drive or performance. With vasectomy, a complete absence of sperm in the semen does not occur immediately, because some sperm still linger in the genital tract below the block. These have to be emptied out by repeated ejaculation, which may take several months, during which time other contraceptive precautions are necessary. Female sterilization, on the other hand, takes effect immediately, since a woman normally produces only one egg during each monthly cycle. Because of its irreversible nature, sterilization is normally performed only on one partner of a couple who have decided they do not want further children.

Abortion

Abortion is not strictly a form of contraception, since it refers to the termination of a pregnancy as opposed to its prevention. An abortion is normally carried out by a gynaecologist after approval by a doctor. The procedure is safer and easier the earlier in pregnancy it is done. If a pregnancy is no more than 12 weeks old, it is usually terminated through the vagina, by one of two main methods. The newest method, *vacuum aspiration*, involves inserting a suction catheter through the cervix and sucking out the womb contents.

If a pregnancy is no more than 16 weeks old, termination may be done by dilation and evacuation (D&E) under a general anaesthetic. For a late termination, drugs may be injected into the uterus, causing it to contract and expel the foetus.

Relative effectiveness

The effectiveness of each method of contraception has been evaluated in a variety of studies, but the results do not always agree. Oral contraceptives and sterilization have been found to be the most effective, followed closely by IUDs. Condoms and diaphragms provide reasonably reliable protection. The highest failure rates are among users of spermicides (alone) or natural methods.

There is continuing conflict between religious beliefs on the rights and wrongs of using contraceptives. But today's social and economic pressures are making their use more widespread than ever before.

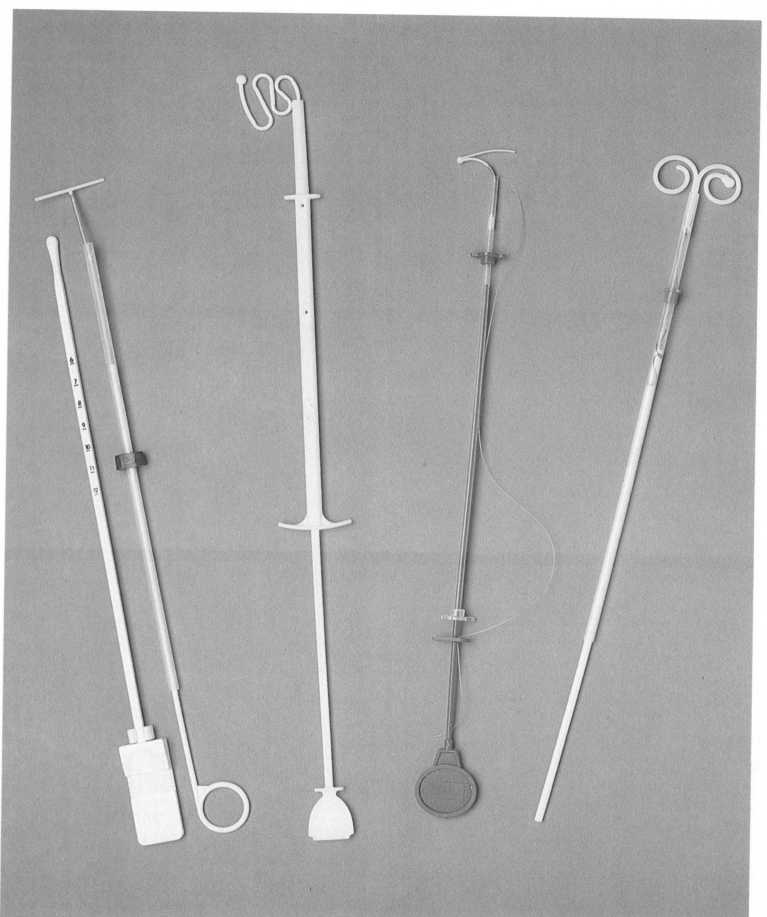

Modern intrauterine devices have revolutionized contraception. As shown (left to right): an intrauterine sound, a probe to measure the direction and depth of the uterus when inserting an IUD; the Copper T, Lippes Loop, Copper 7 and Saf-T-Coil.

Pregnancy

For a woman, the bearing and delivering of a baby can be a richly satisfying experience. The process, however, involves complex and interrelated bodily changes, some physical and some psychological. They do not end with delivery, and often the woman's physical and psychological balance does not return to normal for a year afterwards, especially if she breastfeeds her baby. It is not precisely known in what way many of these changes are brought about, and they become all the more confusing because some changes are undergone by certain women but not others, and even in the same woman different pregnancies may follow different courses.

The course of pregnancy falls into three periods, called *trimesters*, of about three months each. Broadly, each trimester produces its own group of bodily changes, though some changes may occur during any period. Sometimes a woman will feel sensory and emotional changes long before any overt physical changes have occurred. She may notice an odd metallic taste in her mouth, or suddenly dislike the taste of beverages such as coffee which she had previously enjoyed. Her reflexes may become sluggish, judgement impaired and mood variable between irritability, tears and excitement. The woman may easily become tired and depressed, however pleased she is about being pregnant.

The first trimester

The first physical symptom of pregnancy is usually that the menstrual period fails to occur on the expected date. Marked changes in the breasts also take place very early in pregnancy, involving a rapid increase in size together with feelings of fullness, tenderness and tingling in the nipples. The hormones oestrogen and progesterone, produced first by the mother's body and later by the placenta, and possibly others such as prolactin, cause these breast changes by stimulating growth of the milk sacs and ducts, increasing the flow of blood to the breasts and encouraging the storage of a cushion of fat around the milk apparatus.

Feelings of nausea, and sometimes actual vomiting, occur in about one-half of pregnant women. They vary in intensity, and may happen at any time of the day although 'early morning sickness' is most frequent. The cause is obscure but thought to be a reaction to the sudden increase in blood hormone levels. These discomforts usually disappear by the end of the first trimester.

In early pregnancy the kidneys, too, often become over-efficient. The bladder fills with urine more quickly, and the woman frequently needs to pass water. This discomfort disappears by about the twelfth or fourteenth week, only to reappear for different reasons in the last weeks of pregnancy. Constipation is common in early pregnancy, and is due to the action of progesterone which reduces the movements of all smooth muscles such as the gut and the uterus. A similar relaxing effect on the muscles which guard the entrance to the oesophagus from the stomach may allow food and stomach juices to be regurgitated into the oesophagus, especially after a large meal.

Above: Diagrams of a pregnant woman. Each stage of pregnancy is accompanied by changes in the mother-to-be's appearance, outward indications of the development of the baby in her uterus. Pregnancy is divided into three periods known as *trimesters*. The first is from the beginning of the last menstrual period to the 14th week, the second from the 15th to the 28th week and the third from the 29th to the 40th week, around which time the baby is delivered.

Top right: The uterus, or womb, must enlarge to accommodate the developing foetus, which grows from an almost invisible cell to a 6-8 lb infant. It increases in capacity by up to 500 times its pre-pregnancy size. The muscle fibres of the uterus may elongate up to 10 times their normal size, and to prevent the walls from becoming too thin, new muscle fibres may develop to give extra strength and support. After delivery, the uterus can 'shrink' back to its original size within six weeks.

Werner Forman Archive

1½ months

4 months

5½ months

Alphabet & Image

Left and above: Embryology was not established as a science until after 1827. The 19th century drawing from a door in New Guinea (left) and the 16th century woodcut (above) are two earlier attempts to depict the position of the foetus in the womb.

Since the stomach juices consist mainly of hydrochloric acid, this may result in heartburn and unpleasant indigestion. Since levels of progesterone increase throughout pregnancy, these changes caused directly by the hormone tend to persist.

The second trimester

For the pregnant woman the second trimester is often very pleasant. The expectant mother's condition becomes more obvious to the outside world as the growing foetus swells the uterus and pushes out her abdomen. Most of the discomforts of early pregnancy disappear once the pregnancy is well established. Feelings of extreme vitality and well-being are common and the woman in mid-pregnancy is frequently said to have a

special 'glow'. Her hair may become thicker and glossier, and her skin may seem smoother and healthier because of the increased blood flow. The foetus, via the placenta, requires such a large supply of blood that the mother's blood volume is increased by 40%. Circulation of maternal blood is improved in two ways, by an increase in the number of heartbeats per minute and also by an increase in the amount of blood pumped out by each beat. Darkening of the skin often occurs, especially around the nipples, as a 'butterfly mask' on the face, or as a thin line from the umbilicus down to the pubic hair. All of these pigmentation changes return to normal after delivery, except that the nipples often remain slightly darker than before.

During the second trimester the woman

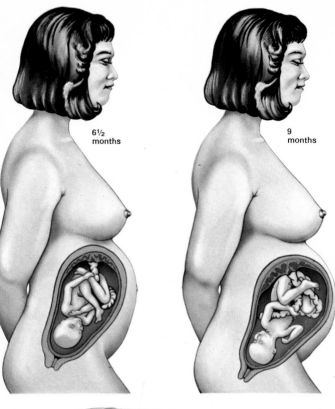

6½ months

9 months

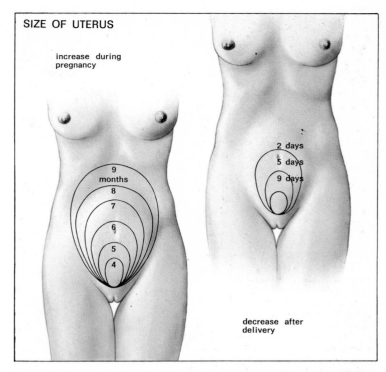

SIZE OF UTERUS

increase during pregnancy

9 months
8
7
6
5
4

2 days
5 days
9 days

decrease after delivery

THE PLACENTA

placenta

us

umbilical cord

amnion

wall of uterus

basal layer of endometrium

maternal blood

chorion

rnal artery

maternal vein

cervix

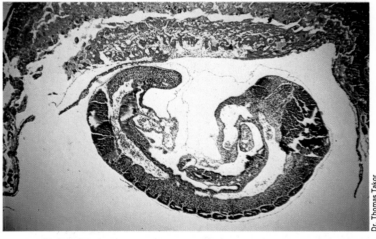

Dr. Thomas Takor

Left: The placenta, the organ of respiration, nutrition and excretion which develops from the embryo's outer layer of cells. Dissolved oxygen and nutrients diffuse from the mother's blood into the infant's bloodstream; carbon dioxide and other waste products pass from the infant to the mother for excretion.

Above: The stage of development which this mouse embryo has reached can be seen from the number of somites present on the placenta. Each of the somites—the bead-like blocks on the outer surface of the placenta (bottom)—is a group of cells which will later be specialized into muscle, bone or nerve.

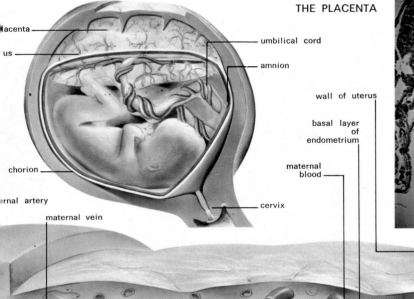

trophoblast

foetal blood vessels

two foetal arteries

Wharton's jelly

foetal vein

umbilical cord

usually feels her baby's movements for the first time. They are difficult to identify at first since the sensation is similar to that of wind or gas moving in the stomach, but by the twentieth week most women can reliably identify their baby's movements. These first movements are known as 'quickening' and it was once believed that the baby became alive only at this time. Later in the pregnancy, there is no problem in feeling the baby move, and the mother may find it difficult to get to sleep if her baby decides to get some exercise when she has gone to bed.

The third trimester

The third trimester of pregnancy, from the twenty-ninth week until delivery, mainly involves the mother's adjustment to the rapidly increasing maturity of her

79

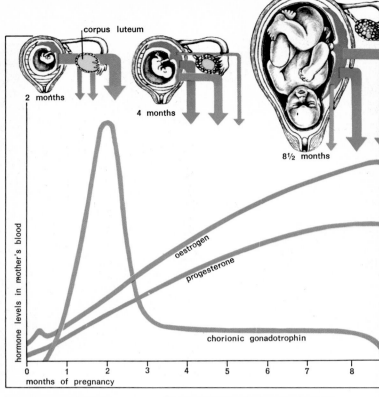

corpus luteum

2 months

4 months

8½ months

oestrogen

progesterone

chorionic gonadotrophin

hormone levels in mother's blood

months of pregnancy

0 1 2 3 4 5 6 7 8

John Watney

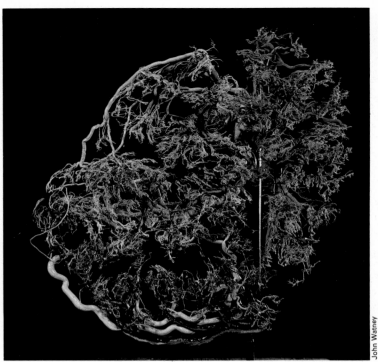

baby and her preparation for labour. Some of this preparation is mental. Even the normally alert and intellectually active mother may become increasingly placid and drowsy as pregnancy advances. Her clarity of thought and precision diminish. The focus of her interest turns inwards to the contents of her womb. She becomes forgetful of matters unconnected with the coming baby. The action of progesterone on the nervous system is thought to be the cause of these mental changes and after delivery the mother's usual powers of thought will return.

Progesterone also softens up muscles and ligaments throughout the body. This softening effect is directed at the pelvis, uterus and cervix, in order to make them more elastic for the birth. Unfortunately it also affects other ligaments such as those in the back. During the last ten weeks of pregnancy the lower part of the body of the uterus stretches and gradually enlarges in order to accommodate the baby's head. The cervix, which is firm and hard before pregnancy, rapidly becomes softer and gradually becomes larger as pregnancy advances. the canal of the cervix fills with a tenacious plug of thick mucous material the purpose of which is to prevent infection ascending from the vagina into the uterus.

Late pregnancy brings a variety of minor discomforts to the expectant mother. Her increasing bulk makes her feel clumsy and awkward and her feelings of tiredness and lassitude become strong. Pressure of the baby on her lungs, at one end, makes it difficult to breathe, and on her bladder, at the other end, elicits a frequent desire to urinate. A sudden upsurge of energy may be a signal that delivery is near. Some women at this time are seized by the 'nesting instinct' and feel compelled to scrub, clean and tidy everything in preparation for the baby who is soon to arrive.

Labour

Like pregnancy, labour falls into three stages, each of which has different characteristics. It is difficult to define

Above: This complex circulatory system was taken from the placenta of triplets. The arteries, which carried oxygenated blood to the three embryos, are stained blue, and the veins, carrying the deoxygenated blood, are red.

Top right: Apart from its main function as the foetus's organ of nutrition, excretion and respiration, the placenta also acts as an endocrine gland for the mother. Hormones that maintain the pregnant state are produced by the corpus luteum—the small body which develops from the follicle from which the ovum erupts in the ovary— until the placenta develops.

Eve Arnold/John Hillelson Agency

THE UMBILICAL CORD

sheath

Wharton's jelly

umbilical vein

umbilical arteries

before birth

at birth

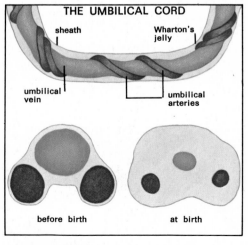

Above: The umbilical cord connects the unborn child with its placenta. It is made up of two arteries twisted around a vein, surrounded by a clear material known as Wharton's jelly. Before birth the blood vessels are distended by the blood flow which passes through the cord at the rate of four

miles per hour. The speed of the blood flow prevents kinking and knotting in the cord. Immediately after birth, the cells of the jelly-like coating swell up, constricting the blood vessels and stopping the flow. The cord can then be cut near the baby's navel and the remaining stump withers and falls off.

Robert Harding Associates

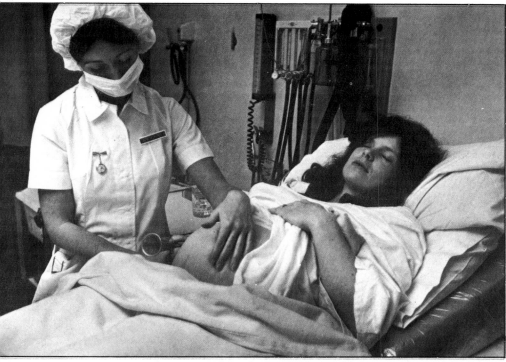

Emotionally, the end of the first stage is often a difficult time for the mother. She may feel drained and exhausted. It is not known what causes these feelings but fortunately they disappear when the second stage is well established.

The second stage of labour lasts from the time of full cervical dilatation until the moment the baby fully emerges. It rarely lasts more than two hours. During this stage, the uterus probably produces stronger contractions than any other human muscle is capable of. The contractions occur once every two to three minutes and last for up to 100 seconds, but some women are able to relax between contractions to summon new energy. The mother feels an overwhelming desire to 'bear down', to actually push the baby out. By taking in a deep breath, tensing her diaphragm and pushing downwards with her abdominal muscles she aids the uterus in its work and significantly speeds up the whole process of birth.

The third stage of labour is the time between delivery of the baby and the expulsion of the placenta from the uterus. Contractions recommence shortly after the baby's delivery and within 20 minutes the placenta is expelled.

Changes after delivery

After childbirth changes continue to occur in the mother's body. Some of these changes are directed towards getting the mother's functions and systems back to their pre-pregnancy state. Some are directed towards the continuing care of the baby. During pregnancy, and for the first three days after delivery, the breasts produce a thick yellowish liquid, *colostrum*. This is rich in protein and antibodies, and provides all the baby's immediate needs. On the third and fourth day of the *puerperium* (time after delivery) the mother begins to produce milk and her breasts may become tender. As the milk supply stabilizes this symptom gradually disappears. Changes in the composition of the milk continue at least until the tenth day when it becomes mature human milk. At each stage the mother's breasts produce exactly what the baby needs.

Breastfeeding speeds up many of the processes by which the mother's body returns to normal, but retards others. For example, milk production delays the occurrence of menstruation so that conception is less likely, although by no means impossible, while a woman is breastfeeding. The baby's suckling also stimulates the release of a pituitary hormone, *oxytocin*, which causes the mother's uterus to contract and hastens its return to a pre-pregnancy size. This *involution* of the uterus is usually complete six weeks after delivery. During this time, the uterus sheds its lining and the blood from the site of placental attachment. This is gradually lost through the vagina rather like a prolonged menstrual period. The loss is known as *lochia*, and generally lasts for about three weeks.

Emotional changes during the puerperium, probably caused by the sudden enormous hormonal changes, may be strong. Nearly all women feel a little shaky and vulnerable, and may easily become weepy and upset. As the mother's hormonal balance gradually readjusts itself, however, her emotional equilibrium will return.

Far left, below left and above: Pre-natal care has improved in many parts of the world but the Brazilian Indian (below left) is still protected more by the supernatural than by antiseptics. The Zulu women (far left) are 'weighing in' at their pre-natal clinic. Most women in industrialized societies are content to give birth in sterile surroundings (above), although the demand for home births is increasing.

Left: A 14th century way of coping with the discomfort of pregnancy.

Right: Pregnancy has fascinated many artists. The art nouveau style of Gustav Klimt (1862-1918) gives the subject a romantic aura.

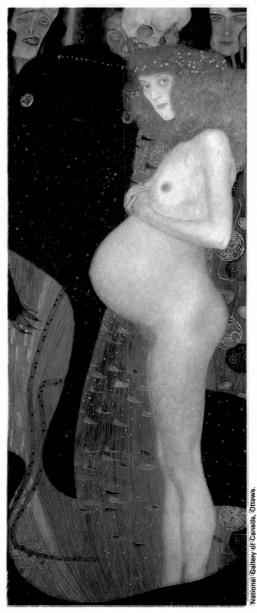

accurately at what point labour begins. Like all involuntary muscles, the uterus contracts regularly throughout life; the change from these mild contractions to the stronger ones of true labour is gradual and subtle. The woman may remain unaware of her contractions until the cervix has opened up enough to release its plug of mucus. This 'show' of thick, jelly-like substance, which may be blood-stained, indicates that labour has begun.

The first stage of labour lasts until the cervix has opened to its full extent. This *dilatation* of the cervix can last about 13 hours for a first birth, and about seven hours in subsequent ones. The contractions grow in regularity from once every 20-30 minutes to once every 3-5 minutes, and in intensity until each may last up to one minute. The mother's main task during this stage is to relax and to avoid tensing other muscles during the contractions. Unnecessary tension not only causes pain but quickly tires the mother. It also interferes with the functioning of the uterus by reducing the efficiency of its contractions, and in this way prolongs labour. Towards the end of the first stage, the amniotic fluid surrounding the baby gushes out through the vagina, and effectively sterilizes the birth canal.

The Mother's Role and Status

Procreation is the result of the urge to reproduce. Charles Darwin and several biologists who came after him have observed that this urge to ensure continuation is present in every species but, in the human species, whether or not it is present in every *individual* may be another matter.

Some of these same observers have noted that biological evolution has a modifying effect on all basic drives.

Animals have no influence over the direction their biological drives take—whether it be towards over-production, thereby exposing the group to shortage of food and space, or under-production, thus reducing their overall chances of survival —but human beings do. Regardless of what is necessary or vital for the human species as a whole, humans can choose to produce offspring or remain childless.

This has given rise to an interesting question in sociological terms—one with which some social scientists have been preoccupied for many years. Is there any longer such a thing as the *need* to procreate? In other words, has it, too, been modified by evolution so that a proportion of the human race no longer has this urge, thereby ensuring that the species will increase at a reasonable rate and not drive itself to extinction through over-population?

Nobody has tried to find an accurate answer to this question in the only way that might be feasible: to interview thousands of people scientifically selected to represent the whole population of the earth.

What most observers have done is to look at particular societies and their attitudes towards related aspects of the problem. For example, what is a society's attitude towards childbearing as a whole and maternity in particular? And does the society regard maternity as synonymous with womanhood, or separate from it?

Childbearing and maternity

In many societies, past and present, the pregnant woman and the mother and her newborn have been powerful symbols in art and religion. They represent eternal themes: the unity of life, the promise of renewal, the never-ending recreation of hope and potential.

In mythology the child is unspoiled and uncorrupted: and somehow this aura of wholeness is transferred to the mother-to-be and the new mother so that together mother and baby form a complete and perfect unit, above the hurly-burly of everyday life.

This fascination with maternity is by no means confined to humans. The work of Harry Harlow with rhesus monkeys— and of other primatologists such as Jane Goodall van Lawick with chimpanzees and baboons—shows that the response to a newborn infant is common to all of the higher primates. The mother's status in the group grows: both males and females pay her and her offspring a great deal of solicitous attention.

As the baby gets older the other adults lose interest in him, but the mother-child bond continues to grow in strength and endures for many years. Indeed, it is this relationship which forms the core of the animals' society. It is stronger than any other bond formed in the group—and the higher the place on the evolutionary scale, the stronger the mother-infant attachment.

The status of the mother

The earliest recorded religions also show the power of the mother. Early man in many societies worshipped a female deity or goddess who took many forms— Universal Mother, Earth Mother and Mother Goddess among them—all of which symbolized her regenerative or procreative power.

The initiates of these religions—the class which held the knowledge and power

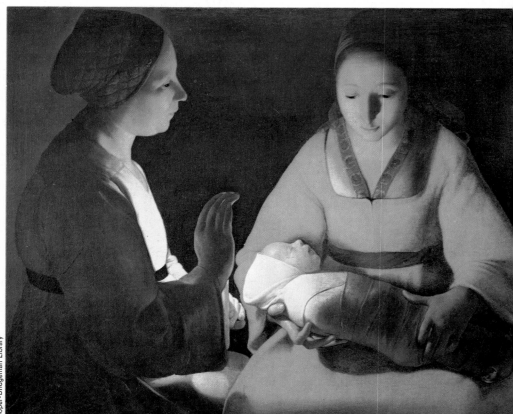

Left and below: Motherhood is regarded as the most essential feminine role in many societies, although attitudes towards mothers have often been ambivalent. The late 16th century painting by Georges de la Tour (below) conveys the simplicity, tenderness and purity he sees as incarnate in all mothers.

The engraving of a peasant woman by Pieter Bruegel, although almost contemporary with the painting, takes a grosser view of the mother's role as a child-rearer.

Above: Preparation for motherhood begins early through toys considered 'feminine' and therefore appropriate for girls.

82

Left: The 'Venus of Willendorf', a neolithic mother goddess figure in sandstone. The fecund, or fertile, aspect of woman is shown in the exaggeration of the breasts and belly. Some contemporary scholars believe— and have uncovered evidence to suggest— that the male priests of some early religious cults helped to tie women to their procreative role by encouraging fertility worship, so rendering women politically powerless.

Below: A wood carving from Northern Yorubaland, Nigeria, part of an altar panel of a fertility shrine.

of the religion—were female priestesses. It has often been assumed that these priestesses did not engage in sexual activity. In fact, 'vestal virgins' and 'temple prostitutes' were the same things, for the essence of the term which is now translated as 'virgin' (sexually inexperienced) originally meant 'not belonging to any man': the priestesses were nobody's property. Several writers interested in woman's position in society— for example, Dr Esther Harding in her book *Woman's Mysteries*—have noted that confusion over the very word 'virgin' may be responsible for the ambivalent attitude towards women which still persists in some Christian societies.

Inheritance of wealth and goods in these ancient societies was matrilineal (through the mother's line) and hence a person's social standing depended on who his mother was: his father's identity was not important.

Later religions, particularly Judaism and—later still—Christianity, worshipped a male deity and the initiates of the religion were men. The reasons why these societies became male-orientated are complex and difficult to assess. However, it has been suggested by some scholars—the American professor Merlin Stone and Dr Harding (a pupil of Dr C E Jung) among them—that the reasons may have derived from evolving property laws. Restrictions on a woman's sexual activity may have been introduced so that a man

Left: 'Suffragettes', depicted in a late 19th century French journal. Although the movement was sparked off by the publication of Mary Wollstonecraft's book

A Vindication of the Rights of Women in 1792, British women did not succeed in attaining the right to vote on equal terms with men until 1928.

Below: A creche in every commune allows mothers in the People's Republic of China to fulfil an equally valuable role as part of the work force.

could ensure that the children to whom he was to pass on his wealth and status or power were his own.

It has been argued that, in providing for their children in this way, women in these early societies sacrificed their independence and, consequently, their equal status with men. In some cases, as the laws became more complex and rigid, it even resulted in subjugation to the point where the entire female population was (and still is, in some Moslem societies) reduced to an inferior status with few, or no, political or social rights.

However, even under these conditions the power of the maternal bond is not completely lost. To the Christian, the Madonna and child symbolize love at its strongest and purest.

In a broad evolutionary and social context, attitudes to the process of child-bearing appear to be universal and un-altered by time. But does the overall view

Left and below: Not all societies have the kind of problems integrating male and female roles prevalent in industrialized countries. This young father from a Central American agricultural community (left) spends as much time looking after his infant son as his wife does. The Shipibo Indian mother (below) carries her baby around with her as she works, fulfilling her roles as mother and woman in a way that is useful to her society.

put forward by a society necessarily represent the feelings or beliefs of its members—and particularly its female members?

In the individual woman, the urge to bear children is a difficult characteristic to define. However, studies by Helen Singer Kaplan (recorded in her *Manual of Sex Therapy*) and by Masters and Johnson—pioneers of the clinical approach to sexual functioning—have established that the procreative urge is different from the sexual urge: only a small proportion of women regard the two as synonymous. In other words, few women, according to these observations, enjoy sex only when they are trying to conceive. But there is, nevertheless, some biological component in the desire for motherhood, or it would not persist.

One of the longest-standing controversies in scientific circles is that of *heredity* versus *environment*. The argument concerns the effects that each of them has on all aspects of human behaviour, but their effect on the maternal instinct in the early years of a child's life has been one of the main issues in question. Some child psychologists, among them Corinne Hutt in her book *Males and Females*, have noted that among three-year-olds there is a definite tendency for girls to act out mothering roles more frequently than boys do. However, the reasons why this should be so are not yet clear. Some observers attribute it wholly to heredity (that is, because they are *born* girls); others to the learning process and the effects of the environment (that is, that they are encouraged to *behave* as girls). Still other researchers have open minds.

Society and the individual

For many years, in Western industrialized societies anyway, it was believed that a woman who had no maternal instinct was abnormal. But it has since been discovered that a woman's response to the discovery that she is pregnant, and, later, to the birth of her baby, is very individual. She can be affected by a variety of factors: her hormonal activity; her intellectual and social needs; her economic status; and even her reactions to her own childhood. And she is influenced not only by her own needs but also by society's view of them.

In some cases—in certain African tribal communities, for example, and some Mediterranean countries such as Greece where the social structure is built around the family—a woman's *only* viable position is motherhood. Childlessness brings social scorn, as well as the woman's own feelings of failure or disappointment. Even in societies where a choice is apparently available, women may be no better off. Ellen Peck contends in *The Baby Trap* that childless women are often pressurized by their family and friends in ways that are equally destructive to their own self-esteem. In the face of such pressures, how can any woman decide whether or not she should have children?

One possible answer is given by Dr Harding in *The Way of All Women*: that this is, for women, what growing up is all about. When women decide what fulfilment really means—is it to be creativity or *procreativity*?—perhaps the male half of humanity will come to terms with their decision. And the result will be happier—and fewer unwanted—children in the future.

The baby's suckling during breastfeeding stimulates the production of *oxytocin*, a pituitary hormone which causes the uterus to contract and hastens its return to pre-pregnancy size.

Margaret Murray

Ageing

Ageing is a process that actually begins from the moment a human being is born. However, the decline in physical and mental functioning which is the popular concept of ageing does not begin until a person is in his early 20s, and the more overt changes do not occur until middle and old age. There is a wide individual and geographical variation in the rate of ageing, and because of this it is difficult to define at what point middle age and old age begin. In western society, the measurement of age purely by 'years lived' gives a convenient definition of middle age as the years between 45 and 65 and old age as the years after 65. However, in countries with a lower life expectancy, a man of 35 may be considered middle aged and a man of 50 old-aged. Hence it is more accurate to describe the various stages of ageing in terms of the physical, mental, and social changes that occur, rather than by 'years lived' alone.

Changes in middle age

Most cells which make up the body are dying and being replaced throughout life, but before the age of 20 there is a net increase in cells, leading to growth. In the early 20s, the cell turnover begins to have an effect on the body and there is a net cell loss in certain organs, in particular the brain. However, few marked physical changes take place until middle age.

Middle age brings certain characteristic physical and social changes. Some of these are undergone by both sexes, and others are peculiar to one sex. For women, there is a distinctive event which clearly draws attention to middle age. This is the *menopause*, also known as the *climacteric* or 'change of life'. The monthly cycles of ovulation and menstruation finally stop, marking the end of the fertile period of female life. The menopause may occur at any time from the age of 40 onwards, but normally occurs around the age of 45. It may take place gradually, or quite suddenly. With the 'closing down' of the ovaries, there is a decline in the body level of the female sex hormones, oestrogen and progesterone, which the ovaries had previously manufactured.

The decline in oestrogen in particular affects the health and appearance of the woman. Individual variations in the rate of its decline account for the fact that some women pass through the menopause with few mental and physical upsets and little external change; while others suffer sagging and a reduction in the size of the breasts, thinning and drying of the vaginal and vulval tissues, increased wrinkling of the skin, and mental upsets like headache, insomnia and listlessness.

Traditional medical therapy or 'treatment' of female menopausal changes involves hormone replacement of the missing oestrogen for a few months after the menopause arrives. This reverses many of the mental and physical changes, but cannot alter the shutdown of the ovaries nor reverse the loss in fertility. By taking progestogen as well, the lining of the uterus is shed periodically; thus most of the potentially dangerous changes to the cervix are eliminated. Hormone

Camera Press

Below left: Mother George, an inhabitant of nineteenth century London, described by the artist as being in her 120th year. Such reports of longevity are usually exaggerated. Since the introduction of birth certificates to authenticate age not one person in Britain for example, has been proved to reach 120.

Below: The process of ageing may be speeded up for those living in countries where poverty, disease and hunger are widespread or where continuous physical labour is required to sustain a living. This mother from Honduras is only in her thirties, but in terms of physical deterioration is 'old' by any country's standards.

Mansell

86

Cornell Capa/John Hillelson Agency

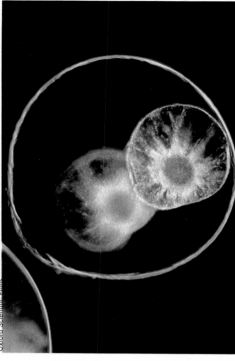

replacement therapy has the added advantage of reducing calcium loss and thus the high incidence of broken bones in older women.

The loss in fertility in middle age takes place at a time of considerable self-reassessment—and possibly some problems of adjustment—for a woman. She may still feel in the mainstream of life, having achieved some of her ambitions but still having other goals to strive for. If she has never married, the menopause may accentuate the fact that motherhood is no longer possible. If she already has and enjoys a family, it may emphasize the fact that, with the children already grown and some even flown the coop, her role as a nurturing mother may soon be over. Conversely, a woman who has felt tied down and unable to flower creatively because of her job as a mother may feel that social freedom is at last available.

Before the menopause, the sexual needs and the patterns of sexual behaviour of an individual woman are reasonably stable. At the menopause, physical, mental and hormonal changes may alter her sexual needs. They may increase, due to her new social role as 'woman' rather than 'mother', or because of her freedom from the possibility of becoming pregnant. Or they may decrease, due to depression and anxiety over 'the change'. This can result in tension and arguments between husband and wife, sometimes even leading to separation and break-up of the marriage. This may be avoided, however, if the couple recognize the basic cause of their problems and can discuss possible solutions. Marriage problems or not, many women find that the menopause coincides with a renewed vigour in a new or previously interrupted career, or in

Above: Many rich and famous people seek to cover up their age by surrounding themselves in glamour, or through cosmetic surgery. Film stars such as Mae West, here seen reclining in a limousine, are notorious for this. She may look fifty, but anyone who made films in the 1920s must have been born by around 1900.

Below: Despite the slow decline in some of their physical functions, many old people remain deft with their fingers, possessing skills that have been developed over a lifetime. This Aymara Indian woman from South America is preparing Alpaca wool ready for weaving without even having to use a spinning wheel.

Below right: After the menopause and the departure from home of their children, many women find satisfaction in a new career or in undertaking voluntary activities in which they can employ their experience with children. This hospital 'granny' is amusing a young patient with an injured arm.

Above: The process of ageing is not universal to all forms of life. When the working parts of these unicellular dinoflagellates 'wear out', they merely divide in two. By abandoning the machinery of their cells but duplicating their nuclei, they can start afresh using the instructions held in their nuclear DNA.

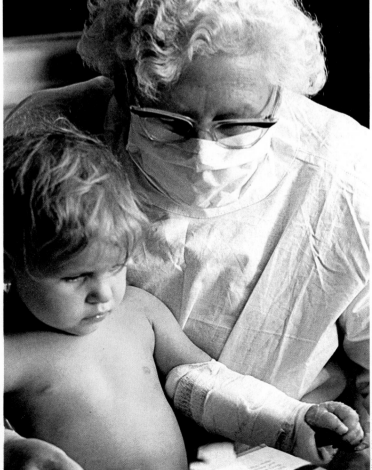

Robert Harding Associates

Oxford Scientific Films.

Michael Hardy/John Hillelson Agency

voluntary activities.

For men, there is no physiological change in middle age directly comparable with the female menopause—the true male climacteric, or loss of the ability to father children, does not occur until the 70s at the earliest. The only marked physical change in middle age for men is a gradual thinning of the scalp which may later lead to baldness. This is widely variable in extent, since it is largely determined by genetic factors. The man's sexual needs may alter, especially if he is less interested sexually in his regular partner (whose appearance and attitudes may have altered) or if his career or social activities are changing. As for women, for many men middle age may be a time for reassessment of past successes and future goals and this may bring an anxiety or depressive reaction. But in general it is a less traumatic time for the male than for the female.

Changes in old age

Changes in old age fall into three categories: physical, mental and social. Physical changes result from the decline in the quality and functioning of certain tissues and organs, through the degeneration or loss of individual specialized cells. Loss of scalp hair, which is more obvious in men but also affects some women after the menopause, continues into old age. Muscles become gradually weaker and thinner, causing a general appearance of weight loss and, later, of frailty. Good nutrition and exercise may delay these changes. The bony parts of the skeleton gradually lose their structural calcium, leading to a greater liability to fractures. The spongy discs between the spinal vertebrae degenerate and there is a loss of spinal mobility. A real loss in height, from the pressing together of the verte-

bral bones, and an apparent loss, from the tendency to stoop, may lead to a shortening of stature. A protruding abdomen or 'paunch' may be caused by obesity in the abdomen and from a lack of tone in the supporting external muscles of the body frame. A gradual decline and loss of elastic tissue leads to wrinkling and sagging of the skin, notably in the face, neck, and arms.

A loss of elastic tissue in the lens of the eye may lead to *presbyopia* or 'old eye', a decline in the ability to focus on near objects; this requires correction by reading glasses. Degeneration of the cells of the inner ear produces a decline in hearing ability, known as *presbycusis*. Reduced mobility in the muscles and cartilages of the *larynx*, the voice box, can produce either a roughened hoarseness or a high-pitched, piping timbre in the voice. The thin quality of the ageing voice is particularly noticeable in professional singers who, with few exceptions, 'lose their singing voice' after the middle 50s.

Stiffness and slowness of movement in old age stems in part from wear and tear in the major joints of knees, hips and spine, because of the loss of cartilage and lubrication. Poor resistance to extremes of air temperature also occurs because of thinner skin, a slower blood flow and the impairment of the reflexes which make us shiver and our blood vessels contract. All these changes can be speeded up by the presence of *atherosclerosis*, the narrowing or obstruction of the arteries caused by the degeneration of the arteries' lining. This process diminishes the supply of oxygen and food reaching the body's organs and inevitably affects most people. The degree of its severity varies tremendously from person to person, and is a major factor in deciding

Above left and above right: Queen Victoria was the longest-ruling British monarch, her reign spanning 64 years from 1837 to 1901. Here she is seen (left) at the start and (right) near the end of her reign. At her death she left a large number of living descendants, including thirty-seven great-grandchildren.

Left: In his poem *Father William*, Lewis Carroll expresses his personal views on old age:
'You are old', said the youth, 'as I mentioned before, and have grown most uncommonly fat; yet you turned a back-somersault in at the door—pray, what is the reason of that:'
'In my youth,' said the sage as he shook his grey locks, 'I kept all my limbs very supple by the use of this ointment—one shilling the box— allow me to sell you a couple?'

whether a 75-year-old looks, talks and behaves like a 58-year-old, a 75-year-old or a 90-year-old. Factors which show atherosclerosis are mainly of a genetic nature. Factors which accelerate it include obesity, high blood pressure, heavy smoking, sugar diabetes, thyroid hormone shortage, excess animal fats in the diet, and lack of exercise.

The second type of change is mental and intellectual. Mental alertness can be well preserved into old age, but there is a slow and steady decline in reasoning and thinking power. The understanding of new situations and ideas, the ability to co-ordinate actions and functions, and the memory for recent events are all impaired. However, people, places and events from the past are often well recalled.

Emotional changes may also appear.

The elderly person may show a narrowed and restricted emotional reaction to people and events, or may tend to depression and apathy, or may reveal an exaggerated form of previous personality traits—aggression, for example, or bonhomie. In some cases, normal mental processes may be irreversibly damaged by a severe degree of brain atherosclerosis, or by accelerated ageing of the brain cells. This pathological state, *senile dementia*, is an abnormal form of mental ageing. It is characterized by loss of concentration and drive; confusion about people and time; loss of control over social habits and hygiene; unstable and inappropriate emotions; and a degree of physical and mental dependency that demands constant care.

Several social changes occur in old age. Once a person retires from an active working life, his goals of ambition and drive towards success may be replaced by a need for personal comforts and satisfaction. He must adjust to the fixed income of retirement, to having a 'non-productive' status, and to having far more leisure time. A decline in physical function and mobility may encroach on the individual independence of a retired person as the years progress. He may have to seek out help from relatives, friends, neighbours and official professional and social services. Hobbies, indoor and outdoor, can be enjoyed and expanded in retirement, and part-time jobs are deservedly popular, too.

The cause of ageing

The ageing process is not well understood, but there are indications that the principal cause of ageing is *cell mutation*. Most cells which die in the body are replaced by the division of other living cells. However, some of these living cells suffer *mutations*, which occur either before or after division. Mutations are caused by exposure over a lifetime to natural radiation from the sun or sometimes by disease or nuclear radiation. They are changes in the structure of a cell's DNA, which controls the functioning of the cell. If a mutation impairs a cell's functioning, it will have an increasing effect as the mutated cells multiply. This will lead to a disorder of the organ of which the cells are the building blocks, and in turn to disorders of the whole body.

Some cells, including nerve and muscle cells, are after a certain age not replaced when they die and this loss can result in a decline in an organ's function. Loss of neurones (nerve cells) from the brain begins in the early 20s and is accelerated in old age by atherosclerosis.

89

Food for Health

No one food contains all the vitamins
and minerals essential for a healthy
metabolism, so a varied diet is needed.
Fruit provides vitamins A, B₁, and
C. Niacin, phosphorus and iron are
derived from nuts.

Cheese and fish are *complete* proteins – i.e. they provide a balanced protein diet. Shortage of protein slows down the metabolism, resulting in tiredness and a lowering of barriers to infectious disease.

Food for Growth

Man's need for a constant supply of protein to provide for the growth and maintenance of his body has had a profound effect on the course of history. Advanced civilizations become possible only when a steady protein supply has been secured; so long as men have to spend their whole day hunting, or growing low-protein crops, little time is left for creating new tools or new surroundings.

The word 'protein' comes from a Greek word meaning 'of first importance'. This is an apt description. All living cells, animal or plant, contain proteins. Some form the cell's structural components;

Left: Domestication of animals can provide a source of both protein and income. Pigs were evidently an integral part of this rural household in nineteenth century Britain. Once 'fattened', every part of them would be used.

Below: Baron Justus von Liebig, a nineteenth century German chemist and biochemist, made several advances in organic chemistry and the science of nutrition. He was the first to classify foods according to their various uses in the human body and, through analysis of blood, bile and urine, clarified many important biochemical processes. He became famous for his special food for infants and for his nutritive meat extracts.

Left: A Bushman from the Etosha plain of South-West Africa out hunting for antelope. If he is successful he will both eat the flesh and drink the animal's blood. Lacking domesticated animals, such nomadic peoples spend most of their time in the search for proteins—necessarily restricting their creative development.

Below right: Famines occur frequently in parts of the world where farming is not varied enough to offset fluctuations in climate. Inevitably, poor people are the most affected due to rising food costs. Here, sufferers from a famine in India in the nineteenth century ask for help from a better-fed British officer.

others are enzymes, the molecules that catalyze the essential cellular processes such as *anabolism* (energy-consuming synthesis of large molecules) and *catabolism* (energy-releasing breakdown of large molecules). When a living organism is growing, it requires a constant protein supply both for new cellular components and for enzymes. Even when the organism stops growing, such as when a person reaches maturity, the requirement for protein does not stop. This is because living cells are not static, but in a state of *dynamic equilibrium*, in which their components are continuously being broken down and replaced. Components of certain organs, such as the heart, liver and kidneys, have a *half-life* of only ten days—that is, after ten days half of them have been replaced, ten days later half the remainder have also been replaced, and so on. After ten weeks the heart, liver and kidneys are virtually 'new'. Other body components such as those of muscle and bone are more stable, having a half-life of five or six months.

A little of the protein which breaks down in the body is reformed into new protein. Some is converted into urea and excreted in the urine, and another part is oxidized and serves as a source of energy. A steady supply of protein is thus required throughout life to maintain the tissues.

Protein in food

Since proteins are found in all living cells, all raw foods, whether animal or vegetable, contain some proteins. Proteins are complicated molecules, consisting of chains of simple substances called *amino acids*; the chains sometimes being

200 or more 'links' long. Twenty-two amino acids commonly occur, but different proteins contain different relative proportions of each amino acid. The sequence in which the amino acids occur in the chain is also variable, and thus an infinite variety of different proteins is theoretically possible. The number used by living organisms is finite, but each type of protein has its own particular properties. Those found in meat and plants are different from those in the human body and may not be suitable for direct use by humans. Thus, the body has to break down the proteins in the diet into their constituent amino acids. This is done by enzymes in the digestive system. The amino acids are then circulated in the blood, from which each organ can select the amino acids required to build the proteins it needs.

Of the amino acids, fourteen, called *non-essential*, can be manufactured by the body, either from other amino acids or from other simple molecules. The other eight, called *essential*, cannot be manufactured by the body and must be directly provided for in the diet. A good diet must therefore contain enough proteins to provide the minimum requirement of these essential amino acids, and also enough extra for the body to be able to manufacture the non-essential amino acids. A protein diet that supplies these needs is called *balanced*. Certain foods, *complete* protein foods, provide this balance and, with the notable exception of the soybean, are mainly of animal origin. Others, called *incomplete*, provide only part of the amino acid requirements, and are mainly of plant origin. This

| dairy products | cereals |
| legumes | seeds |

Left: Combinations in this Z diagram provide a balanced protein diet.

Below: Table of foods containing high protein.

COMPLETE PROTEINS	INCOMPLETE PROTEINS
eggs	powdered skim milk
cheese	wholewheat bread
raw milk	rice
fish	potatoes
meat and poultry	legumes (lentils, beans
brewers yeast	etc)
soybean	corn
wheat germ	

THE ROLE OF PROTEIN IN THE BODY

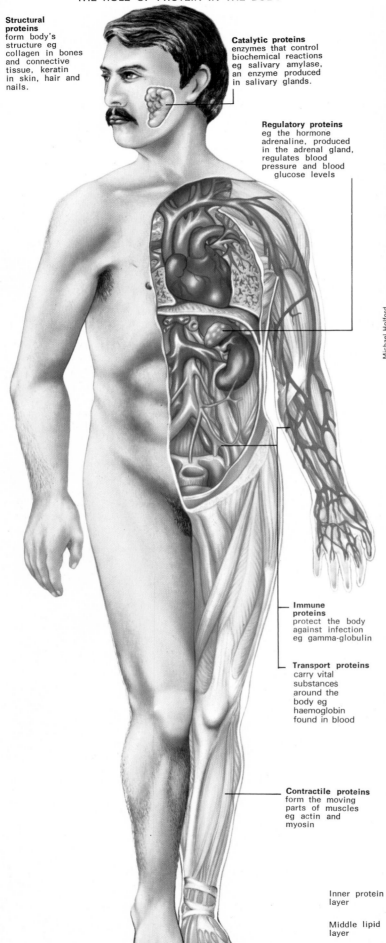

Structural proteins
form body's structure eg collagen in bones and connective tissue, keratin in skin, hair and nails.

Catalytic proteins
enzymes that control biochemical reactions eg salivary amylase, an enzyme produced in salivary glands.

Regulatory proteins
eg the hormone adrenaline, produced in the adrenal gland, regulates blood pressure and blood glucose levels

Immune proteins
protect the body against infection eg gamma-globulin

Transport proteins
carry vital substances around the body eg haemoglobin found in blood

Contractile proteins
form the moving parts of muscles eg actin and myosin

Michael Holford

Brian Seed

Above: Ostriches are bred on farms in certain parts of the world for their highly-prized feathers, but their eggs, the largest of any bird's, are also an important product. This woman on a farm at Oudtshoorn in South Africa is cracking open a three-pound egg which contains as much protein as two dozen hens' eggs.

Above: Apart from the fat on the pork chop in the centre, all these foods, including items both of animal and of plant origin, contain appreciable amounts of protein.

Right: Kwashiorkor, a children's disease caused by deficiency of protein, is clearly marked in these children from Tanzania. It is characterized by a sparseness and lack of colour in the hair, loss of weight, listlessness, and *oedema*, a swelling of parts of the body due to retention of fluid in the tissues.

Left and below: The uses of protein are manifold, both for the whole body (left) and at the level of the individual cell (below).

Dr. Maletuloma/London School of Hygiene and Medicine

STRUCTURAL PROTEIN IN THE CELL

All membranes (orange) contain protein

1 Plasmalemma

2 Mitochondrion

3 Endoplasmic reticulum

4 Ribosomes

5 Lysosome

6 Golgi body

7 Nuclear envelope

The plasmalemma magnified and stained to show three-layer structure. Outer orange bands represent protein

Inner protein layer

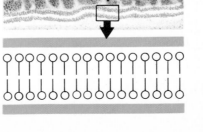

Middle lipid layer

Outer protein layer

Presumed position of protein and lipid in cell membranes

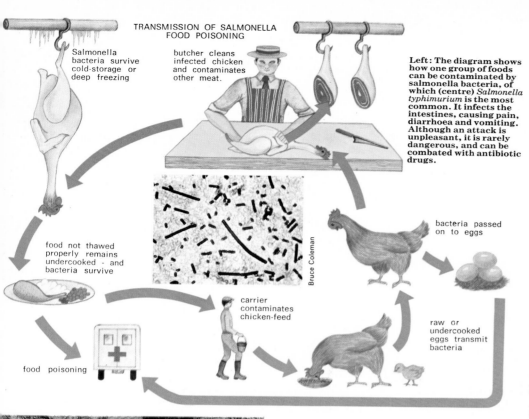

Salmonella bacteria survive cold-storage or deep freezing

butcher cleans infected chicken and contaminates other meat.

food not thawed properly remains undercooked - and bacteria survive

food poisoning

Bruce Coleman

bacteria passed on to eggs

carrier contaminates chicken-feed

raw or undercooked eggs transmit bacteria

Left: The diagram shows how one group of foods can be contaminated by salmonella bacteria, of which (centre) *Salmonella typhimurium* is the most common. It infects the intestines, causing pain, diarrhoea and vomiting. Although an attack is unpleasant, it is rarely dangerous, and can be combated with antibiotic drugs.

A. Pasieka/ZEFA

Above: Crystals of the amino acid *asparagine*, photographed using polarized light, which produces colours that vary with the crystal thickness. Amino acids are simple organic compounds containing carbon, oxygen, hydrogen and nitrogen. They combine to form proteins, but are crystalline solids in the pure form.

Below: Colouring is an important factor in the attractiveness of food. Many people might not find this dyed loaf palatable, although it tastes the same as the white or brown bread they are accustomed to. Similar ideas on what food should look like prompt food processors to dye margarine yellow and peas bright green.

Sunday Times

cereal: for instance, the US Thanksgiving dinner of turkey with corn, Italian lasagna with mozzarella cheese, and British roast beef with Yorkshire pudding. Combinations of cereals with legumes, such as beans or peas, (sometimes with a small supplement of animal protein) include Spanish paella, made from beans and rice, Mexican pancakes, made from fried cornmeal and beans, and the typical Chinese meal of fried rice with vegetables and soya bean curd. The typical Indian dish of curried vegetables with boiled rice, dahl (cooked lentils), chapattis (wholegrain pancakes), yogurt and sesame seeds, is a combination of all four protein groups.

Meat is thus not an essential dietary item, and indeed, about half the world's population survives without eating meat. For many this is due to necessity rather than choice, but there are many people who make a conscious decision not to eat meat for ascetic, ethical, religious and sometimes nutritional reasons. These people are of two types. The first are called *lacto-vegetarians*, for although they exclude flesh from their diet, they eat animal products such as milk, eggs and cheese in addition to vegetable foods. This can be an excellent form of diet and is often favoured by top-class athletes. The second type, *vegans*, eat plant food only. It is possible to eat well this way, but since most plant foods are incomplete protein sources, it may require considerable ingenuity and dedication from the vegan to work out a varied yet complete food combination every day.

Protein-deficient diets
Protein deficiency occurs for one of two reasons. It is due either to a lack in quantity of protein, *undernutrition,* or to an imbalance in the proteins eaten, *malnutrition.* Undernutrition often occurs in areas and at times when food is scarce because of famine; malnutrition in communities that eat almost exclusively a single type of low protein crop, such as cassava, without enough supplementary protein to provide a balance.

A shortage of protein produces a slowing down of the whole person, with resultant tiredness, listlessness and susceptibility to infectious illness. In South America, medical teams have successfully treated widespread protein deficiency with a Z mix of cottonseed flour, sorghum and maize, which gives roughly the protein equivalent of milk.

New protein sources
Protein deficiency is widespread in many parts of the world and there is continuing research to find high-quality substitutes for animal protein. A good substitute would alleviate the world protein shortage since animal protein is expensive to produce, in terms of both money and land. Efforts are being made to make edible protein from wool, grass and even coal and petroleum, but these are in the experimental stage. The most successful efforts so far have been in the production of textured vegetable protein, using the soybean as a base. Having little taste of its own, it takes up the taste of whatever it is mixed with—meat, for example. The total world need cannot be met from animal protein alone, so unless artificial protein can be manufactured, the best solution may be to combine various types of plant protein into the most nutritional dishes possible.

division is not surprising, since animals, being closer to humans in evolutionary terms than plants are, use similar, but not identical, proteins to those used by humans. Thus meat and dairy products contain a close approximation to the human amino acid requirement.

Balanced protein diets
Quality of protein intake is thus as important as quantity. For example, protein makes up 12% of an egg but 25% of a peanut, yet it is the egg which is regarded as nutritionally superior. In fact egg protein provides such a complete balance of amino acids that all other proteins are measured against its standard. And although the peanut contains plenty of protein, a diet consisting exclusively of peanuts would soon lead to a deficiency in certain amino acids.

Eating meat and dairy products is not the only way to obtain a protein balance, and would prove expensive. If incomplete protein foods are analyzed for their amino acid content, however, certain combinations of foods are found to complement each other. For instance, baked beans and wholewheat bread are both incomplete protein foods, but the amino acids lacking in wholewheat bread are found to excess in baked beans, and vice-versa. Their combination gives a surprisingly complete protein snack—baked beans on toast. The addition of an egg to this produces a highly nutritious dish.

This system for providing a balanced protein diet can be represented on a 'Z' diagram. The four basic types of protein foods—meat and dairy products, cereals, legumes, and seeds—are placed at the corners of a Z. Food combinations joined by any line of the Z will usually provide a balanced protein diet.

This idea is not new. The human race has worked it out on a trial-and-error basis over thousands of years and traditional dishes throughout the world consist of combinations contained in the Z diagram. Many of the well-known dishes of the western world consist of a combination of a dairy product or meat with a

The average annual consumption of refined sugar in industrialised countries is an alarming 55 kg per person. The body cannot deal satisfactorily with concentrated sugar and starch—as they are found in biscuits and cakes—and high sugar diets can lead to obesity and its attendant illnesses.

Alan Duns

96

Food for Energy

The human body needs energy for three purposes. First, it needs energy to maintain its *basal metabolic rate* or BMR; that is, to operate vital services such as running the brain and keeping the heart beating. Second, energy is needed to carry out cell activity involved in growth. Third, it is required for daily activities such as walking, working and playing. The body has created ingenious storage and bio-feedback systems to cope with variations in these needs.

The energy value of the foods from which the body derives its energy is measured in units known as *calories*. The original calorie is so small as to be suitable only for laboratory use. In nutritional work, what is used is the 'Big C' *Calorie*—in fact a kilocalorie, since it equals 1,000 'little c' calories.

Calories are measured in a *calorimeter*, which literally burns food and measures the energy released. This measurement does not correspond exactly to the energy produced inside the body by the same food, but it shows that a low calorie food such as a cabbage produces as little as 8 kcal per 100 grams while a herring, which is a high calorie food, produces over 200 kcal per 100 grams.

Energy requirements
People's energy requirements vary with their size and individual variations in BMR. Some people 'burn' fuel more quickly than others. Calorific needs are related to the amount of lean flesh on the body, not to the total weight, including fat. Average minimal basic calorie requirements are 500 kcal a day for an infant, 1000 for a child of eight, 1300 for an

adult woman and 1,500 for an adult man. However, once activity above the minimum is taken into account, the energy consumption varies greatly from 180 kcal per hour with light activity, to 450 kcal per hour with heavy activity such as swimming or mining. Hence a miner doing six hours of actual work would need 2,700 kcal to cover this period alone, to which must be added a further amount to cover the remaining 18 hours of 'normal' living but an office worker might find 2,000 kcal a day sufficient.

Energy can be obtained from almost any sort of food, but foods which contain high percentages of fats and carbohydrates have the highest calorie values. Fat is found in milk, cheese, butter, margarine, egg yolk, oily fish, the fatty part of meat, and in certain legumes such as the peanut and soybean. Carbohydrates are found in cereals such as wheat, rice and maize, root crops such as potatoes, some dried fruits, legumes, nuts, and foods containing sugar, which is pure carbohydrate. A combination of a little of some of these foods will provide a fair part of the daily energy requirement. For instance, a slice of bread will give 80 kcal. When buttered it gives 130 kcal, and if a 50 gram piece of Cheddar cheese is added, the total figure rockets to 350 kcal—15 per cent of many people's needs.

The body can also obtain energy from protein. But protein is used primarily for growth and the body gives this use a priority. Only when there is a surplus of protein, or a calorie deficiency, is it passed to the liver for use as an energy source.

Fats and oils
Fats and oils are highly concentrated energy sources. In addition, since many food flavours are fat-soluble, fats provide much of the palatability of food.

Fats can be divided into *saturated* or

Top of page: François Magendie, a 19th century French physiologist and the founder of modern pharmacology, was the first man to evaluate the components of foods.

Right: The traditional Christmas pudding is a high energy food. This specimen of about 10 kg would supply the average person's energy needs for over a fortnight.

Below: 'Jack Sprat could eat no fat, his wife could eat no lean. And so between them both, you see, they licked the platter clean.'—a good illustration that 'we are what we eat.' However, neither's diet is well balanced. Jack could have done with some additional calories and his wife's fat diet was deficient in protein.

USES OF FAT-LIKE SUBSTANCES IN THE BODY

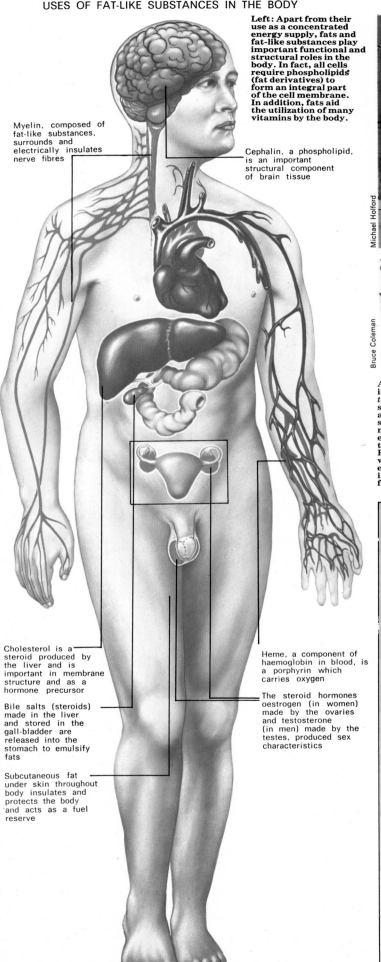

Left: Apart from their use as a concentrated energy supply, fats and fat-like substances play important functional and structural roles in the body. In fact, all cells require phospholipids (fat derivatives) to form an integral part of the cell membrane. In addition, fats aid the utilization of many vitamins by the body.

Myelin, composed of fat-like substances, surrounds and electrically insulates nerve fibres

Cephalin, a phospholipid, is an important structural component of brain tissue

Cholesterol is a steroid produced by the liver and is important in membrane structure and as a hormone precursor

Bile salts (steroids) made in the liver and stored in the gall-bladder are released into the stomach to emulsify fats

Subcutaneous fat under skin throughout body insulates and protects the body and acts as a fuel reserve

Heme, a component of haemoglobin in blood, is a porphyrin which carries oxygen

The steroid hormones oestrogen (in women) made by the ovaries and testosterone (in men) made by the testes, produced sex characteristics

Michael Holford

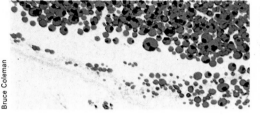

Bruce Coleman

Above: A selection of carbohydrate foods. To provide energy needs, a large proportion of the diet should consist of one of more of these foods, but not so large a proportion that the appetite is satisfied before enough protein and other essential nutrients have been eaten, nor so much as to cause obesity.

Above: Fat stained red in a slice of *adipose tissue* from under the skin, where it acts as an insulator and energy store. One end of a fat molecule, the *hydrophilic* end, attracts water and the other end repels it. Fat molecules cluster with their hydrophilic ends pointing outwards into the watery tissues, forming globular shapes.

Right: A cube of sugar burning and releasing energy. A similar type of process occurs in muscles where glucose is oxidized to water and carbon dioxide, releasing energy for work.

Below: Energy needs vary greatly. Strenuous activity may use up 10 times the energy that is required to sit still.

James Webb

ENERGY EXPENDITURE WITH VARIOUS ACTIVITIES

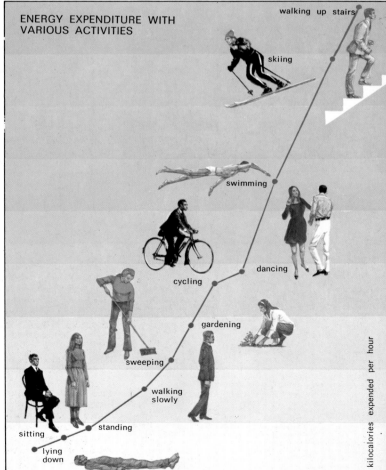

walking up stairs

skiing

swimming

cycling

dancing

gardening

sweeping

walking slowly

standing

sitting

lying down

kilocalories expended per hour

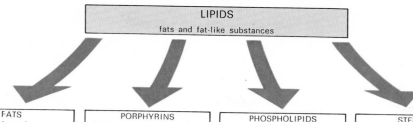

LIPIDS
fats and fat-like substances

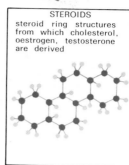

FATS
Contain only carbon, hydrogen, oxygen. Consists of glycerol and fatty acids

glycerol end of molecule

3 fatty acids

14 carbons in each

Tristearin-a saturated fat

PORPHYRINS
Highly complex organic molecules which have a lipid portion in their structure for example haemoglobin, bile pigments

- carbon
- oxygen
- hydrogen
- nitrogen
- phosphorus

PHOSPHOLIPIDS
2 fatty acid chains joined to a phosphate group

head of molecule

fatty acids 17 carbons in each

Lecithin-a phospholid

STEROIDS
steroid ring structures from which cholesterol, oestrogen, testosterone are derived

Above: The term *lipids* refers to all the fats and fat-like substances with the common property of being insoluble in water. Fats are composed of a glycerol end and three *fatty acid* chains (of different lengths in different fats). In phospholipids, one fatty acid is replaced by a phosphate group. Other lipids are more complex.

Below: In the developed countries, most people's sugar intake is far too high—partly, as here, because of the many ways of 'dressing it up' to make it sell.

Bottom: For the Xhosa tribe of South Africa, maize is a staple. It provides carbohydrate, but is deficient in certain amino acids.

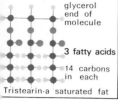

Brian Seed

Brian Seed

unsaturated types according to their molecular structure. Those containing some double bonds in their carbon chain are unsaturated, those with only single bonds are saturated. Animal fats are mainly saturated. The main sources of unsaturated fats or oils are cereals such as corn, seeds such as linseed or sunflower seed and legumes such as soybeans and peanuts.

Fats in the diet are digested in the small intestine. With the aid of bile salts, an ultra-fine emulsion known as *chyle* is produced. It consists of *chylomicrons*, tiny globules capable of passing into the bloodstream and circulating. About 70 per cent appear to go directly into the blood, from which they may be extracted for use by various tissues.

Other chylomicrons are converted in the liver into glycogen and become a part of the carbohydrate distribution system. Any surplus is deposited in the fatty tissues.

When the body becomes deficient in energy, stored fat is further broken down and enters a cycle of chemical reactions called the *Krebs cycle* which releases energy and furnishes simply molecules from which new cell components needed for growth may be manufactured.

The composition of fats in the blood is naturally influenced by the type of fat ingested in the diet. Excess animal fat can produce high blood levels of *cholesterol* which is undesirable in that it is thought to increase the chances of heart disease. A high cholesterol level can be avoided by replacing animal fat in the diet with unsaturated fats.

Carbohydrates
For most people carbohydrates form the main bulk of the diet, being the chief constituent of the world's staple foods such as rice, wheat, maize and cassava. The simplest carbohydrates are *monosaccharides*, of which glucose is the most important. Glucose occurs in only a few foods such as honey and grapes, together with another monosaccharide called fructose. *Dissaccharides* are formed by the combination of two monosaccharides and include sucrose, better known as sugar, and lactose, which is found in milk. The most important *polysaccharide*, formed by the condensation together of many monosaccharide molecules, is starch, the main carbohydrate component of cereals and root crops. Another important polysaccharide is *glycogen*, the substance built up from monosaccharides by the body to provide an energy store.

Carbohydrates, gram for gram, do not provide as many calories as fats. One gram of carbohydrate provides about 4 kcal while a gram of fat produces about 8 kcal or 9 kcal. However, carbohydrate has the advantage that it can be more readily absorbed and used up by the body.

Starch is broken down in the body into glucose molecules. Some of the glucose is released into the bloodstream, where it plays the crucial role of providing an easily metabolized energy source for the nervous system, and some is rebuilt into glycogen for storage. Any surplus may be converted into fat via the Krebs cycle. A surge of excess glucose into the blood causes fat to be deposited. This subsequently creates a drop in the blood glucose causing a temporary shortage of energy.

Every time mankind has learned to concentrate food the result has been beneficial—until concentrated sugar and starch arrived. The consumption of refined sugar in industrialized countries has risen to a staggering 55 kg per person per year. The results can be gauged from a survey of the health of Africans who lived on a sugar-free diet, compared with members of the same families who had gone to live in mining townships, where they ate a western diet containing upwards of 25 kg of refined sugar every year. Whereas heart trouble, constipation, and varicose veins were virtually unknown in the village communities, the people living in the mining communities contracted these illnesses much as western communities do.

One explanation for this is that the human body can cope with sugar and starch only in a 'dilute' form, that is when it is supplied together with plenty of roughage such as the cellulose in bran. It appears unable to deal satisfactorily with starch and sugar in concentrated form, as in biscuits, cakes or sweet drinks. Too much sugar consumed this way may lead to obesity, from which a whole group of more serious illnesses stem.

Calorie deficiency
If the energy input to the body is insufficient, first weight loss and then starvation occurs. During starvation, top priority goes to supplying energy to the brain, then the heart, the eyes and so on. First, the reserve of glycogen in the liver is released as glucose. Then the tissue fat is broken down and passed through the liver for fuel. Up to this point the whole process is quite harmless. However, eventually the body starts using its protein for energy and literally begins to burn itself up. First to go are the muscles of the limbs, and so on until eventually the vital organs themselves are used and death ensues.

In most countries, high energy foods form the basis of people's diet and are fortunately relatively inexpensive. Only when a very large amount of heavy manual labour is done, or in countries where famine is common, is there any risk of a shortage. In industrialized countries, where manual work has been superseded by machines, there is no shortage at all; if anything, there is a surplus of energy foods. But 'energy' in this sense does not refer to the subjective feeling of energetic well-being. This healthful feeling, in fact, does not appear when the so called 'energy' foods are over-supplied—it appears only when the diet is complete in every respect.

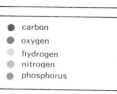

99

Many people live predominantly on food which has been processed, packaged and stored, with a resultant loss of goodness. The best sources of vitamins and minerals are fresh foods, especially plant foods, milk, fish and liver.

Vitamins and Minerals

Today's concept of the healthy diet dates from the work of Sir Robert McCarrison, who used a whole sub-continent for his laboratory. As the head of British medical services in India at the beginning of the twentieth century, McCarrison observed that certain religious and tribal groups had characteristic health patterns. He saw that the Madrassi tended to be thin, the Sikhs and Pathans to be sturdily built, and so on.

He followed these observations with a scientifically controlled experiment in which the diets of the different groups were fed to rats. The rats developed the same health patterns as the human groups using the corresponding diet. The Madrassi-diet rats tended to be thin, the Sikh-diet rats grew strong, and so on. To extend his findings McCarrison placed some more rats on a diet of typical western refined foods. These rats developed illness patterns identical to those of the poorest of Indian diets.

This discovery that there was a relationship between specific foods and health patterns was an entirely new concept. It had been considered enough that a diet contained protein, fat, and carbohydrate. Now it became essential to examine the tiny fraction of food categorized as 'trace' or 'impurity'. And this fraction turned out to contain the minerals and vitamins without which good health is impossible.

Most vitamins and minerals cannot be manufactured by the body. If they are lacking or undersupplied, one or more of a whole range of deficiency diseases—such as *scurvy*, the scourge of sailors until the eighteenth century—can result. Although treatment can yield spectacular results, a supply of the correct vitamin reducing the symptoms within hours, the after-effects may remain.

Vitamins

Vitamins are a group of organic compounds which are essential for normal metabolism. They appear in various quantities in a variety of foods, but no one food contains all of the vitamins together: hence the need for a varied diet. Vitamins do not appear in large amounts in food, but this is of no consequence since their role is often that of *co-enzymes*. That is, they help trigger chemical reactions, but are often left over for re-use after the reactions are completed.

The vitamins fall into two main groups. The first group, vitamins A, D, E and K, are fat-soluble and so are usually found in the dietary fats. They tend to be stored in the body, making it possible to build up a reserve. The other group are water-soluble and include the vitamin B complex and vitamin C, both of which tend to be excreted in the urine, although the body does retain a small reserve of them.

Minerals

Acting in conjunction with the vitamins are the minerals. A lack of these can produce a similar group of deficiency diseases, which also yield to the simple

Constantine Manos/John Hillelson Agency

Above: A Mexican woman treating a *tortilla* (maize pancake) with limewater. This avoids the danger of niacin deficiency, common when maize is a staple food, since it converts the niacin in maize from a non-absorbable to an absorbable form. Niacin can be manufactured by the body from the amino-acid *tryptophan*, but maize contains little tryptophan and a maize diet must thus supply niacin directly.

Below: A microscope photograph of a crystal of vitamin A (retinol), which is a fine yellow powder in its pure form. Its chemical structure is fairly simple and it can be synthesized for use as a food supplement.

James Webb

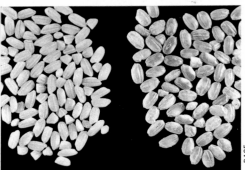

BASF

Above: The disease beri-beri is caused by a deficiency of thiamine, a vitamin which occurs in rice husks. This was discovered in 1901 by a Dutch doctor called Eijkman. Chickens to which he fed polished, huskless rice (left) soon showed symptoms of beri-beri, but they recovered rapidly when their diet was changed to include whole, unpolished rice (right).

Below: A table of the more important vitamins, their sources and uses. The vitamins B_1, B_2, B_{12} and niacin form the most important part of the vitamin B complex. They take part in the same metabolic reactions and are commonly found together in food.

VITAMIN	GOOD SOURCES	IMPORTANCE
A Retinol	Fish liver oils, liver, eggs, butter, milk, green leafy vegetables, carrots, tomatoes, yellow fruits. The body can make Vitamin A from carotenes, the yellow pigments in fruits and vegetables.	Essential for normal functioning of the retina. Lack leads to inability to see in dim light, and diseases of the skin and internal body linings. Children with insufficient vitamin A do not grow properly.
B_1 Thiamine	Yeast, meat, wheatgerm, nuts and beans, milk. Milled wheat and polished rice contain only 30% of the thiamine in the whole grain, but white bread is often fortified.	Essential for oxidation of glucose in the body to give steady energy release. Also needed for growth and nerve and muscle functioning. Lack leads to beri-beri, with muscle wasting, partial anaesthesia, loss of appetite, swelling of the limbs.
B_2 Riboflavine	Wheatgerm, liver, meat, milk, green vegetables, eggs.	Essential for food metabolism. Lack has ill effects on eyes, tongue, mouth.
Nicotinic acid (Niacin)	Yeast extracts, meat, poultry, fish, nuts, corn treated with alkali. Also manufactured by intestinal bacteria.	Needed for growth. Deficiency results in pellagra, characterized by inflammation of skin and mouth and mental disorders.
B_{12}	Raw liver, meat, fish, milk.	Essential for red blood cell formation.
C Ascorbic acid	Citrus fruits, currants, fresh vegetables, milk. Much is lost in preparation and cooking.	Essential for healthy condition of bones, teeth, blood vessels. Lack leads to scurvy, characterized by spongy and bleeding gums.
D Calciferol	Cod-liver oil, cream, egg yolk and liver. Also formed from Vitamin D precursor when sunlight falls on the skin.	Concerned with growth of bones and teeth. Can only function with sufficient calcium and phosphorus. Deficiency in children leads to abnormal bone formation called rickets.
E Tocopherol	Wheatgerm oil, soybeans, liver, butter, egg yolk, oatmeal.	Necessary for normal reproduction, and metabolism of muscle tissue. Lack can lead to sterility and muscle wasting.
K	Green leafy vegetables, pig's liver, eggs and milk. Also manufactured by intestinal bacteria	Essential factor in blood coagulation. Rarely lacking in adults, but newborn babies may suffer bleeding since they lack the bacteria which make the vitamins.

treatment of a supply of the correct mineral. But most of the required minerals appear so widely in foods that only three are commonly in short supply —calcium, iron and iodine.

An adult body contains about 1,300 grams of *calcium*, mainly in the bones and teeth. Calcium is also important in the nervous system. A satisfactory daily supply appears to be 400 milligrams and, for this mineral to be deposited, a supply of vitamin D is also necessary. Since one of the main sources of vitamin D is the effect of sunlight on a vitamin D precursor in the skin, the deficiency disease of *rickets* (soft bones) is most prevalent in industrial slums of cold countries where clothes, buildings and pollution block sunlight from reaching the skin.

Iron is an essential component of blood, being necessary for the formation of *haemoglobin*. A minimum daily intake appears to be about 12 milligrams. In its absence, especially during adolescence, pregnancy or the menstrual period, the deficiency disease *anaemia* (lack of haemoglobin) may appear.

Iodine forms part of a substance secreted by the thyroid gland. Its lack in the diet leads to *goitre*, an enlarged condition of the thyroid. Iodine is found in all sea foods, including kelp. Central areas of continents are known as 'goitre belts', because of the lack of iodine in the crops and the scarcity of seafood, but the use of iodized table salt can overcome such shortages.

The best sources of both vitamins and minerals are natural, fresh foods, especially plant foods, milk, fish and liver.

When mankind learned to preserve and store food against winter hunger, a great advance in civilization became possible. However, by the middle of the twentieth century this technique had begun to backfire. During the preserving of food some of its nutrient value is lost, while still more is lost during storage, especially the vitamin content. Now, large sections of the world's population live almost wholly on packaged, stored food—to which the increase in degenerative diseases is thought to be related.

Two major worldwide foods, wheat and rice, are also commonly subjected to processing which is nutritionally disastrous. Wheat grains undergo high-speed milling which removes the husk and the wheat germ in order to produce white flour. The effect of this is to lose the roughage of the husks, some of the protein, and some of the vitamin B complex and vitamin E contained in the wheat germ. Some doctors think removal of the roughage causes *diverticulosis*, a disease of the intestine, which can be treated by the simple administration of two spoonfuls daily of the bran removed from the wheat by the milling. A similar milling process is used for de-husking and 'polishing' rice, a staple in most oriental countries' diets. This removal of the husks can virtually eliminate the B-complex vitamins from the diet, causing the widespread disease *beri-beri*.

Excessive and badly managed home cooking is also a potent destroyer of nutrients. In the case of vitamins C and E, losses can reach as high as 90 per cent. Cooking of foods containing these vitamins should be as gentle and as brief as possible.

The increase in consumption of vitamin-deficient foods has stimulated the

A. F. Kersting

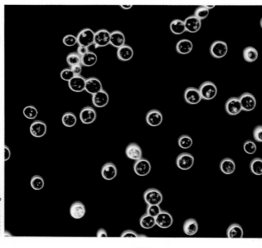

Heather Angel

Victoria & Albert Museum

Above: The Roman baths at Bath, England. Water is discharged from a hot spring at Bath at the rate of half a million gallons every day. The health-giving properties of the minerals in these waters have long been known. The waters are drunk as a medicine as well as being bathed in.

Below: A table of the more important minerals. Some, like cobalt, are required in tiny amounts, but five grams each of sodium and potassium are required daily.

Above right: Yeast cells viewed in polarized light. Yeast and yeast extracts contain plenty of the vitamin B complex and iron. Yeast is also a good protein source and can be grown as a protein supplement for humans and animals.

Right: A dish decorated with flowery symbols in the Chinese *yin* style. Chinese superstition holds that nutrients from the flowers are absorbed by food in the dish and so consumed by whoever eats the food.

MINERAL	SOURCES	IMPORTANCE
Calcium	Milk, egg yolk, shellfish, green leafy vegetables.	Constituent of bones and teeth; required for blood clotting, hormone synthesis, membrane integrity and muscular contraction.
Phosphorus	Dairy products, meat, fish, poultry and nuts.	Needed for normal bone and tooth structure. Plays an important part in muscle contraction and nerve activity, and is a component of many proteins and enzymes, ATP, RNA and DNA.
Iron	Meat, liver, shellfish, egg yolk, legumes, nuts and cereals.	Essential component of haemoglobin (which carries oxygen to cells) and of coenzymes involved in ATP formation.
Iodine	Iodized salt, seafood and cod liver oil.	Required by thyroid gland to synthesize thyroxin, the hormone which regulates metabolic rate.
Copper	Eggs, wholewheat flour, beans, beets, liver, fish, spinach and asparagus.	Required, with iron, for synthesis of haemoglobin. Component of the enzyme needed for melanin pigment formation (skin colour).
Sodium	Widespread in foods. Table salt is sodium chloride.	Necessary for conduction of nerve impulses. Strongly affects the osmotic movement of water, for example in kidney tubules.
Potassium	Contained in most foods.	Functions in transmission of nerve impulses and muscular contraction. Required for growth
Chlorine	Contained in most foods, also table salt.	Important in the acid-base balance of blood, water balance and formation of hydrochloric acid in the stomach.
Magnesium	Contained in most foods.	Required for the normal functioning of muscles and nerves. Participates in bone formation, and is a constituent of many enzymes and coenzymes.
Sulphur	Beef, lamb, liver, fish, poultry, eggs, cheese, beans.	Component of many hormones (eg. insulin) and vitamins (eg. thiamine) so is involved in the regulation of various body activities. Also a component of the contractile protein of muscle.
Zinc	Widespread in foods.	Important component of some enzymes. Needed for normal growth, and insulin formation.
Manganese	Traces present in green plants.	Activates several enzymes. Needed for haemoglobin synthesis. Required for growth, reproduction and lactation.
Cobalt	Traces present in green plants.	As part of vitamin B12, is needed for red blood cell formation.

Left: Lime juice being distributed to prevent scurvy aboard the British ship 'Alert' during an Arctic voyage. Scurvy, caused by a lack of vitamin C, frequently affected whole crews on long voyages, and was fatal for many. The nickname 'limey', applied to the British, came from some British captains' insistence on their crews drinking lime juice as an anti-scorbutic, a measure that was rarely popular.

Right: Although what could be scurvy appears in ancient records, the first definite accounts of it are found in descriptions of the crusades, for instance the crusade to Tunis in 1269 by Louis IX (Saint Louis) of France, which is depicted here.

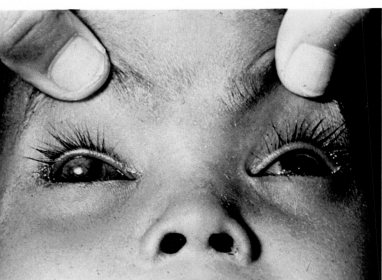

Left: A child suffering from serious vitamin A deficiency. The opaque cornea of his right eye indicates blindness. This deficiency also harms skin and teeth, although in mild cases only night blindness is experienced. When rice and cassava, which contain no vitamin A, are staple foods, the deficiency is common.

Below: A Japanese boy suffering from Minamata disease, which affected several hundred people in the fishing community of Minamata in the 1950s. The cause was traced to mercury outflow from a nearby industrial plant into Minamata bay. The mercury was converted into an organic form, became a constituent of marine plants in the bay and was concentrated in fish which ate the plants. When humans ate these fish, the organic mercury built up in them, causing nerve disorders, seizures and death.

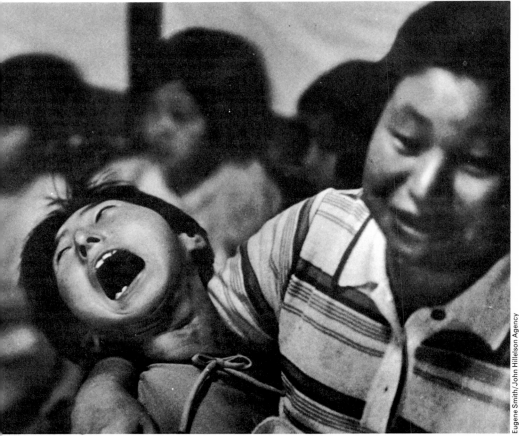

production of vitamin and mineral supplements, created synthetically in laboratories or concentrated from extracts of the natural food source. The virtues of the synthetic products are that they are often more stable, more exact in their dosage, and cheaper. However, natural nutrients may be better absorbed by the body. This improved absorption is thought to be due to *intrinsic factors*— substances which accompany a vitamin in its natural source. Vitamin C, for example, is always found accompanied by the intrinsic factors *rutin* and the *bioflavonoids*. Reliable manufacturers recommend that supplements such as vitamin C pills should be taken only at mealtimes so that there is a better chance of the correct intrinsic factors being available to improve the vitamin absorption.

Food contamination

Since the human body can be so beneficially affected by chemicals in the small amounts that are provided by vitamins and minerals, it follows that the reverse effect can take place if even small amounts of unwanted chemicals are absorbed from foodstuffs.

The first source of food contamination is from additives used in the food industry to preserve or improve the appearance of products. Each country has its own regulations to control food additives since, in the past, some have been proved to be *carcinogenic* (linked to cancer).

The second source of contamination arises from industrial pollution, particularly from the contamination of the environment with organochlorine pesticides such as DDT. Pesticides used on fields drain into estuaries and lakes where some fish have their breeding grounds. For instance, the salmon in Lake Michigan became uneatable after organochlorine sprays had drained into the lake. The average daily human consumption of DDT is estimated at 0.10 micrograms. The amount considered harmful is upward of 10 micrograms daily per kilogram of body weight, since the human body is better able to rid itself of these chemicals than are fish.

Modern food processing means that man has simply substituted one set of problems for another. But certain basic rules can still produce healthy eating. As far as possible, fresh food, plenty of mixed vegetables and fruit, and a supply of complete protein should be eaten. Also, the diet should include a plentiful supply of roughage, and excess sugar and starch consumption should be avoided.

Fitness

Fitness, in its most general sense, is the ability to cope with one's environment. For primitive man, fitness was essential for survival since it was required to escape predators, obtain food, combat illness and endure adverse climatic conditions. Primitive man remained fit for two reasons. First, unfit individuals died young and did not reproduce; hence, only 'fit' genes passed on to the next generation—'the survival of the fittest'. Second, the necessity to hunt prey for food required a great deal of physical activity, which promoted fitness.

By contrast, among people living in the industrialized world, physical fitness is the exception rather than the rule. Food, transport, shelter and treatment for illness are all easily bought as long as one has a source of income from a job, from one's family or in some cases from the state. Most jobs neither require nor promote physical fitness. Only for those individuals whose occupations involve strenuous physical activity, such as miners or professional footballers, is fitness essential.

However, in the long run, fitness is a valuable asset. The fit person is better able to resist illness, cope with stress, and enjoy activity than the unfit person, and is likely to achieve a greater sense of well-being. Fitness is indeed admired, as can be judged by the enthusiasm with which the Olympic Games and other exhibitions of physical ability are watched, and the adulation that is poured upon sporting champions. Many people regard fitness as attainable only by a dedicated minority through gruelling exercise, but this is a misconception. Fitness can be achieved without the need for several hours of training daily—for many, a reasonable level of fitness could be obtained merely by giving up detrimental habits such as smoking.

Components of fitness

Fitness is not a single attribute, but a complex combination of various factors. These factors are developed to various extents in different types of athlete. For instance, a weightlifter has well-developed muscular strength, a gymnast rates highly on joint flexibility and agility, while a marathon runner relies on efficient respiration and muscular endurance. These various factors are interdependent: no one factor can reach its optimum unless the other factors are also at an efficient level.

The central component of fitness is the performance of the muscles and joints. In the human body there are more than 600 muscles, groups of which work together to enable us to walk, stand, sit, run, look around, chew food and carry out all other types of physical activity. The performance of a muscle depends on two factors, *strength* and *endurance*. Strength is a measure of the maximum force a muscle can apply in one action, and there are two types: *isometric* strength, the force applied against a fixed resistance, and *isotonic* strength, the force applied through the full range of movement of the muscle. Both kinds can be seen in arm-wrestling. To begin with, as the opponents' arms lock

Above: Two peppered moths, *Biston betularia*, resting on lichen-covered bark. In this particular environment, the darker, *melanic*, moth is the less fit, since a predator could spot and catch it more easily than its camouflaged companion. However, on a darker background, the melanic moth might be considered the fitter of the two.

Right: Russian athlete Juriy Zurin receiving oxygen after a 5000 m race in Mexico City, where oxygen in the air is eight per cent less than at sea level. In this situation, athletes cannot obtain enough oxygen during a long race, with the result that a severe oxygen debt occurs, requiring immediate treatment.

motionless against each other, isometric strength is being applied. When one person starts to force his opponent's arm to move downwards, isotonic strength is being applied. The two factors are partly independent. Isometric strength is directly proportional to the number of fibres in the muscle, while isotonic strength, since it involves movement, is also dependent on the efficiency of the relevant joint or joints.

Muscular endurance is the ability of a muscle to go on working over a period of time. It relies on the efficiency with which the muscle uses its energy reserves as much as on sheer muscle size, but strength and endurance are closely interrelated. A muscle capable of a maximum force of 50 kg will go on working longer against a resistance of 10 kg than will a muscle that has a maximum force of 20 kg.

In most joints of the human frame, the bone ends are prevented from rubbing against each other by a lubricant-filled sac, the *synovium*, and also by a gristly material called cartilage on the bone ends. Stability of the joints is achieved by means of *ligaments*, strong bands of fibrous tissue binding the bones together, as well as by the muscles and tendons. In a fit person, the synovium and cartilage are in good condition and function efficiently to lubricate the joint, and the ligaments are strong and elastic enough to allow a full range of movement of the joint without the risk of undue strain or injury.

As well as the muscles that work the joints of the skeleton, the internal muscles must also be in good condition. The heart, for example, which is regularly

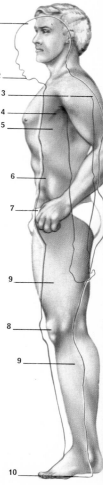

Right: Diagram shows the difference between a fit person (solid) and an unfit person (superimposed). The unfit person suffers from the following :-

1 Effects of ageing, such as balding. are speeded up.

2 Drooping head due to bad posture and reduced feeling of well-being.

3 Weak back and shoulder muscles lead to rounded shoulders and back pain.

4 Bad posture reduces chest capacity, and internal muscle weakness prevents lungs being fully emptied, so that they cannot work at full capacity. Respiratory efficiency is thus reduced.

5 Weak heart muscle has to work harder to provide the same blood flow as a fit person's heart. Clotting time of blood is increased, adding to the chances of atherosclerosis.

6 Sagging abdomen due to weak muscles and poorly balanced diet.

7 Excess fat results in the body carrying an extra burden, which can strain the hip and knee joints.

8 Reduced joint flexibility through lack of exercise and weakness of associated muscles.

9 Atrophied leg muscles.

10 Flat feet, caused by obesity overstretching the ligaments in the foot.

Left: *Satan Rousing the Rebel Angels,* by the 19th century English artist William Blake. Satan is here depicted as the epitome of fitness with his ideal male form—a perfectly proportioned structure, well-defined muscular development and a fine sense of balance.

Right and below: A Polish athlete having his fitness tested at the Institute of Sports Medicine in Warsaw. Three electrodes are taped to his chest which pick up electrical changes in his heart and monitor his heart beat. He then does a standard amount of exercise, such as a 400 metre run. After a pause, the electrodes are connected via a lead to a machine (below) that records the small electrical currents from the electrodes on a graph, called an electro-cardiogram. This shows the rate of his heart beat. The speed at which this rate decreases is a measure of his circulo-respiratory fitness. Any abnormality in heart functioning is easily recognizable on the electrocardiogram, so it can also be used as a diagnostic tool.

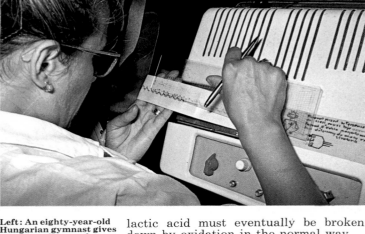

Left: An eighty-year-old Hungarian gymnast gives a display of strength and agility. Although the ageing process leads to a gradual decrease in muscular, respiratory and nervous performance, regular exercise can delay or slow down the changes, allowing an octogenarian to perform feats of which many teenagers are incapable.

contracting throughout life, must remain strong to keep the blood flowing round the body. If the heart stops, even for a few minutes, death can result. It therefore needs exercising, normally best done by exercising the rest of the muscular system. Similarly, the smooth intestinal muscle acts to move liquified food along the intestinal tract, while the bowel muscles act to excrete waste. 'Fitness' implies the correct action of these muscles too.

Energy supply

Muscles cannot work without an efficient supply of energy. This is supplied by *glycogen*, a carbohydrate like starch which is stored in the muscle and acts as a fuel. As the glycogen is broken down, first to glucose and ultimately to carbon dioxide and water, considerable amounts of energy are released. Under normal conditions glucose is broken down in many small steps and through many intermediate compounds, notably *pyruvic acid*, to release the energy needed to work the muscles. The process (respiration) requires oxygen and this is supplied by the blood which picks it up in the lungs.

At times of extreme exertion, however, the bloodstream may not be able to supply oxygen fast enough for normal respiration to supply all the muscles' energy requirements. When this happens, pyruvic acid is converted to *lactic acid*, a reaction which does not require oxygen, and this allows the breakdown of glucose to continue, with release of energy. This process, known as *anaerobic respiration*, can last for only a limited period, for the

lactic acid must eventually be broken down by oxidation in the normal way.

Anaerobic respiration can be seen in a sprinter, who may not take a breath during a 100-metre dash. He quickly builds up an *oxygen debt*—an excess of lactic acid in his muscles and bloodstream. The lactic acid in the blood acts on brain centres to increase respiration and heart rate, thus supplying oxygen at a faster rate to oxidize the acid. Hence the sprinter will find, after his dash, that his heart rate and depth of breathing are greatly increased.

The amount of work and the length of time for which the muscles can perform depends on the efficiency of the heart and lungs in supplying oxygen. This is called *circulo-respiratory efficiency.* A fit person has a greater lung capacity and a stronger heart than an unfit person, and his energy reserves are more efficiently metabolized—that is, his work output for a set amount of energy input is greater because of improved functioning of his metabolic systems. It has been calculated that the average person is only about 20 per cent efficient. The other 80 per cent of his energy input is not turned into useful work, but is lost as heat. On the other hand, very fit 105 people may achieve 50 per cent efficiency —a better performance than that of many man-made machines.

Another important component of fitness is the performance of the nervous system. Nervous impulses initiate muscle activity. Co-ordinated movement, agility and quick reactions all depend on the correct and integrated functioning of the nervous system.

The fit and the unfit

Variations in fitness are due either to variations in potential fitness or to impairment of its components. Even if all people were as fit as possible, their physical abilities would not be equal since potential fitness is limited by factors such as age and sex. The ageing process decreases the efficiency of the whole body, but different aspects of fitness reach peak potential at different ages. Speed is greatest in the early twenties, strength in the late twenties, and endurance improves up to middle age. The different distribution of muscle and fat on men and women imparts different types of fitness to the two sexes.

Below: The siege of the castle of Mortaigne, in the French province of Poitou, which was held by the English during Richard II's reign. In medieval times, fitness often meant 'fighting fitness', the ability to survive such a battle.

Right: An 'Apparatus designed to afford the advantages of mountain climbing without leaving one's apartment.' Exercise on this type of machine probably improved the heart, lungs and leg muscles, despite its tediousness.

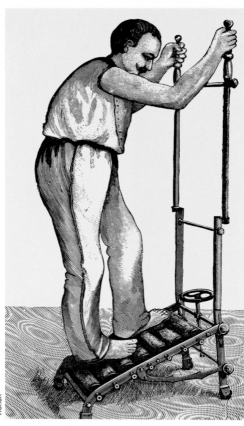

Ronan

SPORT AND FITNESS

● considerable effect

◗ some effect

- cardiovascular and respiratory performance
- muscular endurance
- strength
- power
- agility

	cardiovascular and respiratory performance	muscular endurance	strength	power	agility
SOLO ACTIVITIES					
archery		●	◗		
bicycling	●	◗	◗		
canoeing	●	●	◗		
gymnastics		●		●	
hiking	●	◗			
running	●	◗			
sculling	●	●	◗		
skipping	●	●			
skiing	●	●		◗	
swimming	●	●	◗		●
TEAM SPORTS					
basketball	●	●			●
hockey	●	●		◗	
rowing	●	●	◗		
soccer	●	●		◗	
volleyball		◗			●
OPPONENT SPORTS					
badminton	●	◗			
bowling		◗			
golf	◗			●	
tennis	●	◗			●
skating	●	●		◗	
skiing	●	●		◗	

British Museum

Women are constitutionally fitter—they are better at withstanding extremes of environment, and have a longer life expectancy. Men are specifically fitter in terms of muscular power and speed.

Fitness depends on so many components that it may be impaired by a wide variety of causes. Muscles, like many other organs, become less efficient if not frequently used. They tend to atrophy; that is, they become smaller and weaker and respond less rapidly to nervous stimulation. Weak muscles 'complain' and become stiff after exercise has been taken by someone normally inactive.

Like muscles, joints must be used regularly to remain functional and strong and to prevent injury to the lubricating system. This may occur with increasing age in the weight-bearing joints of hips and knees, when the cartilage may be damaged, and the synovium may degenerate, leading to painful and restrictive arthritis.

Anything which reduces the reserve capacity of the lungs or heart impairs fitness. This may occur as a result of a lung disease, such as bronchitis, an inflammation of the air tubes. Smoking helps to cause and worsen bronchitis. Tobacco smoke also produces carbon monoxide, which is a potential poison, weakens the heart, and is taken up by blood haemoglobin in preference to oxygen, thereby reducing the quantity of oxygen available to the tissues. No-one who smokes is completely fit.

An unbalanced or inadequate diet can also impair fitness. Malnutrition produces weak muscles, though this is not often seen in developed countries, where an excess intake of food, leading to fat deposition, is the main problem. Excess fat affects the action of muscles and throws a greater strain on certain joints. The liver, which controls the metabolism of glucose and glycogen, may be impaired by fat deposits or by excessive alcohol intake, resulting in reduced efficiency of the glucose supply to the muscles. An unbalanced diet combined with too much alcohol may also lead to inadequate nerve functioning.

Finally, fitness or the lack of it affects the way the individual feels in himself. An unfit body produces many aches and pains and this may lead to an unfit state of mind—often displayed in irritability, anxiety and introspection about health. This in turn may lead to excessive indulgence in food, tobacco or alcohol— and possibly to the development of physical and psychological illness which could have been avoided by keeping fit.

Daily Telegraph Colour Library

Left: A chart showing the effect of different activities on components of fitness. *Power* **is a measure of the amount of work the muscles can do in a certain time, while** *strength* **is the instantaneous force the muscles can produce.**

Above, below and below right: Three varieties of fitness. Mr Paul Grant (above) prepared himself for the 1972 Mr Universe contest by lifting weights for three hours every day for several years. He also swallowed a daily

total of 624 pills. During a bath in the Ganges river, a Brahmin yogi (below) performs *pranayama,* **a conscious control of the breathing which improves the economy of respiration and other bodily systems. At the 1976**

Olympics, Nadia Comaneci (below) was the first gymnast ever to be given a perfect score by the judges for her performance on the assymetric bars. Here we see a display of her agility on the floor.

Paolo Koch

Don Morley/Allsport

Exercise

The importance of exercise in the maintenance of both physical and mental efficiency has been recognized throughout history, and has often been encouraged by states, often to keep their citizens in a state of military readiness. In the Greek state of Sparta for instance, children from the age of seven would undergo an education that consisted largely of physical exercise, with the arts and literature taking a subordinate role. In medieval England, regular archery practice was obligatory for the male population, in order to preserve England's military monopoly with the longbow.

In the twentieth century, regular exercise is still encouraged, and sometimes enforced, in schools, since it is seen as being beneficial to health and providing an enjoyable release of energy. For many people, however, leaving school provides a welcome relief from the 'P.E. teacher', and as this often coincides with the beginning of a sedentary job, regular exercise is often discontinued or severely curtailed. The prevalence of inactive use of leisure time, exemplified by the popularity of spectator sports and television, may contribute to a vicious circle in which lack of exercise leads to reduced fitness, which in turn leads to a reduced desire to take exercise. This tendency can be counteracted only through regular exercise.

Types of exercise

The type of exercise a person takes in order to improve or maintain his fitness can vary with age, sex, time and facilities available, and personality—he may prefer to take exercise by himself, or with other people. The two main types of exercise are sports, which usually involve a competitive aspect and exercise the whole body, and 'keep-fit' schedules, which involve no competitive aspect and usually develop only particular components of fitness.

The main advantages of sports are that they are more sociable, and provide the competitor with the satisfaction of seeing his efforts rewarded with an improvement in skill. Sports can be divided into team sports, such as football, hockey and cricket, which involve some team co-operation, and individual sports, such as tennis, squash and golf. The individual variety is often favoured by competitive personalities who prefer to depend on their own skill and effort to decide the outcome of a contest rather than relying partly on the efforts of others.

The degree of activity that a sport requires varies and is related to the amount of time the sport takes up. For instance, squash, ice hockey, and rowing are highly strenuous and take place in short bursts of from a few minutes to half an hour. Slightly less strenuous are sports such as tennis and badminton, which last for an hour or more, while cricket, in which games may last for several hours or days, and golf are considerably less strenuous, although requiring an occasional burst of effort. The most suitable sport for the individual depends on the time he has available, and the degree of activity he requires and can withstand. A very busy, but fit,

Left: A dish from the Agora museum in Athens, depicting a wrestling bout. The ancient Greeks encouraged exercise through the Olympic games, traditionally founded in 776 BC. In those days, the games lasted for up to seven days, and included track and field events, boxing, wrestling, and chariot racing. Winners of the games became heroes, and their feats are recorded in art and poetry. The Greek preoccupation with physical fitness contributed to their military successes against the Persians and other invaders.

Right: The southern Nuba of the Sudan believe in a dynamic life-force which can be tapped for the community's benefit through ritual sports. In two villages, this takes the form of fights between young men, who strike at each other with heavy brass wrist bracelets, as can be seen here. Fight rules prevent serious injury.

Right: Workers at the Mitsubishi shipbuilding yard at Nagasaki in Japan doing their daily 'keep fit' exercises. Companies in Japan tend to exert more control than those of western states over the welfare, including the fitness, of their employees. As can be seen from the picture, not everyone is enthusiastic about this. But by increasing physical and mental efficiency the group exercise may contribute to the high productivity generally found in Japanese industry compared with that in other industrial nations.

Below: Joe Bugner, who became British and European heavyweight champion in the 1970s, is seen here improving his strength and aim with a punch-bag. Many regard boxing as a barbaric sport, but it can provide a controlled release for those with aggressive tendencies, as well as a means of getting fit.

Above: This Indian's balancing ability is his source of livelihood. The development of such ability involves years of practice and much suffering, but the doctrine of *asceticism*, requiring strict self-discipline, may have helped him overcome these difficulties.

Left: 4000 participants set out on the Engadine ski marathon, which takes place yearly at St Moritz in the Swiss Alps. Skiing is a most strenuous sport. When going downhill at speed, the legs have to work like pistons to control the skis on an uneven surface, while pushing oneself uphill is even more tiring.

Below: A good cyclist requires exceptional strength and endurance in the legs. In order to get rid of the excess heat being produced by the calf muscles, the leg veins enlarge to such an extent that they stand out from the legs.

individual will favour a sport such as squash, a retired person with plenty of time but reduced fitness may favour golf, while a partially fit person with limited time available may have to find a compromise such as tennis.

'Keep fit' exercises suffer from the drawback that they are somewhat repetitious or boring, and provide little immediate reward for the individual since they develop only pure physical ability and have no skill component. However, they may be the only type of exercise available for the person with very limited time, such as only a quarter of an hour a day, or for people who have just started getting fit after a long period of inactivity and for whom any sport would be too strenuous. 'Keep fit' classes, where a group of people go through a schedule of exercises in unison, are of psychological benefit to individuals who might give up regular exercise at home after a few days. They also add a degree of sociability to this type of exercise. 'Keep fit' exercises are of two types. *Isotonic* exercises involve contraction of the muscles through their full range, and can be used to develop particular groups of muscles. They are useful for increasing joint flexibility and stretching the ligaments, and also improve circulorespiratory efficiency. For instance, press-ups develop the arm and shoulder muscles, improve respiration and exercise the elbow and shoulder joints. Sitting up to touch one's knees from a lying position is good for the muscles of the back and abdomen and the flexibility of the backbone. Stepping up and down on a bench improves the leg muscles and their associated joints and ligaments.

Isometric exercises, on the other hand, involve the application of force by a muscle against a fixed resistance. An example is an attempt to lift an immovable object, or holding the arms out sideways and stationary. Various types of machine have been devised to provide a means of performing isometric exercises. They are particularly suitable for increasing strength in the shoulder, arm and chest muscles, but do little to increase circulorespiratory efficiency or joint flexibility.

Exercises are best combined in a schedule in which each exercise develops a particular component of fitness or muscle group. One type of training which does this is weight training, in which bars with weights on either end are used in a series of graded exercises, starting with light weights and gradually building up. Schedules have been devised to exercise all the major muscle regions.

Another type of schedule that systematically stimulates the whole body is part of the physical system of yoga, called *hatha* yoga. Here the emphasis is on gentle physical and mental relaxation, as opposed to exertion, through a series of postural exercises. Some of these postures, called *asanas*, are static and are held for a certain length of time, while others are dynamic, requiring movement of either the whole body or parts of it. Breathing is also important in yoga, the aim being to use the respiratory system to its full extent, with a resultant increase in efficiency and respiratory control. Through the practice of quiet meditation in conjunction with the physical aspects of the system, the experienced yoga practitioner acquires both mental and physical fitness, and

THE BODY DURING EXERCISE

John Hillelson Agency

1. Heat is lost from the skin by radiation and sweat production.

2. Blood capillaries near the skin surface enlarge to enhance heat loss from the blood. This accounts for the reddening of the face.

3. Lungs respond to the greater demand for oxygen and build-up of carbon dioxide by increasing depth of breathing. Ventilation may rise up to 12 times the resting rate.

4. Rate and volume of heartbeat increase to hasten the transport of oxygen, nutrients and waste products by the blood.

5. Muscles require more oxygen. If the supply is not great enough, they can function anaerobically (without oxygen) for a time, but this leads to accumulation of lactic acid (oxygen debt).

6. Liver works harder to convert waste lactic acid to glucose. This maintains blood glucose levels and slows the build-up of oxygen debt.

Left: Changes that occur in the body during exercise, many of which are brought about by the release of the hormone *adrenaline* into the bloodstream from the adrenal glands. During an emergency, when the body must move fast to escape danger, this occurs automatically as a response to signals from the brain.

Above and below: Cross-country running, or jogging, can provide a chance of seeing the countryside while getting fit. Some (above) find that doing this in a group is more sociable and hurries along the less fit individuals, while British athlete Alan Rushmer (below) prefers to set his own pace during training.

Right: Many people's idea of a holiday is to move from a sedentary existence at their jobs to a sedentary existence on a beach. These German holidaymakers, however, have been jerked out of their inactivity by an enthusiastic beach entertainer, and are taking their partners for a dance around the sandcastles.

Gerry Cranham

indicates a poor level of fitness. People with an index this low who wish to get fit should start off with light exercise in the home and build up gradually to more strenuous forms.

A good way to start exercising is by doing standing press-ups against a chest of drawers at chest height. When about 30 of these can be performed without difficulty, an object 18 inches lower is used, such as a table or a sideboard, and the exercises repeated. Continuing in this fashion the muscles will become strong enough in a few days to start press-ups on the floor. Other types of exercise, such as sitting up to touch the knees, first from lying on a board at an angle of 45 degrees to the floor and then from progressively lower angles, should be performed together in a daily schedule. In this way the hardest of exercises, which appear impossible at first, are within the reach of anyone with determination.

To quantify progress, the pulse recovery index and resting pulse should be measured at regular intervals. These will improve encouragingly. Once the resting pulse is down to 80, and the recovery index up to 25 per cent, one is well on the road back to full fitness and can begin strenuous sports and exercises.

Dangers of exercise

Although sport and exercises are on the whole harmless, certain injuries do occasionally occur. Apart from the risk of cardiovascular strain, specific sports and exercises carry with them the chance of various types of injury. Knee and ankle injuries are common in ball games and cycling, head and neck injuries are common in rugby football and wrestling, while tendon and muscle injuries are common in athletics, tennis (*tennis elbow*), and squash. The simplest kind is a strain, affecting the muscle, tendon or joint, which responds to rest for 48 hours and a gradual return to the sport. This type of injury can be avoided by 'warming up' the muscles and ligaments through a few moderately strenuous exercises before the game commences.

A more serious type of injury is tendon or muscle rupture, or cartilage damage, which may require sophisticated treatment and a more delayed return to the game.

Certain types of exercise also carry with them an environmental danger. Hill climbing, mountaineering, skiing and scuba diving can all be dangerous unless a high degree of training is first acquired. *Hypothermia*, or *exposure*, is not uncommon in these activities, occurring when an accident exposes the individual to bad weather and the body temperature falls to dangerous levels. Anyone suffering from hypothermia, which is characterized by shivering, giddiness, and reduced mental awareness, must be warmed up as quickly as possible. This can be done by immersing the victim in a hot bath, wrapping him in warm clothing, or if nothing else is at hand, by cuddling him.

Most types of exercise, however, can only be beneficial. Much of the benefit is in the increased strength of the lungs and heart. Since these are the organs which most often fail in middle and old age, keeping them in good shape makes sense. A new world of enjoyment, exhilaration and relaxation opens up to the fit person, producing a healthy mental and physical balance.

Above: Pupils at the North London Collegiate School for Girls taking some mild gymnastic exercise in 1882. Great physical ability was thought 'unladylike' in those days, but women have since taken an increasing role in sport. Top women gymnasts, for instance, especially those from the USSR and Eastern Europe, have become famous sporting figures in recent years.

Below: A summary of the factors that promote the occurrence of cardio-vascular disease, which accounts for 50 per cent of deaths in developed countries. Regular exercise and a good diet radically reduce the chances of incurring the two main factors, high blood pressure and high cholesterol levels. Exercise can also help relieve other factors such as mental stress.

- mental stress
- high cholesterol levels and high blood pressure
- effect of smoking on lungs and arteries
- overeating and overdrinking
- obesity

CAUSES OF CARDIOVASCULAR DISORDERS

develops slender muscles, good posture, a supple, efficient body, and a sense of well-being. Yoga is an excellent form of exercise for those who wish to develop all-round fitness, rather than just brute strength.

Exercise for the unfit

For the unfit person, sudden strenuous activity after a long period of inactivity may be dangerous, since it may overburden the heart. Anyone with a history of heart or lung disease should have a medical check-up before recommencing strenuous exercise, and for others a simple test of one's own fitness is a good idea before deciding on a schedule for getting fit. This can be done by measuring one's pulse rate and its recovery after exercise. At rest the heart normally beats between 60 and 100 times per minute, (the lower this *resting pulse* the fitter the person), but with exercise it rises to between 140 and 160 times per minute.

The speed with which it returns to the resting level, called the *recovery index*, and usually expressed as the drop in pulse after 90 seconds as a fraction of the maximum pulse, is an index of fitness. For instance, if the pulse immediately after exercise is 160, and this drops by 40 after 90 seconds, then the fractional drop is 40/160, or 25 per cent. Someone with this index is fairly fit and can begin moderately strenuous exercise without fear of strain or damage. Someone with an index of 30 per cent or more is in very good condition and could undertake the most strenuous of activities. On the other hand an index of 15 per cent or less

Obesity

Many citizens of all ages in many countries are obese. A person can be defined as obese if his weight is 10 per cent or more above the ideal weight for his height, sex, age and frame size. This 'ideal weight' is the weight which, statistically, gives the individual his longest life expectancy. The best known tables of these ideal weights are those published by the Metropolitan Life Insurance Company of the United States. Anyone who claims his obesity is due to big bones may find that such an excuse is not valid if he consults these tables, for they take into account frame size—small medium, or large—as well as age, sex and height. However, most obese individuals do not have to consult tables to know that they are overweight. Their main problem is to discover the cause of their obesity and ways of counteracting it.

Causes of obesity

There are at least five approaches to the problem of why obesity develops in some people but not in others. These different approaches consider different factors: mechanism of fat metabolism; family influences; personality influences; glandular disorders; and social factors.

The first approach involves examination of the nature of fat itself, its production, storage, and movement in and out of the tissues. Fat is not fixed or inert material. Its chemical content of *triglycerides* is constantly being moved in and out of the body cells. This movement and deposition is controlled chemically by a range of hormones, such as *growth hormone*, *noradrenaline* and *thyroxine*, and also by unknown factors. Fat is stored in the body in fat cells called *adipocytes* which are present both in the layers of fatty tissue under the skin and in deeper body tissues and organs.

The number of adipocytes increases steadily in the normal individual from the first year of life up until sexual maturation at puberty. However, constant overfeeding of an infant in the first year of life may increase the number of adipocytes at a more rapid rate, and a similar increase may occur with excess food intake at puberty. This leaves a permanently enlarged number of fat cells for the rest of the individual's life. Obese children and adolescents are hard to treat for obesity in later life as a result of the excess adipocytes. One way to avoid obesity is thus to prevent overfeeding in the first year of life and subsequently through childhood to puberty.

The body lays down more fat if there is plenty of sugar, starch and other carbohydrates available to provide body energy. Conversely, restriction of carbohydrates in the diet reduces the amount of fat laid down. Hence, an unbalanced or high carbohydrate diet, rather than a high fat diet, is the main dietary cause of obesity.

A second way to consider how obesity arises looks at the influence of the family, in both genetic and environmental terms. Obesity often appears to run through a family, down the generations and across brothers and sisters. Research has been undertaken to look for a genetic influence on metabolism which might lead to

obesity, but the only type of altered metabolism that has been found with a possible genetic cause is one which predisposes some individuals to the opposite of obesity—thinness. People under this influence tend to be 'fast burners' in that, however much they eat, the body metabolizes it so quickly that fat storage is barely affected and they remain the same light weight.

The majority of people are not 'fast burners', and as no 'obesity gene' has been identified, it seems that among these people, obesity is mainly caused by overeating, and not by genetically altered fat metabolism. Obesity which runs in families can thus be explained as being a result of social habits and customs within the family—an environmental, rather than genetic, cause. Examples of habits

that run in families which may lead to obesity are: heavily sugared tea or coffee drinks; a regular intake of sweets, candies and chocolates between meals; the enlarging of meals with plenty of bread, pie crusts, biscuits, puddings and other high carbohydrate foods; and the custom of eating, or drinking alcohol, on a regular basis to provide hospitality.

Alongside this, a family's income level may influence the tendency of its members to obesity. Sugar and starch foods have long been cheaper than protein foods. People on low or fixed incomes may therefore become obese because carbohydrate food is all they can afford.

A third approach is a consideration of the mood, personality, and mental state of obese individuals. The idea of the 'jolly, fat person', perpetuated by fat

Left: Brazilian Agnaldo Galdino weighed a normal 3.5 kg at birth, but more than doubled his weight in each of his first three years of life. He weighed over 35 kg at age three, when most children weigh about 15 kg. Such children's greatly increased number of fat cells, due to overfeeding, may make weight reduction very difficult in later life.

Right: An American housewife preparing a vast quantity of meat pies for her family. The tendency for obesity to run in families is caused mainly by common patterns of diet within the family rather than by any genetic influence. Children become used to the types of food that are provided by their mothers, and if these include excessive amounts of carbohydrate food, obesity will commonly result.

Below: Some people, such as these Japanese *sumo* wrestlers, cultivate obesity for professional reasons. Champion sumo wrestlers weigh up to 170 kg and rely as much on their vast bulk as on strength to push their opponents out of the ring.

Right: Susceptibility to obesity is thought to be determined partly by body type. American psychologist W. Sheldon classified body types according to their relative content of three variables, called *ectomorphy, mesomorphy,* and *endomorphy,* the main characteristics of which are seen here. A person's body type stays constant throughout life and a predominantly endomorphic person, with a rounded and stocky body, is more susceptible to obesity than the muscular and athletic mesomorph or the thin, angular ectomorph. This is thought to be due to differences in the rates of food metabolism by the different types.

Below right: Daniel Lambert, an 18th century jail-keeper of Leicester, led an active life but died aged 39 weighing 336 kg and wearing a waistcoat measuring over 255 cm at the waist. His name became a synonym for immensity in 19th century England, but his British weight record was overtaken in 1878 by a Scotsman weighing 341 kg.

Below: Widespread obesity is not unique to the 20th century. Many people in 19th century England were fat, as seen in this cartoon of 1831. Improvements in road surfacing at this time, and the resulting popularity of stagecoach riding instead of more active means of travel, may have initiated the obesity problem.

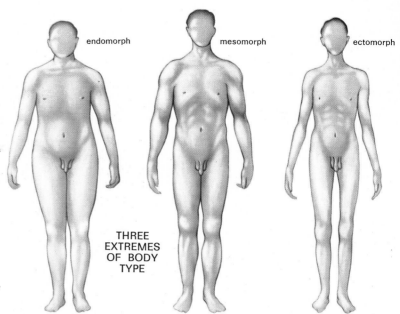

endomorph   mesomorph   ectomorph

THREE EXTREMES OF BODY TYPE

"Just room for three insides Sir"

figures of fun such as Santa Claus, is often inaccurate. Anxiety and depression is common in obese individuals and for such people, food and drink—especially sweet food and alcohol—provide a warm and pleasurable feeling and help to soothe the anxious mind and soften the depressed mood. Food and alcohol may also be used as a substitute (however ineffective) for the stimulus and excitement of life's experiences which may not be available in a boring job or in a monotonous home life. Excess intake of food and alcohol is also seen in emotional problems of puberty and adolescence, and in sexual disturbance in marriage. The risk of obesity is increased when a depressed mood leads to apathy, lethargy, and a reduction in physical activity and energy output.

Many fat individuals claim that the cause of their obesity is their 'glands'. A variety of glandular hormones are known to play a role in weight changes and fat deposition, but glandular disorders, such as Cushing's syndrome (due to excess cortisol production), Stein-Leventhal syndrome (in association with ovarian cysts), or male sex hormone deficiency, are very rare. Their existence in an individual can be readily excluded or confirmed by a careful medical examination, and anyone who claims that his obesity is due to 'glands', without medical confirmation, may simply be not facing up to the truth.

The fifth approach to the cause of obesity is to consider it as a symptom of certain countries and social groups, rather than as a symptom of particular individuals. Different races, societies and occupational groups vary in their susceptibility to obesity, but since there is no genetic influence at work, it must be the differences in life styles of these groups which leads to the differing extents of their obesity problem. For instance, affluent societies of Europe and North America have a major problem with obesity—the result of the exercise-reducing habits of the affluent: driving rather than walking; taking lifts rather than walking upstairs; watching television rather than playing active games. Within the affluent society, particular occupational groups are particularly vulnerable to weight gain, often because their work patterns do not allow a correct balance of food intake over energy output. Business executives are one such group. Business lunches, official dinners, a 113

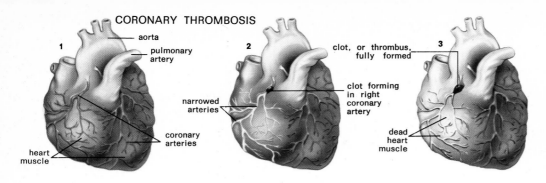

CORONARY THROMBOSIS

1
- aorta
- pulmonary artery
- coronary arteries
- heart muscle

2
- narrowed arteries

3
- clot, or thrombus, fully formed
- clot forming in right coronary artery
- dead heart muscle

Above: The course of coronary thrombosis, caused by *atherosclerosis*, which is common in obese people. (1) In normal hearts the arteries are clear. (2) Deposition of plaques, consisting largely of cholesterol and other lipids, narrows the arteries. (3) This leads to formation of a clot, which closes off the blood supply to part of the heart muscle. This then ceases to function, resulting in a heart attack.

Right: A Chinese businessman riding to his office in Hong Kong in a rickshaw, rather than walking. He is tending towards obesity, while the rickshaw operator, whose work involves physical activity, manages to remain slim.

Bryn Campbell/John Hillelson Agency

Popperfoto

Thomas Hopker/John Hillelson Agency

Left: A Bavarian sits down to a traditional feast of roast pig, pretzels, sausages, and *knodel* (potato dumplings flavoured with liver and bacon). In addition to their immense appetite, Bavarians average 50 gallons a year in their beer consumption. It is not surprising that many of them are obese.

Above: Danish politician Per Haekerrup drinking a beer while on holiday. Alcohol is broken down in the liver to carbon dioxide and water and can provide significant amounts of energy. If a heavy or moderate beer drinker does not expend this energy in active work, he may develop obesity, often as an abdominal 'paunch'.

sedentary pattern of work and excess consumption of high-calorie beverages such as wines and spirits, all combine to make weight maintenance difficult.

Disadvantages of obesity

The adverse influence of obesity on the life, health and welfare of twentieth century men and women has led some doctors to describe obesity as a disease rather than a weight problem. In men, obesity can shorten the normal expectation of life (about 68 years in industrialized countries) by up to 25 per cent in a given individual. The effect on the life expectancy of women is much less significant—but this is counterbalanced by a greater preponderance of obesity-associated illnesses in women.

114   Direct ill-effects of the increased weight

load carried by an obese person, and of his altered shape, include varicose veins, in which the one-way valves in the return blood flow from the legs become incompetent, and osteoarthritis, in which the weight-bearing joints of spine, shoulders, hips and knees show increasing stiffness and discomfort due to wear and tear of the cartilages. Poor balance, with the risk of falling and breaking bones, reduced chest expansion, and increased risk of chronic bronchitis developing are other effects.

Fatty deposits in the blood vessels account for the association of obesity with heart attacks, *angina pectoris* (chest pain), and high blood pressure. There is also an association between obesity and the occurrence of *diabetes mellitus*, a disease involving impairment of the ability of muscles to use glucose, caused

by underproduction of the hormone *insulin* by the *pancreas*, and resulting in high glucose levels in the body's fluids.

The increased number of skin folds in obese people can also create problems of hygiene. Excessive sweating in hot weather, and resultant skin irritations under the breasts in women and in the genital area in both sexes, are common.

Social concern over obesity is mainly a matter of fashion. Admiration of the rotund and grossly curvaceous figure beloved of classical painters has given way to fashions in both outerwear and undergarments which are designed for the slimmer individual. Slimness also tends now to be considered sexually more appealing, at least in the West. Emotional aspects of obesity are tied in with this social unacceptability of being too fat. In particular, the obese adolescent may suffer from psychological doubts, and even social rejection by members of his own age group. Older obese individuals may fall into a vicious circle in which obesity leads to anxiety, often relieved by eating, and leading to further obesity.

The understanding of the medical dangers of obesity and the changed attitude of society to fitness has led to a greater interest in weight reduction and control in the affluent countries. The main approach to 'curing' obesity is still a dietary one, but psychological treatment to strike at the causes, rather than the results of obesity may be more effective in the long run. In particular, medical attention to the problems of anxiety or depression, and joining slimming groups in which the obese individual can share the resolution of his problems with others, are most beneficial.

Slimming

Perhaps the first person to appreciate the consequences of over-eating and the benefits of slimming was the Greek scientist Hippocrates. In about 400 BC he observed, correctly, that 'those naturally very fat are more liable to sudden demise than the thin'. Slimness, however, is a matter of fashion as much as of health, and therefore it has not always been considered a desirable attribute. For instance, plump women were considered more attractive in sixteenth and seventeenth century Europe.

Twentieth century interest in slimming has grown in parallel with the affluence of developed societies and the sharp rise in the percentage of people in these societies who are overweight. There are two important reasons why people are encouraged to slim, namely to conform to society's concept of the beautiful body shape and to improve health. The dictates of fashion in clothes have placed increasing emphasis on the slimmer figure. This began in styles for teenagers and later spread to adult clothes, crossing both class and national boundaries. Slimming is now also seen to be of increasing importance for health reasons, and people professionally concerned with health and health education have supported this trend.

Effective means of slimming

A person who sets out to slim may be grossly overweight, only mildly above the ideal weight, or even a normal weight, but in all cases, weight reduction can only be achieved when energy output exceeds energy input in the form of food. This goal is beset with difficulties. For example, if an individual is eating too much because of an anxiety state or depression, then medical help will be required in addition to an effective diet. The person with a 'sweet tooth' may be asked to eliminate sugar and sweets from his diet and must replace these with non-sugar artificial sweeteners. The individual who claims not to eat anything all day until the evening meal, yet cannot lose weight, may not realize that the small nibbles of food taken during the day constitute a definite energy intake.

Any diet which reduces carbohydrate intake or reduces the total calorie intake, including carbohydrate, fat and protein, is an effective means of slimming. The principle of the low carbohydrate diet is that restriction of carbohydrates causes the body to convert fats to energy instead of storing them.

The low calorie diet simply alters the energy balance towards excess energy output instead of intake.

The low carbohydrate diet is most suitable as a mild way of slimming for those who are not more than 15 per cent overweight. Sheets describing a diet of this type usually stipulate that no more than 120 grams of carbohydrate should be taken daily. Those who do not wish to weigh their food can simply eliminate sugar-containing foods such as sweets, cakes, most processed foods and alcohol, and avoid deep-fried items such as french fries and crispy packaged snacks as well as fatty meats such as pork, lamb and some cuts of beef. Although officially carbohydrates, potatoes and wholemeal bread and pasta are excellent for dieters as 'fillers' as they contain a great deal of dietary fibre, which helps constipation.

For those who have to eat out as part of their work, a low carbohydrate diet can be observed by avoiding sugar in any form and welcoming unbuttered vegetables and salads, ordering grills but ignoring fried food, and drinking clear rather than thick soup. Instead of wine, low-calorie long drinks can be taken; if wine is considered mandatory, dry wine is preferable to sweet wine. Extras such as rolls and butter should also be avoided.

For those who do not find a low carbohydrate diet effective, or for those more than 15 per cent over their ideal weight, the alternative diet is a low total intake

Courtesy Wrangler

Right and below left: Changes in society's concept of the beautiful female body shape are reflected in variations in the style of outer clothing in different eras. The representation (right) of the Roman lady Lucretia, who was considered a beauty in her time, reveals the fashionable body shape prevalent at the time of the artist, the 16th century Venetian Lorenzo Lotto. The model's plumpness is emphasized by the voluminosity of her dress at the arms and hips. In contrast, the tall slim figure of one 20th century symbol of beauty, the model Verushka (left), is emphasized by the skin-tight blue jeans and shirt she is wearing. The desire to attain a body shape like this motivates many 20th century women to slim.

Below: These French ladies are participating in a dietetic cruise. Isolated at sea, they can only eat the closely controlled diet provided by the ship, and are made to exercise to aid slimming. However, the lady on the left appears to be putting rather less than her full effort into this.

National Gallery

Raymond Depardon/John Hillelson Agency

115

ENERGY VALUE OF SOME COMMONLY EATEN FOODS	Kilo-calories in 100 g of food
Bread and flour	
White bread	253
Wholemeal bread	241
Wheatgerm bread	237
White flour	348
Toast	299
Other cereal foods	
Rye crispbreads	318
Cream crackers	557
Cornflakes	365
Boiled rice	122
Sweet foods	
Mixed sweet biscuits	496
Boiled sweets	327
Plain chocolate	544
Milk chocolate	578
Honey	288
Jam	262
Marmalade	261
Sugar—white demerara	394
Ice cream	192
Black treacle	257
Fats and oils	
Butter	793
Margarine	793
Lard	894
Olive oil	899
Suet	894
Dairy produce	
Cheddar cheese	412
Cream cheese	813
Milk	65
Sweetened condensed whole milk	322
Egg	158
Double cream	449
Single cream	189
Meat and fish	
Fried back bacon	597
Grilled beef steak	304
Grilled lamb chop—lean and fat	500
Fried pork sausage	369
Fried sheep's kidney	199
Fried calf's liver	262
Roast beef—lean and fat	385
Roast lamb—lean and fat	292
Roast pork—lean and fat	455
Steamed cod	82
Fried cod	140
Soused herring	189
Grilled kipper	108
Salmon, canned	133
Fruit and vegetables	
Eating apples	45
Bananas	76
Grapes	60
Pears	41
Oranges	35
Dates	248
Dried sultanas, raisins, currants	248
Baked beans	92
Fresh peas—boiled	49
Dried peas—boiled	100
Boiled cabbage	8
Boiled old potatoes	79
Potato crisps	559
Potato chips	236
Miscellaneous	
Peanuts	586
Cocoa	446
Spirits, 70° proof	222
Red wine	67

Note: Figures are based on edible portions.

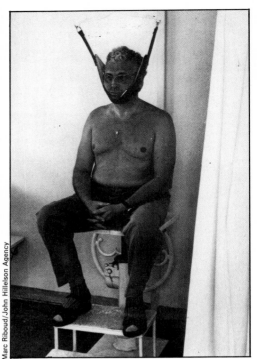

Marc Riboud/John Hillelson Agency

Camera Press

Left: A middle-aged Czechoslovakian having his chin massaged by a vibrating apparatus in an effort to remove his facial fat. There is little evidence that machines like this are of real use in slimming.

Far left: Slimming involves avoidance of high energy foods.

Above: A Spanish mother taking mild exercise with her daughter in an effort to slim her waist. Mild exercise alone is ineffective in weight reduction as it burns off only about 15 grams of fat per hour, but is useful as a supplement to dieting and tones the muscles, producing an attractive appearance.

Right and below: Control over feeding is thought to be exerted by a brain mechanism called an *appestat*, centred around the *hypothalamus*. If an area called the *lateral nucleus* of a cat's hypothalamus is cut, the cat will stop eating, while if another area, the *ventromedial nucleus* is cut, the cat will overeat. This indicates that in a normal cat, the lateral nucleus exerts a stimulatory effect on the appetite, and the ventromedial nucleus an inhibitory effect, the two effects acting as a balance. Overeating may inhibit the effect of the lateral nucleus, causing feeding to stop, while reduced feeding inhibits the effect of the ventromedial nucleus, and stimulates eating. A similar mechanism exists in humans and must be overcome if weight reduction is to be achieved by the slimmer.

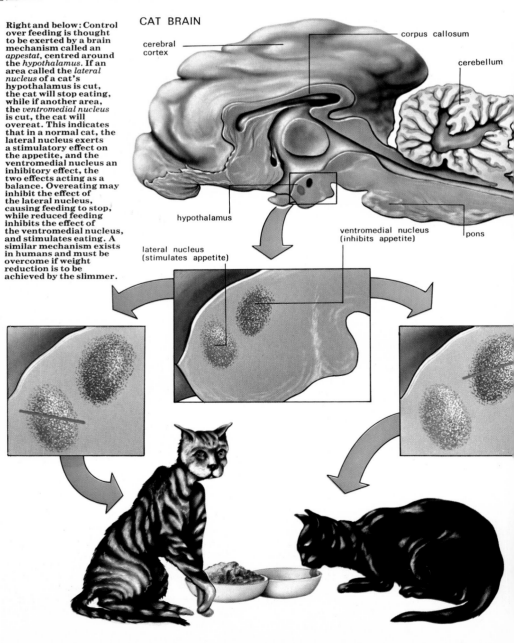

CAT BRAIN

cerebral cortex

corpus callosum

cerebellum

hypothalamus

ventromedial nucleus (inhibits appetite)

pons

lateral nucleus (stimulates appetite)

A CORRECT VIEW OF THE NEW MACHINE FOR WINDING UP THE LADIES

Above: The fashion for extremely slim waists, brought about by wearing increasingly tight-fitting corsets, reached its peak of popularity in Britain around the 1880s. This humorous cartoon of the period only mildly exaggerated the situation, since waist measurements down to 33 cm (13 in) have been recorded in women of normal height.

Right: A selection of health foods. There is a common misapprehension that these foods provide a short-cut to weight reduction. They are good sources of vitamins and other nutrients, but slimming requires a reduction in quantity of food intake more than improvement in quality. Only health foods which are low in calories are of use to the slimmer.

of daily kilocalories—no more than 1000 kcal in a day. This allows a better balance of liked and less-enjoyed foods, but requires periodic adjustment by a dietary adviser, both to avoid monotony and to ensure there is no deficiency of vitamins or an imbalance of protein. For either diet, the slimmer should weigh himself no more than once a week, since daily fluctuations in weight are normal and frequent weighing may give a false picture. Consistent and gradual weight reduction is more effective than rapid reduction in the long run. The aim is to lose half to one kilogram each week.

Grossly obese individuals with a persistent inability to slim with any diet can undergo treatment of a medical or surgical variety. One treatment involves total starvation as a hospital in-patient, with only vital salts, fluids and vitamins permitted. Surgical methods include cosmetic fat removal from the abdomen, splint wiring of the teeth to allow only fluid intake, and operations on the digestive system designed to 'by-pass' parts of the intestinal tract responsible for digesting food products. Each of these approaches has its risks and can be carried out only under strict medical supervision.

Effective slimming is difficult to undertake alone and group support can prove helpful. National and local slimming clubs can help in keeping and adjusting diets. For the well-to-do, temporary success in weight reduction can be achieved at health farms.

Slimming myths

Because of the difficulties inherent in slimming, people are constantly looking for short cuts to fast weight reduction. For example *thyroxine*, a hormone which is known to exert some control over metabolism, has been tried as a weight reducing drug. In a healthy person with a normally functioning thyroid gland, this hormone is ineffective and may produce dangerous side-effects. *Amphetamine* drugs, which act to increase energy expenditure, have also been tried, but have been discredited since they are highly addictive and have not been found to produce weight loss. However, there are a few drugs which have been developed since the 1960s which can help, on a short-term basis only, to support a slimmer. For example, *fenfluramine* helps some people to control their appetites without wild swings in their emotions. The slimmer who depends on drug support is liable to

relapse and gain weight when he or she stops taking the drugs.

Another alleged short-cut to weight reduction is the so-called 'crash diet'. This involves eating only one or two items each day. Common combinations are bread and butter, banana and milk, grapefruit and coffee, and eggs only. Such diets do produce a quick temporary weight loss because the food, and therefore energy, intake is very low. However, diets of this kind are monotonous, fail to produce proper attitudes to long-term weight reduction, and are often nutritionally unbalanced, producing vitamin lack, excess cholesterol or protein deficiency over long periods. The same holds true for patent formula foods which are not recommended over long periods.

Neither is there any scientific evidence for the use of such substances as cider vinegar, acetic acid vinegar, herbal extracts, vegetable extracts or lemon juice to 'slim a person down'. There is no such thing as a slimming food since every food has some energy content.

Water loss to reduce weight can be induced by tablets or injections, or by sweat loss in Turkish or sauna baths but this is not an effective way to slim since the water is quickly replaced once the individual starts drinking.

Another disappointing approach is the use of hypnosis. The idea of this is that the slimmer is put into a hypnotic trance and given suggestions on subsequent diet. Once out of the trance, the post-hypnotic suggestion is supposed to reduce food intake. Relapse is common even in those subjects who can be hypnotized.

Exercise alone is normally insufficient to produce a steady weight loss, since a great deal of activity is required even to lose a few grams a day. However it can be useful to supplement weight loss through dieting. There is no scientific evidence that passive exercise applied by massage or machines of an automatic nature can help weight reduction.

Contemporary interest in slimming has highlighted a disorder which appears to be a result of 'slimming excess'. The disorder is known as *anorexia nervosa*, and involves persistent aversion to food intake on the part of the sufferer. It usually occurs only in teenage or young adult girls. Over weeks and months, the individual starves herself in the most severe fashion. She insists that she feels quite well but becomes increasingly emaciated, despite the inevitable encouragement to eat given by worried parents, relatives and friends. For those not brought under medical and psychiatric care for treatment, death due to starvation or lack of resistance to infection is a serious risk.

It is now thought that anorexia results, at least in part, from over-protective parents who can seem repressive to their daughter. She seems to conform perfectly to her parents' ideal, only to cover up her basic lack of self-confidence, self-esteem and any true idea of herself as a person. Very often this is accompanied by a secret dread of the demands that are part of becoming an adult. The girl's emaciation returns her body to a child-like state, and menstrual periods will become sporadic and then will cease altogether. These are deep disorders and will need medical help, psychological support and often hospital care, before the weight is returned to normal.

Chapter 5
Thought and Behaviour

A sports crowd whose thoughts are concentrated on a single event are capable of acting in unison to a considerable degree. The individual may submerge his personality in the atmosphere created by the occasion and the crowd around him.

Human Adaptation

Man is the most adaptable of all animals, being able to live in a great variety of environments. This is not because he has a particularly adaptable body. It is because he has a vast learning capacity, allowing him to protect himself against nature's extremes by using both natural materials from the environment and objects which he himself creates.

The successful exploration of such alien environments as the depths of the ocean and outer space has necessitated subjecting volunteers to conditions of unprecedented severity. But there are limits to the extent that technological innovation can compensate for man's physiological limitations. Beyond them, technological 'success' might spell human disaster.

Heat and cold

The range of man's tolerance to extremes of the environment can be judged from the temperatures of some of the places he inhabits. At one extreme, people live in polar regions where temperatures drop as low as —40°C. These people cannot survive direct exposure to such temperatures, for below —15°C more heat is lost from the surface of the body than the heat produced by the tissues. To survive, man either has to insulate his body by wearing heavy protective clothing or raise the temperature of his environment through the use of shelter and fuel. Eskimos, the most permanent inhabitants of northern polar regions, do both. In addition to their unusual amount of body fat, they protect themselves in seal skins, and have devised an ingenious type of shelter, the igloo, for use where normal building materials such as wood are usually absent. In addition, eskimos have genetically adapted to their environment in that their body shapes tend to be short and rounded. This means that the surface areas of their bodies, compared with their mass, is relatively small, reducing the rate at which their skin surface loses heat.

At the other extreme, people live in tropical or desert climates where temperatures can reach 50°C. In such environments, the body's main problem is to lose enough heat to keep its temperature at the normal level of 37°C, but even people tested at 50°C on a treadmill have managed to prevent overheating. This is achieved by the exudation of sweat, the subsequent evaporation of which from the surface of the skin removes considerable amounts of heat from the body. The rate at which the body can lose heat through sweating depends to some extent on the amount of water vapour already in the air. In humid climates sweat evaporation is far more difficult than in desert climates where the water content of the air is low.

Water lost by sweating, which may be up to 10 litres per day in extreme conditions, has to be replaced, since the loss of more than five litres of water leads to dehydration and damage to the tissues, and the loss of more than 10 litres causes death. Loss of salt from the body in sweat similarly, can cause heatstroke, in which cramps and sometimes collapse are

Above, above right and left: Two groups of people who were forced to adapt to highly adverse conditions. The efforts to survive of the 1912 South Polar exploration party (above) led by Captain Robert Scott were in vain. Having been the second to reach the pole, their return was halted just a few miles from a food depot by severe blizzards. Scott and his companions died soon after Scott wrote the last entry in his diary, seen here. In contrast, many of the Uruguayan rugby team that crashed in the Chilean Andes in 1972 (left) did manage to survive—but only by eating flesh from the corpses of companions killed in the crash.

experienced. A further problem in hot climates is protection from ultra-violet radiation from the sun, which can damage the skin. In the wet tropics, vegetation and cloud cover provide protection, but in desert regions light clothing must be worn.

High altitudes

Climbing high above sea-level exposes man to cold, wind, increased ultra-violet radiation and oxygen deficiency. For every 5,500 m (18,000 ft) rise in altitude, the air pressure, and hence the pressure of oxygen, decreases by half. There comes a point when it is impossible to breathe in enough oxygen for the cells to carry out their normal metabolic functions and an oxygen supply must then be carried.

More than 10 million people live permanently above 3,500 m (11,500 ft) mostly in the Andes and Tibet. It is possible to ascend to higher altitudes for short periods, and most healthy young people should be able to survive at 8,000 m (26,000 ft) for a short time. Complex changes in respiration occur as a sea-level dweller ascends to high altitudes. The rate and depth of breathing increases and is maintained until return to sea-level. This is accompanied by an increase in the amount of haemoglobin in the blood to increase the blood's oxygen-carrying capacity.

Anybody who ascends rapidly to above 4,250 m (14,000 ft) from sea-level without slowly acclimatizing will suffer from acute *mountain sickness* within a few hours. The most prominent symptoms are

Popperfoto

Right: A diver explores a reef near the Canary Islands off the West African coast. One of the greatest problems involved in *free* diving —that is, without an air supply from the surface— was in providing divers with air at pressures that varied with depth. This was solved by the French diving pioneer Jacques Cousteau, who invented the aqualung. This consists of a valve which delivers air from a tank strapped to the diver's back at a pressure equal to the external water pressure.

Below: At the Ames research laboratory in the US, an astronaut acclimatizes to the effect of very high acceleration forces. By enclosing him in a capsule and swinging this round in circles, it is possible to subject the astronaut to high centripetal forces, very similar to the acceleration forces experienced during rocket take-off. In this way, the astronaut's heart, lungs and blood supply can adapt to the conditions expected at take-off and scientists are able to observe the effect on the human body of high accelerations.

ZEFA

Below: British climber Nick Estcourt nearing the summit of a mountain in the Kashmir region of the Himalayas, which contain numerous peaks over 8,000 metres high. At these heights, the air pressure is reduced to about one third the pressure at sea level, making it necessary to use oxygen tanks when climbing for long periods.

Photri

severe headache, nausea, dizziness, weakness and lack of judgement. These begin to subside after two days and usually disappear within a week. By ascending slowly and spending days or weeks at intermediate altitudes, mountain sickness can be avoided. No drugs, hormones or other chemical treatments overcome the need for slow adaptation, or improve performance at high altitudes.

In space
Modern jets and spacecraft have pressurized cabins to protect the occupants from the low pressures outside, and are provided with an oxygen supply. Should the window or door of a modern jet blow out at 15,000 m (50,000 ft), it would take several minutes for the cabin to depressurize completely, probably causing little harm to the occupants as long as oxygen was provided and the plane descended. In a spacecraft, however, the pressure outside the cabin is zero, and sudden depressurization gives the astronaut only five or six seconds to take any corrective action. After this time he will lose consciousness, his lungs will burst, and his blood will begin to boil. This is because the gases inside the lungs will expand very rapidly, and those which are normally dissolved in the blood will bubble out.

Another problem with spaceflight is the effect of accelerational forces on the body. For a rocket to escape the gravitational force of a planet as large as the Earth, the accelerational forces are so high that the astronauts are subjected to ten times the normal gravitational force for short periods of time. This means that the astronaut's body, including his blood, will be ten times heavier than usual, causing a severe strain on the pumping mechanism of the heart. If the astronauts were upright as the rocket accelerated, the increased weight of the blood would cause it to 'pool' around their feet. Their brains would not receive enough blood and they would become unconscious. To overcome this, astronauts lie transversely to the direction of the rocket, but even so, distortion occurs to loosely-attached body organs such as the eyes and heart.

A similar problem will arise if man ever lands on any of the larger planets of the solar system. Planets and satellites within relatively easy access such as the Moon, Venus and Mars all have a lower gravity than Earth's, but Jupiter and Saturn, for

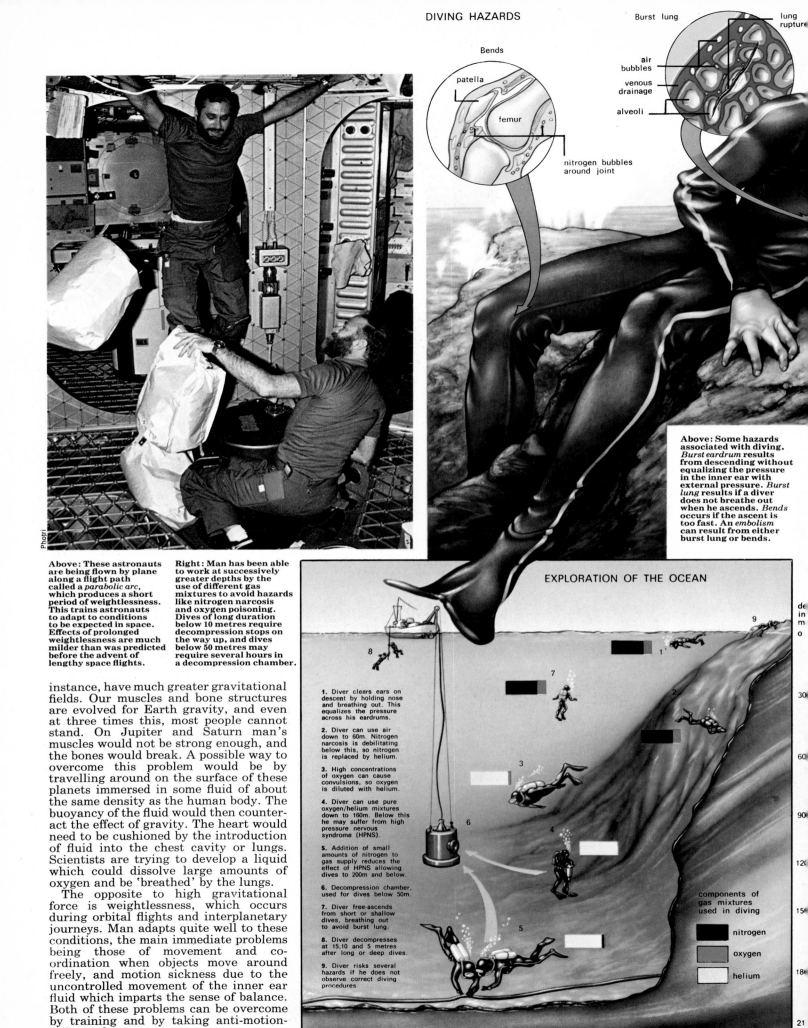

Burst lung

lung
rupture

Bends

air
bubbles

venous
drainage

alveoli

patella

femur

nitrogen bubbles
around joint

**Above: Some hazards
associated with diving.**
Burst eardrum results
from descending without
equalizing the pressure
in the inner ear with
external pressure. *Burst
lung* results if a diver
does not breathe out
when he ascends. *Bends*
occurs if the ascent is
too fast. An *embolism*
can result from either
burst lung or bends.

**Above: These astronauts
are being flown by plane
along a flight path
called a *parabolic arc*,
which produces a short
period of weightlessness.
This trains astronauts
to adapt to conditions
to be expected in space.
Effects of prolonged
weightlessness are much
milder than was predicted
before the advent of
lengthy space flights.**

**Right: Man has been able
to work at successively
greater depths by the
use of different gas
mixtures to avoid hazards
like nitrogen narcosis
and oxygen poisoning.
Dives of long duration
below 10 metres require
decompression stops on
the way up, and dives
below 50 metres may
require several hours in
a decompression chamber.**

instance, have much greater gravitational
fields. Our muscles and bone structures
are evolved for Earth gravity, and even
at three times this, most people cannot
stand. On Jupiter and Saturn man's
muscles would not be strong enough, and
the bones would break. A possible way to
overcome this problem would be by
travelling around on the surface of these
planets immersed in some fluid of about
the same density as the human body. The
buoyancy of the fluid would then counter-
act the effect of gravity. The heart would
need to be cushioned by the introduction
of fluid into the chest cavity or lungs.
Scientists are trying to develop a liquid
which could dissolve large amounts of
oxygen and be 'breathed' by the lungs.

The opposite to high gravitational
force is weightlessness, which occurs
during orbital flights and interplanetary
journeys. Man adapts quite well to these
conditions, the main immediate problems
being those of movement and co-
ordination when objects move around
freely, and motion sickness due to the
uncontrolled movement of the inner ear
fluid which imparts the sense of balance.
Both of these problems can be overcome
by training and by taking anti-motion-
sickness drugs.

EXPLORATION OF THE OCEAN

1. Diver clears ears on
descent by holding nose
and breathing out. This
equalizes the pressure
across his eardrums.

2. Diver can use air
down to 60m. Nitrogen
narcosis is debilitating
below this, so nitrogen
is replaced by helium.

3. High concentrations
of oxygen can cause
convulsions, so oxygen
is diluted with helium.

4. Diver can use pure
oxygen/helium mixtures
down to 160m. Below this
he may suffer from high
pressure nervous
syndrome (HPNS).

5. Addition of small
amounts of nitrogen to
gas supply reduces the
effect of HPNS allowing
dives to 200m and below.

6. Decompression chamber,
used for dives below 50m.

7. Diver free-ascends
from short or shallow
dives, breathing out
to avoid burst lung.

8. Diver decompresses
at 15,10 and 5 metres
after long or deep dives.

9. Diver risks several
hazards if he does not
observe correct diving
procedures

components of
gas mixtures
used in diving

nitrogen

oxygen

helium

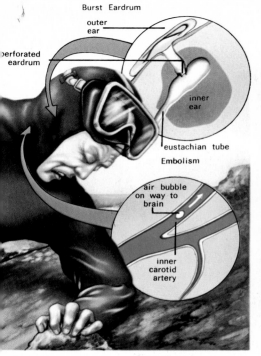

Right: This scientific balloon flight in 1862 by two high-altitude experimenters, Glaisher and Coxwell, nearly ended in disaster. At a height of 11,000 metres | Glaisher fainted due to oxygen lack but Coxwell summoned the strength to pull the release valve, thus saving their lives. Later flights carried their own oxygen supply.

The most worrying problem of weightlessness is the loss of calcium from the bones. In normal conditions calcium is constantly being removed and laid down on the bones in response to the stresses placed on them by movement and gravity. When these stresses are removed, the bones lose calcium but do not replace it. They therefore become weak, and when the astronaut returns to normal Earth gravity his bones are liable to break under the strain. The answer to this problem seems to be to simulate during the flight the normal stresses placed on the body on Earth. If spacecraft could be made large enough and rotated during flight, the astronauts would experience a centripetal force from the walls of the spacecraft, simulating gravity.

Undersea environments

The undersea continental shelf comprises an area about the size of Africa, and is full of mineral and biological resources but has, as yet, been only sparsely explored. Man's main problem in working there is with pressure, which increases by one atmosphere for every 10 m (33 ft) increase in depth. Hence at 30 m (100 ft) the pressure is four atmospheres. To prevent the chest being crushed by this pressure, the lungs must contain air at the same pressure.

The high pressure of air in the lungs causes large amounts of gases (oxygen, nitrogen and any other gases present) to dissolve in the blood. This is quite harmless as long as the diver stays at the same depth, but when he begins to come to the surface after extended periods below 10 metres, the pressure decrease causes gas to come out of the blood at a faster rate than it can be exhaled through the lungs. The blood begins to fill with gas bubbles which interrupt the blood flow, causing agonizing pains, and in bad cases paralysis or death. This decompression sickness is sometimes called the *bends*, since the pain caused by bubbles in the knee, shoulder and elbow joints can be eased only by contorting these joints. To avoid decompression sickness, divers must ascend to the surface slowly, stopping at intervals to allow the gases in the bloodstream to be exhaled through the lungs. Dives to depths greater than 50 m (160 ft) require several hours, or even days, of decompression, and for this purpose *decompression chambers* are provided. The diver seals himself into the chamber, is hauled to the surface, and is decompressed by gradual decrease of the pressure through external control.

Another diving problem is that, below 30 metres, increased concentrations of nitrogen in the bloodstream act on the central nervous system as an intoxicant causing lack of concentration and confusion. This *nitrogen narcosis* becomes debilitating below 60 m (200 ft)—at which depth some divers have been known to offer their air supply to passing fish. The problem is overcome by replacing nitrogen in the air supply by helium, a gas that does not produce the same intoxicating effect. The use of oxygen/helium mixtures allows dives to depths of 100 m (330 ft) and deeper.

As man continues to adapt himself to ever more hostile environments, further problems are bound to arise, but judging from past experience, he should be able to overcome these with his ingenuity and uniquely adaptable brain.

Left: A Tuareg camp in the Sahara. The Tuareg live constantly in areas where temperatures often reach 50°C. They survive by hiding from the sun during the day, by their domestication of desert-adapted animals such as goats and camels and by their intimate knowledge of the location of water sources in the desert.

Below: Eskimos from the north-west territories of Canada crossing sea ice with their dogs. Living in areas where winters last for nine months and are extremely cold, the Eskimos have adapted by making full use of the only resources available to them—seals and polar bears for food, clothing and fuel, snow houses for shelter, and their husky dogs as a means of transport.

Biorhythms

Human life is constantly influenced by the rhythms of the universe. The Earth rotates on its axis once every day, subjecting its inhabitants to cyclical changes of light and darkness. The seasons change as the Earth orbits the Sun; the tides ebb and flow in time to the phases of the Moon. People are surrounded by rhythmical changes in light, temperature, gravity, electromagnetic radiation, and air pressure. Life on Earth has grown attuned to these rhythms of nature. Together with plants and animals, man has adapted to a 24-hour cycle of activity. This biological rhythm is called the *circadian rhythm*, the name coming from the Latin *circa dies* meaning 'around the day'.

People are often aware only of the most conspicuous of their circadian cycles—those of sleep and wakefulness. Yet people's temperature, pulse, blood pressure, respiration and indeed most of their other life processes also fluctuate regularly in time with an invisible clock. The health of the body depends on the co-ordination of these rhythmical timekeepers which direct periods of activity and rest and influence moods and dreams. The rhythms vary from person to person, and manifest themselves in individual preferences for early or late mornings, work and rest routines, and the way people order their lives within the cycle of light and darkness.

Circadian rhythms

One of the most easily observed fluctuations in the daily cycle is that of body temperature. Each day a person's temperature systematically rises and falls by one and a half to two degrees, following an internal clock unaffected by activity or by long periods of isolation. The high point in the temperature cycle usually occurs in the afternoon or evening for a person who sleeps at night, and this often coincides with a person's favourite time of day. The low point occurs during sleep, with temperature generally rising towards awakening. People who are very bright and active when they get up tend to have a temperature rise that occurs earlier than normal. Those who wake slowly and get up unwillingly have a temperature cycle which is only just beginning to rise when they get up.

Along with the peak in the body temperature goes the peak in pulse rate, which also follows a circadian rhythm. It rises to a maximum during the afternoon, and drops along with the temperature during the night. The activity of the adrenal glands also fluctuates over a 24-hour period. The level of the adrenal hormones, which regulate blood-sugar levels and energy production, drops at night and rises to a peak in the morning. When the level is high a person feels alert and active and is able to deal with stressful situations. When it is low he feels tired and lazy.

The body's rate of urine production also varies over the day, although most people only notice this when the rhythm is disturbed and they are annoyed to be awakened from sleep in order to urinate. People usually do not have to urinate at night even if they drink more during the

Heather Angel

Heather Angel

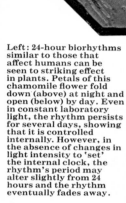

Roland & Sabrina Michaud/John Hillelson Agency

Left: 24-hour biorhythms similar to those that affect humans can be seen to striking effect in plants. Petals of this chamomile flower fold down (above) at night and open (below) by day. Even in constant laboratory light, the rhythm persists for several days, showing that it is controlled internally. However, in the absence of changes in light intensity to 'set' the internal clock, the rhythm's period may alter slightly from 24 hours and the rhythm eventually fades away.

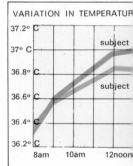

VARIATION IN TEMPERATURE

37.2° C		
37° C		subject
36.8° C		
36.6° C		subject
36.4° C		
36.2° C		
8am	10am	12noon

Above and below: People show variations in the pattern of their daily rhythms according to their temperament. In the chart above, subject A showed a temperature peak (averaged over 20 days) at noon, but subject B showed his peak at 6 p.m. In the chart below, the hand steadiness of the subjects is shown. This was tested by asking

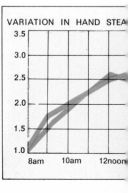

VARIATION IN HAND STEA

3.5		
3.0		
2.5		
2.0		
1.5		
1.0		
8am	10am	12noon

Above: Ancient Chinese philosophers recognized the influence of the rhythms of the universe on the behaviour of man. Part of this belief is encapsulated in the Chinese symbol of yin and yang, seen in the centre of this design. Yin, the black part, symbolizes Mother Earth and her inhabitants, and yang, the white part, symbolizes the ruler, or father of the heavens. The cyclical interaction of the two was seen as the basis of harmonious human existence.

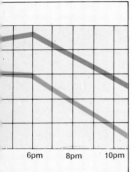

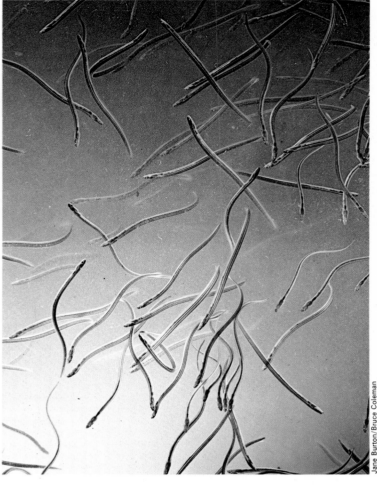

Jane Burton/Bruce Coleman

Above and below: Young eels (above) migrating up a river and flamingos (below) migrating to warm African climates are examples of animals that rely on their own biological clocks to navigate. Ocean voyagers are able to navigate with precision from one continent to another by reference to the position and movement of the Sun, provided they have a clock and a sextant. Animals are also able to fix their position by observing the arc of the Sun across the sky and its position above the horizon at a certain time of the day. But not having mechanical clocks, they have to tell the time by reference to their own internal state. Knowing their position, they can then navigate by moving in a certain direction relative to the Sun's position. In this way birds migrate thousands of miles to their winter residences, and all eels find their way back to the Sargasso sea to breed. The accuracy of these migrations is an indication of the precision of the clocks.

the subjects to place a stylus in a tiny hole—if the stylus touched the sides of the hole, they failed the test. The scale on the left is a measure of their success rate. Again, subject A reached peak performance at noon and subject B at 6 p.m. Subject A appeared to be a 'morning type' of person while subject B preferred the evening.

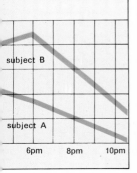

Bruce Coleman

evening than during the day. The kidneys are responsible for producing urine, and do this under the control of a hormone secreted by the pituitary gland, situated underneath the brain. The level of this hormone fluctuates in a pronounced circadian cycle, cutting down the flow of urine during sleep.

The urine itself undergoes cyclical fluctuations in its chemical components which act as a mirror of the body's chemical processes. Each chemical has its own daily rhythm to follow, yet they are all in tune together giving an overall feeling of steadiness in bodily functions.

The senses are not immune from daily cycles. Their sensitivity varies during the day, rising to a peak of awareness usually between five and seven in the evening. This is the time of day when most people's sense of taste, smell and hearing are at their best, so good food, drink and music are more appealing then than earlier in the day. On the other hand, unpleasant noises and bright lights sometimes become more irritating as a person becomes more sensitive in the evening.

The effects of the circadian rhythms dramatically change the body's reactions to physical or chemical disturbance at different times of the day. Experiments on animals have shown that a dose of a particular drug, virus or exposure to X-rays which might kill an animal at one time during its circadian cycle only annoys or makes it sick at another time. Similarly, a high-flying aeroplane pilot who might become unconscious due to lack of oxygen at 4 p.m. would be much less affected under the same conditions at 4 a.m. Understanding the circadian rhythms may solve such problems as determining the best time for administration of a particular drug or deciding whether a surgical operation should be performed early or late in the day.

The constancy of circadian rhythms has been shown by volunteers who have lived for up to six months in deep caves or simulated space capsules. In these isolated conditions of constant light and temperature, the body still maintains its circadian rhythms, although in the absence of any cue to 'set' the internal clock, the length of the average person's cycle tends to increase to about 25 hours.

Some conditions do upset the circadian cycles temporarily. Changing from a day to a night shift at work, for example, means that the body's hormones and temperature cycles are completely out of phase. The person in this situation is attempting to work with his body temperature and hormones at the normal sleeping levels. While asleep he will have high blood-sugar levels and may have to periodically get up and urinate since the cycles take some time to adjust to the newly imposed schedule.

Similarly, international jet travel causes gross disturbances in the internal clock. A businessman arriving in central Europe from New York might attempt to conduct his business affairs at 10 a.m. central European time, but his body would be functioning as though it were 4 a.m., the time in New York. He would be sleepy, wide awake or hungry at the wrong time of day since his systems would be totally out of synchronization with local conditions. Travellers adjust to a new circadian cycle at the rate of about one hour per day, so a New York businessman might take six days to adapt to Euro-

125

Heather Angel

Bruce Coleman

air conditioner
and heater
maintain constant
temperature

soundproof walls
reduce auditory
stimuli

Left: Biorhythms with different periods are sometimes combined. This is illustrated by limpets, which actively feed every 12.5 hours whenever the tide covers their part of the shore, and also every night—even at low tide—since then the rocks are not dried out by the heat of the sun. These activity cycles are maintained even if the animals are kept in constant conditions.

Above: Female grunions show precise biorhythms in spawning activity. They bury eggs in the sand every two weeks, just after the high point of a spring tide. The eggs stay buried for two weeks until washed out by the next spring tide in time for hatching.

pean time—sometimes just in time for his return trip to New York, there to find himself waking up six hours too early.

Symptoms of fatigue often accompany these phase shifts. It has been noticed that rodents which have been subjected to phase-shift experiments are more vulnerable to various poisons and stresses. Inversion of their light-dark cycle once a week results in a small, but significant, reduction in their life span. It is possible that people may suffer similar ill-effects from disturbance of their biorhythms.

Monthly, annual and seasonal rhythms

Circadian cycles are only one of the rhythms of life. Underlying the circadian rhythms are cycles of electrical activity in the brain and nerve cells which last for mere microseconds. At the other extreme there are monthly, seasonal and annual cycles. The most noticeable monthly cycle is the female menstrual cycle which involves dramatic monthly hormonal changes affecting a woman's emotional and physical state. An estimated 60 per cent of women suffer from some form of pre-menstrual stress which can affect their sight, respiration, susceptibility to infection and behaviour.

Men are also susceptible to monthly rhythms. Although these are not quite as conspicuous as the menstrual cycle, they are nevertheless measurable. Monthly episodes of psychosis have been discerned among adolescent boys, and have their counterparts in men who undergo emotional cycles in which their mood rises and falls in a regular cycle. The cycle varies from person to person, from

David Hurn/John Hillelson Agency

Left: British miners emerging from a coal pit after working the night shift. After a few days on a night shift their biorhythms settle down to a 12-hour *phase reversal*—they relax in the morning and sleep in the afternoon. However, continual disturbance of biorhythms because of frequent changes in work shift can cause stress.

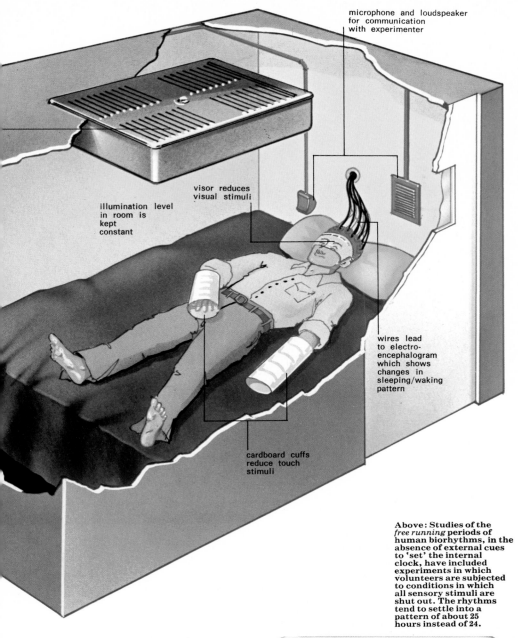

microphone and loudspeaker
for communication
with experimenter

visor reduces
visual stimuli

illumination level
in room is
kept
constant

wires lead
to electro-
encephalogram
which shows
changes in
sleeping/waking
pattern

cardboard cuffs
reduce touch
stimuli

Above: Studies of the *free running* periods of human biorhythms, in the absence of external cues to 'set' the internal clock, have included experiments in which volunteers are subjected to conditions in which all sensory stimuli are shut out. The rhythms tend to settle into a pattern of about 25 hours instead of 24.

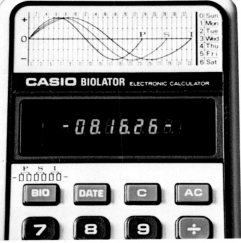

Left: With no watch or radio, David Lafferty begins an attempt to beat a stay-down record in a cave in Somerset. His only contacts with the outside world were occasional phone calls in which he stated his estimations of the time. His estimates soon became inaccurate as the span of his biorhythms began to deviate from normal.

Above: One make of electronic calculator is claimed to compute a person's intellectual, physical and emotional state on any day of his life, on the assumption that these are biorhythms with fixed periods. The method also assumes that at a fixed reference point, the date of birth, the value of each state is equal for all people.

four weeks to as long as 13 weeks in duration. Diseases which often occur periodically are well-known by doctors, common ones being manic depression, epilepsy, migraine and some illnesses characterized by fevers or swellings.

Seasonal and annual rhythms are more difficult to study, and hence there is much less data available about them than about the shorter cycles. Nevertheless it is now known that the thyroid gland secretes something known as a 'summer hormone' which helps to reduce body heat. The hormone's release is somehow triggered in anticipation of hot summer months. Another seasonal rhythm is a strange winter madness called 'arctic hysteria' which affects some Eskimos. This is a hallucinatory type of experience which lasts for a few hours or days. It is thought to be related to fluctuations in the Eskimos' bodily content of calcium, which is known to affect the nervous system. During the summer months there is continuous sunlight in the high latitudes where Eskimos live, and this stimulates the formation in the skin of vitamin D which enhances the absorption of calcium from food. This results in an excess of calcium during the summer but a rapid loss of calcium in winter, when sunlight is absent for several months.

In tune with the universe

Various reasons have been suggested for the occurrence of biological rhythms. Studies of the development of children have indicated that the evolution of many rhythms might be brought about by the physical and social environment. Infants develop rhythms of sleeping, waking and urination only slowly, being unpredictable for the first weeks of life. It seems that to some extent the 24-hour clock is learned rather than inherited; an infant might learn a completely different routine of sleeping and waking if taught differently early in life.

Some scientists believe that people are sensitive to rhythmical changes in the universe far removed from their immediate vicinity, including changes in electrical fields, cosmic radiation, magnetism and gravity. Evidence for this theory comes from the study of some mental patients who become excitable, hostile and sometimes violent whenever there is solar flare activity (sunspots) on the Sun. Solar flares change the magnetic field on Earth, and can occasionally move a compass needle. There are indications that the brain is at least as sensitive to magnetism as a compass, and may respond to these changes in the magnetic fields of the Earth.

The study of time and the cycles of nature has helped to mould the history and culture of many civilizations. Chinese astronomers and philosophers saw relationships between the cycles of the Sun, the Moon and human behaviour: 'The Sun at noon is the Sun declining; the creature born is the creature dying'. Ancient doctors usually took into account the cyclical events of the Sun and Moon, both when prescribing cures and when diagnosing illnesses. Yet it is only since the early 1960s that western science has begun to investigate the importance of biological rhythms in man, and it seems likely that the findings of this research will increasingly influence medical practice and the organization of society in the future.

127

Sleep and Dreams

A baby born in an industrialized country can expect to spend 23 years of its life fast asleep. At first, babies follow a one-hourly pattern of sleep which continues irrespective of night or day, and a larger portion of the 24 hours is spent asleep than awake. Gradually the sleep periods lengthen and fuse together and eventually the sleep takes place at night and waking activity during the day. A minority of people break this pattern—there are a few who can survive on as little as two hours of sleep a day. But for the vast majority of people just under eight hours of sleep at night is the average.

Until well into the twentieth century, the descriptions of poets and philosophers were the only guides to the nature of sleep. However, all early sleep research foundered on one simple problem: the lack of an objective test of whether someone was fast asleep or not—without actually waking them up and involuntarily ending the experiment. Only after World War II did sleep researchers gain the tool they needed. This was the *electroencephalograph*, or 'eeg' machine.

The importance of 'brain-waves'

As far back as 1875, an Englishman named Richard Caton had discovered that animal brains show continuous changes in electric potential. The eeg machine picks up these tiny changes in potential and magnifies them sufficiently to cause them to operate a series of pens on a continuously running belt of paper so that the brain quite literally writes its own characteristic pattern as a series of 'brain-waves' of various shapes.

Recordings on the eeg reveal that there are several different patterns of electrical activity during sleep. As the sleeper closes his eyes, fairly regular electrical waves with a frequency of about 10 cycles per second appear. These are called *alpha* waves. As the subject becomes drowsy, these disappear. They are replaced by more irregular waves which eventually slow down to about 1-3 cycles per second and are intermittently interrupted by short, sharp busts of faster waves called sleep 'spindles'. The subject is now in the *slow-wave* type of sleep. After a while the eeg changes again, the slow waves being replaced by much faster waves, similar to those recorded during drowsiness. At the same time, the eyes begin to execute rapid movements. This type of sleep is called *rem* (rapid eye movement) sleep.

The exact function of these two phases of sleep is not clearly understood but some clues have been provided by waking subjects during sleep. This has shown that if a person is continuously wakened at the start of periods of rem sleep, so that over the night he is getting only the slow-wave type of sleep, then on the first undisturbed night he experiences longer periods of rem sleep than normally, as though to compensate for the rem sleep that he missed on the previous nights.

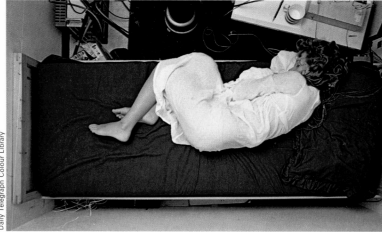

Right and below right: In a sleep experiment, a subject is connected to an *electroencephalograph* (eeg) by wires leading from metal cups attached to her face and scalp (below right). Some of these pick up changes in electrical potential in her brain. Others detect electrical changes caused by eye movement. These electrical changes are magnified by the machine and traced by pens on a moving sheet of paper as 'brain-waves' or as changes in eye-movement frequency. The subject goes to sleep on a couch (right) and is observed simultaneously with the eeg tracings. During sleep, people move every six minutes on average. Movements are most frequent during *rem* sleep, when the eyes make rapid movements.

Left: *Flaming June* by the 19th century English painter Baron Frederic Leighton. Outwardly, sleep appears a serene and relatively uneventful experience, as this painting well expresses. But within the mind, the unconscious third of people's lives is a time of great activity, full of bizarre and dramatic surprises.

Right: Eeg recordings from a subject during different sleep phases. As a person drops off, his eeg changes from the regular alpha-rhythm to irregular waves during drowsiness, and then to slow-waves interrupted by short fast bursts called sleep *spindles*. The eeg traces during rem sleep are similar to those during drowsiness.

Similarly if the subject is deprived of slow-wave sleep, this occurs for longer periods on subsequent nights. It has been surmised from this that both types of sleep are essential, but that their functions in maintaining health are different.

Studies of this type have also shown that if people are asked to report whether they were dreaming when wakened, dreams are reported more often during rem sleep than during slow-wave sleep. For some time rem sleep became known as 'dream' sleep—and the rapid eye movements were thought to be the result of the dreamer scanning the events occurring in his mind. However, current opinion is that dreaming occurs during any period of sleep, but that the most vivid and well-remembered dreams occur during periods of rem sleep.

The sleep mechanism

As a whole, sleep mechanisms seem to be adjusted to the survival needs of a particular animal; sleep is triggered only when the necessity for vigilance is reduced. Thus ruminants, which are prone to attack by predators, sleep very little, whereas gorillas, which are subject to virtually no such attacks, can apparently sleep indefinitely. Man has to seek a protected place to sleep, free from sensory stimuli such as loud noises and bright lights. Nevertheless, although people can normally exert conscious control over when they sleep, they may, in cases of extreme sleep deprivation, fall asleep even in bright, noisy or dangerous situations. There thus appear to be two systems that influence when we sleep. One, the *sleep-triggering* mechanism, exerts a positive influence which increases in strength the longer we stay awake. The other, the *alertness* system, inhibits sleep and is stimulated by sensory inputs from the environment.

Studies have shown that the 'alertness' system is centred around an area in the *brainstem* called the *reticular formation*. When this area is in an 'excited' state, it passes nerve impulses up to the cerebral cortex, the area of the brain responsible for thought and consciousness, and thus keeps the brain in an alert state. Various factors act to keep the reticular formation excited. Nerve pathways from the sense organs have direct connections to the reticular formation, so that sensory stimuli such as noises and lights directly excite it. Nerve pathways also lead directly from the sense organs to the

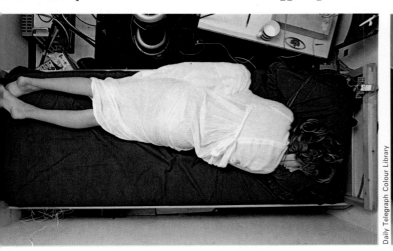

Daily Telegraph Colour Library

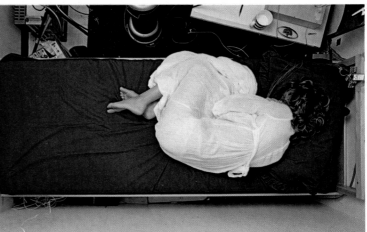

Daily Telegraph Colour Library

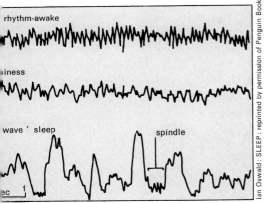

Ian Oswald: SLEEP; reprinted by permission of Penguin Books

Below: Sleep deprivation or boredom is often accompanied by yawning. A slight increase in heart-rate occurs during the yawn, which seems to be an attempt to raise blood-flow to the brain.

Right: The mechanism which causes people to sleep seems to be triggered by security and a lack of sensory stimuli such as noise. This Nigerian has apparently found such conditions.

Mansell

Mark Edwards

129

cerebral cortex, where they are analyzed. Signals from the environment of special significance stimulate the cerebral cortex to send messages down to the reticular formation, thus exciting the alertness system. In this way, if a person is asleep, he may be wakened by signals of particular significance to him.

The sleep-triggering system appears to function mainly through chemical means. That most people start feeling sleepy at certain times of day indicates that the mechanism is affected by changes in the body's chemical and hormonal levels, which fluctuate rhythmically in a 24-hour cycle. Also, since the sleep-triggering mechanism increases in strength the longer a person is kept awake, it seems probable that there is a build-up of some chemical during wakefulness that stimulates the sleeping mechanism.

Two chemicals that have been postulated to be sleep inducers in this way are *serotonin* and *noradrenaline*. Serotonin is located in a group of nerve cells called the *nuclei of raphe* in the brainstem. In one experiment, the administration of a drug that inhibits the manufacture of serotonin led to several days of insomnia in cats. However, the administration of the same drug, called PCPA, to humans did not induce insomnia, so that serotonin has not been firmly established as a sleep inducer.

Noradrenaline is concentrated in an area of the brainstem called the *pons*, and is known to be important in the transmission of nerve impulses. During rem sleep in cats the pons fires off electrical messages to the cerebral cortex, but this does not occur during wakefulness or slow-wave sleep. The pons is thus thought to exert primary control over rem sleep, the phase of sleep in which vivid dreams are most common. The pons also exerts an inhibitory influence on the muscles of the body, to prevent them acting out the content of dreams. When the French sleep-researcher Jouvet destroyed a tiny part of the pons in cats, they began to act out their dreams—lapping non-existent milk off the floor, for example.

Sleep deprivation
Insomnia, lack of sleep, appears to be almost as much a state of mind as an actual condition. When sleep deprivation approaches 100 hours cortical control begins to break down, accompanied by hallucinations, impaired judgement and burning eyeballs. Yet even with this extreme deprivation of sleep, early tests showed that the brain retained an extraordinary ability to deal with problems. It was only when the subjects were given continuous work tests that their performance dropped dramatically.

Eventually it was realized that so highly does the human mechanism prize sleep that sleep-deprived subjects indulge in 'micro-sleeps'—tiny emergency bursts of sleep during which their eyes remain open. During these micro-sleeps the immediately preceding mental activity is forgotten and concentration is impossible, so that a continuous task cannot be performed.

It is not only acute sleep deprivation that can induce these micro-sleeps. Experiments have shown that one of the most effective methods of inducing micro-sleeps, or putting people to sleep altogether, is to feed in a continuous pattern of similar and boring signals. The dangers

Right: Sleep takes place in cycles during which *slow-wave* **('deep') sleep alternates with** *rapid eye movement* **(***rem*** or 'light') sleep, with intermediary phases similar to the state of drowsiness. The slow-wave phases, characterized by reduced movement, heart rate and blood pressure are longer during the first few hours of sleep, while rem phases are longer during the last hours. Dreams may occur during any phase but are most vivid during the rem phases, and most dreams that are remembered occur during the final extended period of rem sleep. Several dreams with widely different themes may be experienced during a single night's sleep.

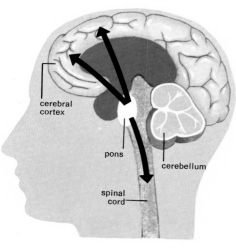

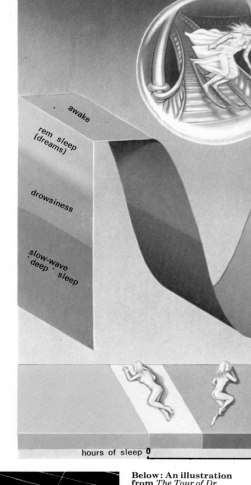

awake

rem sleep (dreams)

drowsiness

slow-wave deep sleep

hours of sleep 0

Above: The *pons*, **located in the brainstem, is thought to exert control over dreaming. It sends excitatory messages to the cortex to start dreams and inhibitory messages to the muscles to prevent physical enactment of the dream.**

Below: *Chrysis*, **a dream painting by the French surrealist Delvaux. Some** people dream frequently of walking around naked without reaction from onlookers. Psychologists say such people often suffer inhibitions due to being scolded as children for their exhibitionism. The dreams reveal the cause of their inhibitions and indicate that their behaviour could be less reserved without fear of social disapproval.

Below: An illustration from *The Tour of Dr. Syntax in Search of the Picturesque* **by the 19th century writer William Combe. The doctor, having spent an evening reading in a library, dreams he is walking the banks of the River Thames, with humanoid books flying all around him. Especially in the first few hours of sleep, dream content tends to be moulded around prominent events or objects from the day, in this case the books. Many psychologists see this as evidence that dreaming is a procedure for sorting out and filing the day's events.**

Left: A 15th century woodcut depicting, in a medieval setting, the biblical figure Joseph interpreting Pharaoh's dream. In ancient times dreams were thought to be prophecies of future events rather than manifestations of past or present circumstances. Pharaoh's dream of seven fat cattle devoured by seven thin cattle was correctly interpreted by Joseph as indicating seven years of plenty followed by seven years of famine. The famine was avoided by storing grain, and as a result Joseph was made second in command over Egypt.

of this for tired motorists, who may start indulging in micro-sleeps while driving along a featureless motorway, have been recognized.

Millions of people take sleeping pills each night to combat insomnia but their effect can actually appear to be the same as sleep deprivation, since they reduce or even eliminate rem sleep. Often these tablets are combined with the use of amphetamines, which also eliminate rem sleep, in combating depression. When either or both types of pill are stopped an enormous increase in rem sleep can result, often accompanied by nightmares.

The function of dreams
There have been several approaches to the question of the function and meaning of dreams. The first approach, the mystic or occult, maintained that man may have access to different times and places during dreams. Hence the importance given in the past to 'prophetic' dreams.

The second approach maintains that dreams are generated out of an individual's daily experience and are manifestations of attempts by the unconscious mind to express repressed thoughts and wishes. The main proponent of this line of thought was the psychoanalyst Sigmund Freud, who maintained that dreams consisted of a universal 'language', consisting mainly of sexual symbols. Although dreams are still seen to have a 'language', this is thought to be an individual, rather than a universal language, and is not necessarily sexual in nature. Thus a dream about a stallion is no longer interpreted as a sexual symbol—it may just be a dream about a horse. Nevertheless, there is a connection between rem sleep, in which dreams are most vivid, and sexual activity. Dreams of a sexual nature are common in both sexes, and in men, erection of the penis often occurs during rem sleep, sometimes resulting in orgasm and sperm emission—the 'wet dream'.

The third approach maintains that dreaming is a means of removing tension from the brain and 'sorting out' information collected during wakefulness, primarily on an unconscious level. The conscious dream (one that can be remembered) may be a method of bringing to the mind a situation or difficulty which needs urgent attention because it might disturb the body's balance or endanger survival. If people are continuously deprived of vivid dreams by being wakened during rem sleep, disintegration of their personalities and impairment of their mental functioning soon follows. Thus, as with sleep generally, dreams play an essential role in health and indeed in survival.

131

Perception and Deception

The patterns of light and sound which arrive at the sense organs, and are transmitted as coded signals to the brain, are of little use in themselves. We need a system of interpreting the signals so that we can react to them correctly. The means by which we do this, deriving our knowledge of the world about us from the information collected by the eyes and ears, is known as *perception*.

Perceptual constancy

The human brain immediately recognizes any familiar object, however it is viewed and from whatever distance. A book, for example, looks like a book whether we see it laid flat, upright or on edge. Yet the shape and size of the image that the book produces on the retina of the eye varies a great deal. For instance, if we hold a book flat, and up close to the eyes, the image it produces is of a greatly foreshortened trapezoid, much narrower at the back than at the front. But we still 'see' it as rectangular, because the brain adjusts automatically to the varied image the book produces. This phenomenon is called *perceptual constancy*.

Our mechanisms for producing perceptual constancy can most easily be demonstrated by situations that produce a *non-constant* effect. For example, if we stare at a bright light for a few seconds, our retinas retain an *after-image* when we look away. This after-image, caused by fatigue and recovery in certain retina cells, has a fixed size, shape and position on the retina. But if we then look first at nearby and then at more distant surfaces, the after-image seems to shrink and swell, seeming largest when we are looking at the most distant object. This is because a real object casts a smaller image on the retina when it is further

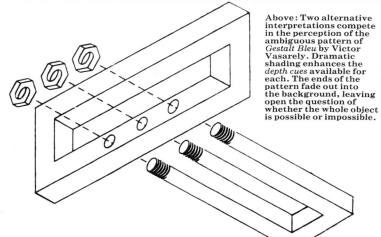

Above: Two alternative interpretations compete in the perception of the ambiguous pattern of *Gestalt Bleu* by Victor Vasarely. Dramatic shading enhances the *depth cues* available for each. The ends of the pattern fade out into the background, leaving open the question of whether the whole object is possible or impossible.

Above: Perception is a form of problem-solving. Sometimes, as with this 'impossible' object, the problem has no solution. *Perceptual hypotheses* can be made to interpret different local parts of the object, but as the lines of the drawing are followed along it is found that the different perceptual hypotheses are incompatible.

Left: In this ambiguous illustration, *Blossom and Decay*, two perceptual hypotheses of equal validity can be formed. The illustration is perceived either as a skull or as two people seated in front of an arched gateway. The two interpretations rival each other and are hard to perceive simultaneously.

Right: Perception is a personal phenomenon. People may perceive sensory stimuli such as colour, music or pain in quite different ways, due to modification of their perception by experience. For instance this Balinese dancer's perception of the 'feel' of fire on his foot is quite different from the painful feeling most people would perceive, because of his experience at fire-walking.

Mary Evans

Alphabet & Image

John Hillelson Agency

away, and to maintain perceptual constancy the image is 'scaled up' by the brain in a process called *constancy scaling*. The same scaling effect is applied to after-images, producing changes in their apparent size.

The mental processes that perform this 'scaling' are unconscious and effortless; we automatically perceive the real, or *veridical*, shape and size of objects. In fact, to consciously perceive objects exactly as they are presented on the retina requires mental effort and training. This can be seen from the drawings of small children, which are 'flat' and lack *perspective*; the small child draws not what he sees, but what he knows is there. The same lack of perspective can be seen in the art of such otherwise advanced people as the ancient Egyptians (who drew people with their heads in profile, but their bodies face-on) and Chinese (in whose paintings nearby and more distant objects were all the same size, with no attempt at scaling down).

To carry out constancy scaling, the brain requires information about the distance of objects. This three-dimensional information is extracted from the two-dimensional image on the retina by a variety of means, called *cues*. One of the most important is *binocular disparity*—that is, the difference between the views seen by the two eyes, which produces slightly different signals from the two retinas. This cannot be the only cue to distance and depth, however, since if one eye is closed the world does not appear 'flat'.

Motion parallax is another effective depth cue; if the head is moved from side to side, nearby objects move further across the retinal image than do more distant ones. Another powerful factor is *interposition*; if one object is partly obscuring another one, we know instantly that it is nearer.

Further information comes from *perspective* cues. In man-made environments, the convergence of parallel lines as they become more distant (railway lines, for example) gives us an immediate sense of depth. Perspective works in natural environments, too. Since most natural surfaces—grasslands, pebble beaches, arrays of tree trunks—are textured, *gradients of texture*, such as the steadily shrinking size of beach pebbles as they get further away, provide a 'frame of reference' within which we can perceive the distance of any object in the outdoor scene.

Ambiguous figures

Perceptual cues are normally effective even when they are fundamentally ambiguous. If railway lines make a converging pattern on our retinal image, we 'read' them as converging parallel lines. But we interpret quite differently the same retinal pattern when it is produced by genuinely converging lines viewed head on—the outline of a church steeple, for example. We are rarely aware of such alternative interpretations; instead, the brain's perceptual mechanisms take the evidence provided by the eyes and interpret it in a way that makes sense.

The interpretations chosen most often by the brain's perceptual mechanism are those having right angles and straight lines. And this is where illusions can be created. The experimental 'Ames room', for example, is so constructed that, although its walls and corners are bizarrely angled, they produce from a fixed viewing point the same perspective image as a normal, rectangular room. A person viewing the room from this point cannot help but perceive it as rectangular.

In some special cases, we can draw two —apparently equally valid—deductions from the same sensory pattern. Such patterns are called *ambiguous figures*.

Left and below: Two examples of *mimicry*. The well-known French mime Marcel Marceau (left) interacts with imaginary objects on an empty stage, creating a context in which the spectator virtually perceives real objects. The hairstreak butterfly *Spindaris ella* (below) mimics a slightly larger insect through the false head incorporated in its rear wings—its real head is here facing to the left. This illusion confers a survival advantage on the insect. If a predator approaches the insect from behind, it may be scared off when it perceives the insect as larger than it really is. If the predator attacks, it may only damage the insect's wings instead of fatally wounding it in the head.

B.B.C.

NHPA

Left: An example of the importance of *context* in perception. Identical shapes are perceived as the letters 'H' and 'A' in different words. The brain selects the most probable of the possible letter combinations this particular pattern is intended to convey. It rejects the improbable combinations 'The cht', 'Tae cat' and 'Tae cht'.

Below: An experiment in *perceptual learning*. The movements of the passive kitten are controlled by the other, active kitten. They experience the same visual input, but only for the active kitten is this associated with its own actions. The passive kitten's co-ordination and visual development are retarded compared with the active one's.

active kitten

passive kitten

Two different scenes seem to alternate in our perception, in a way over which there is no conscious control, even though the 'input' via the eyes does not vary.

Still other patterns have been drawn which fit no possible interpretation. In these 'impossible objects' each segment of the pattern provides cues to our perception of form and distance—but the deductions we make are immediately contradicted by the cues coming from other segments of the pattern. Here, too, perceptual alternation may occur, as first one part of the drawing, then another is scrutinized. But in this case the alternation occurs not because there are two possible interpretations but because the interpretations conflict.

Once the brain has formed a *perceptual hypothesis*—that is, a preliminary interpretation of the information the senses are feeding to it—this determines how the whole sensory pattern is interpreted. In this way, once the Ames room is perceived as rectangular, then the two corners of the rear wall must appear to be the same distance from the viewer.

This is one example of the importance of *context* in perception. We do not perceive, or interpret, an object merely from the information provided by its own sensory pattern. We also take into account the information provided by the object's surroundings. And what we perceive is the object (or event) that, experience has taught us, is most likely in a particular context.

Thus, when a spoken word is transmitted against a background of interfering noise, it is heard correctly more often if it is a common word rather than a rare word, or if it is a word that fits the rest of the sentence rather than one that is out of place.

This illustrates the fact that the brain can produce correct perception even when its 'inputs' from the senses are fragmentary or indistinct; but it also means that improbable events are sometimes not picked up. An example is the misprint that goes unnoticed; the misprinted word is an improbable combination of letters—such as the someti*n*es in the last sentence—which is perceived as the probable, correct, word.

Visual artists through the ages have exploited the properties of perception to achieve their effects. Skilful use of the depth cues of perspective and texture gradient can create, from a flat canvas, the illusion of depth. What is most striking about representational art is how powerfully the artist can create the impression of real objects with simple and even sketchy patterns. The effectiveness of many cartoon drawings with an extreme economy of line, or of the scenes hinted at in patterns of light and colour by the Impressionists or by Turner in his watercolours, demonstrates how perceptual mechanisms can derive hypotheses of the outside world from the most fragmentary input.

Perception and experience

How we manage to interpret sensory information so effectively has been the cause of much argument among philosophers and psychologists. Traditionally, *nativists* believed that perceptual ability is inborn; *empiricists* that all human knowledge is acquired through the senses, and hence that our perception of the world around us comes solely from

Alphabet & Image

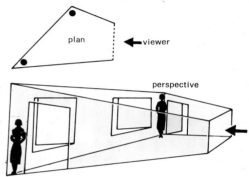

plan ← viewer

perspective

Above and right: The bizarrely angled shape of the Ames room, a plan and perspective drawing of which are given at right, produces the same perspective pattern at the viewing position as a normal rectangular room. Perceptually, the rectangular interpretation is preferred and as a result the two women are misperceived as being the same distance from the viewer. The size of the woman on the left is thus not 'scaled up' by the brain, and as a result she is misperceived as smaller than the other woman.

Below: The 'real' ex-US President Nixon in this picture is perceived normally since the brain scales up the perspective foreshortening produced by the camera. But in the background Nixon looks distorted because the poster is itself a foreshortened perspective. The brain cannot correct for this double effect.

Below right: *Dynamism of a Dog on a Leash* by Giacomo Balla. The illusion of movement is created by superimposing successive images—a technique borrowed from photography.

AP

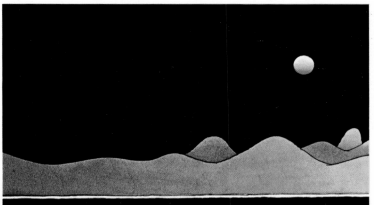

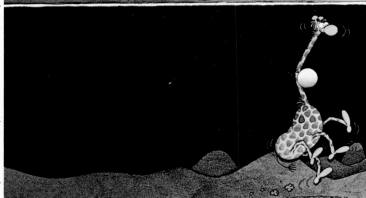

Above: In *An Autumn Landscape with a View of Het Steen* by the Flemish painter Peter Rubens, the artist has created the feeling of depth on a flat canvas by the use of a *texture gradient*. The foreground is roughly textured while the background is given a smooth texture.

Right: Our perception is conditioned to interpret a round, white object in the night sky as the moon. But as this cartoon by Mordillo illustrates, human (and giraffe) perception can sometimes be misled.

our experience of that world.

Some research has favoured the empirical approach. It has shown that perceptual learning is possible—that long experience in making subtle perceptual distinctions allows the expert to use cues in the sensory input which are not recognized by the novice. Examples are naturalists who can identify the species of a bird from just a fleeting glimpse; and wine tasters who can recognize the vineyard and vintage of a wine from one sip.

Experience can also modify the relationship of one sense to another—for example the connection between vision and the sense of touch. Volunteers made to wear special goggles that turn the visual image upside down are unable at first to coordinate their inverted visual world with their movements and sense of touch. However, as they continue to wear the goggles for days or weeks, co-ordination develops until they can perform tasks as delicate as riding a bicycle. When the goggles are removed, they are again disoriented, and have to re-learn how to use normal vision.

These experiments have shown how experience can affect perception in an adult. Presumably similar processes occur in a baby as he learns how to use sensory information for the first time. However, babies do not come into the world completely without perceptual abilities—it is difficult to see how a baby could learn anything if his sensory input was not initially organized in some way. Studies of babies only a few weeks or few months old show that they already have the capacity to recognize certain patterns and to make some response to the way objects are arranged in space. Thus, neither pure nativism nor pure empiricism seems to fit the facts: human beings have some inborn perceptual abilities, but these can be developed to fit the visual world to which they are exposed.

Much of this perceptual development is in the co-ordination of vision, touch and movement. In particular a person must learn to form mental links between changing visual patterns and the body movements that cause these changes.

A special example of the co-ordination of vision and movement occurs in eye-movements. The eyes make movements several times a second, making an image of the exterior world sweep across our retinas. But no motion is perceived when this happens; the perceptual apparatus, in interpreting the sweeping of the image across the retina, takes account of the commands the brain has sent to move the eyes.

The relationship between vision and movement is two-way. On the one hand, knowledge of his own movements allows a person to see the outside world correctly. On the other hand, vision is vital in controlling those movements. Even the most basic example of motor control—keeping our balance when we are standing upright—involves the use of visual information. Experiments in which the visual surroundings are artificially moved show that such movements cause body sway and even loss of balance, even though the floor underfoot remains stationary. The much greater demands placed on perception in high-speed driving or flying, or fast-moving ball games, show how rapid and exact the complex processes of interpreting the sensory pattern must be.

Basic Mental Skills

Once information about the outside world has been obtained through the senses and interpreted by perception, this information can be used, through a variety of *mental skills*, to determine a person's reaction to events or circumstances in the future. Through *attention*, the brain can select the most important pieces of information to be retained; through *memory*, information can be stored in the brain; through *learning*, mental links are formed between specific memories; through *recall*, memories can be brought back to consciousness, and through the use of *language*, information can be communicated to other people.

Although these skills are largely taken for granted, they operate by means of electrical messages circulating in the most complex wiring system imaginable. There are approximately 10 thousand million nerve cells in an adult human brain, and the connections between the cells number 40 million per cubic centimetre. As yet an exact understanding of the function of even one cell in one person's brain has never been achieved. The processes that underlie these skills are beginning to be understood, however.

Attention

If a person is at a crowded, noisy party, he can decide which of several conversations he is going to listen to. But once he starts listening to one conversation, he cannot listen to any of the others simultaneously, although information about these conversations is continuously entering his brain. This is the selectivity of *attention*. To some extent, attention works through the brain 'latching on' to the physical characteristics of the voice that is being listened to—for instance its tone or pitch—but there is more to attention than this.

If a person listens to a tape recording of two voices, one speaking a meaningful sentence and the other talking gibberish, and suddenly the 'meaningful' voice starts talking gibberish and the 'gibberish' voice finishes off the meaningful sentence, the listener immediately switches from one voice to the other to attend to the meaningful sentence. In this case the brain is attending to which of the two messages is most significant, not to a particular voice. The brain must make some analysis of the 'gibberish' voice, in order to switch attention so rapidly when this voice began to make sense. It is important that the brain makes some analysis of all the information reaching it, since concentrating on just one 'channel' of information is useful only as long as we are interrupted immediately something more important occurs.

Psychologists have suggested that each information channel has an *attenuator*, a mechanism which allows only the most important parts of the information through. The brain can affect how rigorously each attenuator is operating. If a succession of important or significant messages comes through one 'channel', the brain will relax this channel's attenuator to allow an increased amount of

Cartier Bresson/John Hillelson Agency

Charles Harbutt/John Hillelson Agency

information to come through and be attended to.

Memory

Memory is considered a three-part system: *sensory information store* (SIS), *short-term memory* (STM) and *long-term memory*. The SIS forms an instant, but very temporary, storage of every piece of information that comes in. Information can last for only about three-tenths of a second in the SIS. If it has not been selected and transferred to short-term memory within this time, it fades away.

Short-term memory is used for carrying information a person needs for a few seconds, but can afford to forget later, for instance a telephone number about to be dialled. Two characteristics of short-term memory prevent its use as a permanent information store. First, concentration is required to maintain a particular piece of information in it. Switching concentration to something else or performing another mental task completely wipe out the information previously held in the STM. Second, it is able to store only six or seven items. A seven-figure telephone number is easily stored, but few people can rapidly memorize a ten-digit number.

For any information to be permanently

Ronan

Left and below: Various animals tabulated according to learning ability, measured by how many actions they can memorize and perform in sequence to obtain a reward. The numbers indicate the relative abilities of the animals in each group. Man, and other primates, can learn complex action sequences but animals further down the table are less capable of associating present actions with future rewards. Man's discovery of the rewards to be gained from the use of tools was a key factor in his ascendancy.

primates

1

2

3

ores

2 1

ungulates

1

2 3

bians

Mansell

Above: The Rev. W. A. Spooner was famous for his *spoonerisms* —his occasional transposition of the initial letters in adjacent words—for instance, 'I have just received a blushing crow.' Studying defects such as this has contributed to an understanding of mental skills.

Below: A prediction of how learning may take place in the future. Animal experiments have suggested that specific memories may be transferred by injecting brain *homogenate* from one animal into the brain of another animal, presumably because memories are to some extent coded chemically. There is no evidence that memories can be induced in the brain through artificial stimulation with specific electrical patterns. However, since this is the basis by which natural memory processes are thought to operate, it is a theoretical possibility.

stored, it has to be passed from short-term to long-term memory by the mechanism of *rehearsal*. The more often an item is rehearsed or occurs repetitively in short-term memory, the more likely it is to get transferred to long-term memory. Much of this rehearsal takes place automatically and unconsciously, but it can also take place consciously, as when a person is learning his lines for a play.

The third part of the system, long-term memory, has a virtually unlimited capacity. It allows a person to remember events that have happened years before, and also stores the memory 'links' formed through learning. Long-term memory probably takes place through permanent chemical or structural changes in nerve cells, caused by patterns of electrical activity in these cells. The longer an electrical pattern relating to a particular memory has been taking place, the stronger the chemical or structural basis of this memory.

It has been suggested that each memory is stored in a *unique cell* in the brain. One objection to this theory is that the number of events a person memorizes in a lifetime exceeds the number of nerve cells in the brain. However, if each memory was stored by a unique *pattern* of cells, linked in a characteristic electrical circuit, it would be quite possible for the number of cell patterns to exceed the number of events to be memorized.

Another objection to the unique cell theory is that specific memories are not stored in specific places in the brain. This was discovered by a psychologist called Lashley in the 1930s. He taught various tasks to an animal and then surgically destroyed parts of the animal's brain, hoping to find that memories for specific tasks could be erased. Instead he found that although the animal's ability for a particular task decreased as more of the brain was destroyed, no specific memory could ever be completely erased. The fact that memory is so diffuse has suggested to psychologists the idea of a memory *hologram*, similar to the technique of storing a three-dimensional

EN L'AN 2000

Mary Evans

Left: British actor Albert Finney playing the leading role in Shakespeare's *Hamlet*. This requires committing about 1,500 lines of Shakespeare to *long-term memory* and recalling them again (in the right order) night after night on stage. The only way to do this is by frequent rehearsal of the lines in *short-term memory*. Retaining information in long-term memory is easy compared with the difficulties in getting the information there in the first place.

PAULO
EXPERIM

Above: How the Russian physiologist Pavlov demonstrated *classically conditioned* learning. Normally, a dog salivates only when presented with food. By ringing a bell whenever he fed the dog Pavlov *conditioned* it to salivate whenever a bell was rung, whether food had been presented or not. The dog had formed an association between food and bell-ringing.

Right: Gulls demonstrate classical conditioning in associating the sight and sound of a tractor with increased chances of food on the ground. But they also show instrumental learning— by trial and error they have learned that looking for food behind the tractor is the most rewarding behaviour.

Above left and above:
Most skills consist of
series of chained actions
leading to an eventual
reward. The reward can
take a variety of forms,
from writing ability
for the Tibetan taking
a handwriting lesson
(above left) to physical
protection for the
Ethiopian roofing his hut
(above). In developing
a skill, new links in
the series of chained
actions are formed
mentally by *instrumental
learning*, in which
actions with desirable
outcomes are repeated.

Right: The basis of the
Struwwelpeter stories is
that actions resulting
in, or just threatening,
punishment should be
avoided. Here Conrad
Suck-a-thumb is being
chastized by the red-
legged scissor man.

picture of an object on a photographic
plate by superimposing laser images of
the object. Superimposed memories might
mean that each brain cell takes part in
hundreds of memories.

Learning

There are two basic types of learning.
Classically conditioned learning was first
recognized by the Russian physiologist
Pavlov, who showed that animals form
memory links between events in the
external world. A dog will salivate when
given food, but if a bell is rung whenever
food is given, the dog forms a link between
food and bell ringing, and eventually
salivates whenever a bell is rung, whether
food is presented or not.

In *instrumental learning*, a memory link
is formed between an action and the
outcome of this action, together with a
classification of whether the outcome was
desirable or undesirable. This is sum-
marized by the *Law of Effect*, which states
that 'an action leading to a desirable
outcome is likely to be repeated in similar
circumstances'. Similarly, an action
leading to an undesirable outcome is less
likely to be repeated—we learn from our
mistakes as well as our successes.

In most animals, actions and outcomes
have to be closely associated in time for
links to be formed between them. Thus, a
seal will keep balancing balls on its nose
only if it is given instant rewards of fish.

Humans, and to some extent apes, can
go further than this and form links
between present actions and rewards in
the future, by the mechanism of *chaining*.
If a chimpanzee must press a button on a
machine in order to obtain a banana, it
will soon learn to do this by trial and
error. Being able to press the button
becomes a desirable reward in itself, and
if the chimp has to pull a rope in order
for the button to appear, it will soon learn
to do this as well. Similarly, it can learn
to operate a switch in order to get at the
rope, and so on. The chimp memorizes a
series of *chained actions* in order to
obtain the eventual reward of a banana.

Human learning is essentially similar.
Through modification of the memory
store by the addition of new links, whole
programmes of actions can be formed to
obtain a reward. These programmes range
from simple ones such as the series of
three or four chained actions required to
make a cup of tea, to highly complex
programmes which may take years to
form such as those required to play a
musical instrument well or make a
beautiful pottery vase.

Recall

Storing information is of little use unless
it can be readily retrieved for dealing
with the situation at hand. When a
person loses his memory, a condition
called *retrograde amnesia*, the recall
system has been impaired. Information
is recalled through a search mechanism
in the same way that data might be
retrieved from an enormous cross-indexed
filing system. A mental 'probe'—an
image with the basic characteristics of
whatever is trying to be recalled—is
formed. The brain searches through the
memory system for a pattern that matches
this probe. If this procedure does not find
the memory, additional information may
be added to the probe. For example, if a
person is trying to recall on which date a
certain event occurred, information about
what happened just before, or after, the
event may be added to the probe to help
in the retrieval, since when the event was
memorized, links will have been formed
between the event and other events closely
associated in time.

Language

Once memories have been recalled they
can be transmitted to other people through
language. Language is the ability to form
links between the physical action of
producing a sound in the vocal chords and
the mental image of what this sound
means—for instance, the link between the
sound 'dog' and the mental image of a
dog. Like any other ability, language has
to be learned and the language 'links' are
themselves laid down in the memory.

One result of language experiments was
the discovery that language ability is
developed almost entirely in just one of
the two *cerebral hemispheres* of the brain,
usually the left hemisphere. This is most
clearly seen in people who have *split
brains*, in which the bundle of nerve
fibres, called the *corpus callosum*, connecting the two hemispheres has been
cut. Split-brain patients display abnormalities when presented with an object in
the left hand side of their field of view.
All the visual information about this
object goes to the *right* hand hemisphere,
which recognizes the object by comparing
information about it with memorized
information. But since the right hemisphere does not have any language ability,
the split-brain person—although he
knows what the object is—is unable to
say what it is.

Thought and Creativity

Rationality, the capacity to think, has often been described as man's defining attribute. Yet although history has produced many great thinkers—Plato, Aristotle, Leonardo da Vinci, Newton and Einstein among them—none of these has ever produced a convincing explanation of the nature of thought and creativity. This is partly because the word 'thought' is so ill-defined, being applied to several different mental activities. Studying thought is also difficult because it is the ultimate case of 'diamond cut diamond'—when a man thinks about thinking he can only examine thought by his own thoughts.

The Greek philosopher Plato wrote that the creative thinker loses himself at the moment of creation and becomes the agent of higher powers: 'God takes away the minds of these men and uses them as his ministers'. Albert Einstein, one of the 20th century's greatest scientists, was unable to produce a scientific explanation of the nature of thought. He claimed that there is no logical path to a great scientific discovery: 'the mind has to make a jump, much like that of a poet or a painter.'

These men were only considering the more advanced forms of creative thought leading to great scientific discoveries or original works of art. Only exceptionally gifted individuals are able to engage consistently in these forms of thought. Yet thought is continually required in everyday life and no study of psychology would be complete without a scientific analysis of how everyday thought processes operate.

In one type of thinking, called *concept attainment*, the goal is to produce a satisfactory explanation of a number of observed facts. Examples of this type of

Dr. Georg Gerster/John Hillelson Agency

Royal Library, Windsor Castle

Above: A Los Angeles wall painting by Kent Twitchell. As well as the inspiration required in conceptualizing an idea such as this, considerable motivation and artistic ability is needed to carry it out.

Left: Some sketches by Leonardo da Vinci, one of history's greatest creative thinkers. It is not known whether the sketch at left is a self-portrait. Those at right, comparing water eddies with human hair, remained a unique record of the behaviour of flowing water until the advent of slow-motion photography. In addition to his ability to make penetrating scientific observations, Leonardo was a famous artist, military engineer and medical researcher.

Ronan

Left: Sherlock Holmes gives his associate Dr. Watson a summary of a case he is handling. In Holmes's thinking style, various *concepts* would be formed to explain the different, and seemingly unrelated, aspects of a case and these would be combined into a *hypothesis* to fit all the facts. The validity of a hypothesis would be ascertained by testing it against any new facts that might emerge or could be uncovered as the case was investigated. Once a hypothesis proved valid within reasonable doubt, Holmes would present it as the correct solution— usually to Dr. Watson's utter astonishment.

Right: Considerable thought is required in both the compilation and comprehension of this story about a man and his unruly pig. To translate it, the concept that each picture is intended to convey must be found. The correct concept is the one whose associated language sound best fits the context of the story. As a clue, the correct concepts for the last two pictures in the second line of the story are 'hen' and 'sum'.

THE OLD MAN & HIS UNRULY PIG.

SIX-PENCE.

Mary Evans

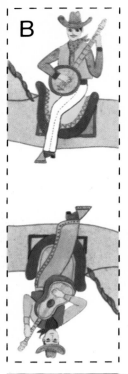

B

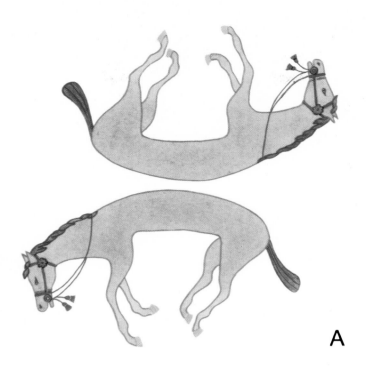

A

Left and above right: Two puzzles that can be solved by a straightforward approach. In the mosaic (above right) is hidden a regular five-pointed star which has to be found. In the maze (left) a path must be found between the centre and the cul-de-sac in the left bottom quarter. Either puzzle can be solved by a trial-and-error approach based on fixed assumptions.

Above and right: In contrast, two puzzles that require some *insight* to solve. The strip with the cowboys drawn on it (above left) has to be placed on top of the horses in such a way that both cowboys are riding a horse. The six matches (right) have to be assembled in such a way that they form four equilateral (equal sided) triangles, in which the sides of each triangle are equal to the length of a match. The solution to these puzzles will come in a 'flash' rather than by a step-by-step logical approach. Making fixed assumptions about the method of solution must be avoided, since these may be misleading.

thinking are a scientist's efforts to find a theory to fit a set of experimental facts or the detective work of Sherlock Holmes and other sleuths.

Another type of thought is required in making *decisions*, whether in a work or a social context. This requires projecting the outcomes of one's own and others' actions, and evaluating their consequence. In resolving *problems*, evaluation of the causes or structure of the problem must be made and a solution found either through the step-by-step method of *logical analysis* or through *insight*, requiring a less conventional approach to the problem. Finally, most people engage in *imaginative* thinking in which new juxtapositions of old experiences or concepts may produce useful, aesthetic or entertaining ideas.

The use of concepts

Psychologists recognize that *concepts* are an important tool in human thinking. The use of concepts in thought is an extension of their use in perception and the way in which concepts operate is best explained by first seeing how they work at the perceptual level.

The concept of a flower is formed from a person's experience of objects he has been told are flowers. If the only flower a person has seen is a buttercup, his concept of a flower will include only the attributes of a buttercup. This concept would be of little use in identifying a poppy as a flower, since poppies have different attributes from buttercups, but by *modifying* the concept so that it includes only the attributes of both poppies and buttercups—green stalks

with attached coloured petals—the concept becomes generalized to be of use in identifying other flowers in the future.

This process of *concept formation* occurs all the time in a developing child as he learns to classify objects he encounters. With experience, a whole range of generalized concepts are developed. When entirely new objects or situations are encountered, several concepts may have to be sifted around and combined to form a satisfactory explanation of a set of observations or facts. This is the process that occurs in thought. The new combination of concepts formed, the solution to the problem, becomes a generalized concept in itself and can be used for dealing with similar situations in the future.

An example of the use of concepts in thought comes from a case presented by Scotland Yard to Sir Arthur Conan Doyle, the inventor of Sherlock Holmes. A man had vanished after withdrawing all his money from the bank and foul play was feared. He had left a music hall at 11 p.m. and after changing his clothes at a hotel had departed in a hurry. To a man of Conan Doyle's experience, the withdrawal of the money indicated that the disappearance was premeditated. His changing clothes near midnight indicated

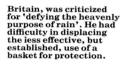

Above: Man's capacity to think relies to a great extent on the brain's ability to pattern the jumble of events occurring in the external world into a meaningful whole. This patterning behaviour is reflected in the symmetry of many of the objects man creates, such as the pattern of this printed fabric.

Above: In Shakespeare's *The Merchant of Venice*, Bassanio chooses between caskets of gold, silver and lead to win Portia's hand in marriage, the inscriptions on the caskets being his only clues to the correct choice of the lead casket. Decisions often involve a choice between several actions, with little information about their consequences.

Above: Creative ideas are often derided if they are contrary to established beliefs or methods. Jonas Hanway, who pioneered the use of the umbrella in Britain, was criticized for 'defying the heavenly purpose of rain'. He had difficulty in displacing the less effective, but established, use of a basket for protection.

a journey of some sort, and his hurried departure indicated an appointment. Juggling the concepts of premeditation, a journey, and an appointment suggested an overall solution to fit the facts. After ascertaining that the only trains leaving London after 11 o'clock were the expresses to Scotland, Conan Doyle announced that the man could be found alive and well in Edinburgh or Glasgow. The man was found in Edinburgh. It was a case worthy of Holmes himself.

Decision making

People are making decisions all the time. The decisions range from the trivial, as when deciding what to eat in a restaurant, to the more taxing, as when choosing moves during a game of chess or making life decisions such as choosing a career or marriage partner.

Logical decisions require an evaluation of all the possible outcomes of possible courses of action and an assessment of which action would result in the most advantageous outcome. The more far-reaching a decision is, the more unknown factors there are which might influence the outcome, and thus the more difficult it is to decide which action to take. In addition, evaluating the relative advan-

Above and right: The urge to express oneself by creating artistic patterns out of a few basic raw materials is a common factor among people throughout the world. The Brazilian Indians (above) are decorating themselves in preparation for a tribal ceremony, while the Panamanian woman of the Cuna tribe (right) is making herself a *mola*, a colourful type of embroidered blouse, in preparation for the Cuna Indians' yearly feast. In addition to providing personal satisfaction, creativity has the advantage of attracting social approval, particularly if the artistic patterns created are of an aesthetically pleasing or original nature. In common with other types of thinking, the thought required in creative art involves the combination of ideas or concepts into a satisfactory product. But unlike the type of thought involved in logical analysis or problem solving, creative art has no fixed rules applied to either its practice or its products, and thus allows great freedom for personal expression.

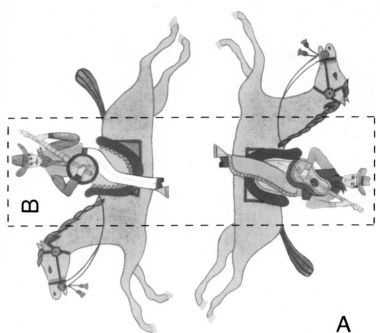

B

A

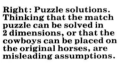

**Right: Puzzle solutions.
Thinking that the match
puzzle can be solved in
2 dimensions, or that the
cowboys can be placed on
the original horses, are
misleading assumptions.**

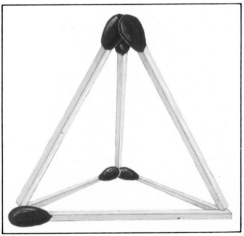

tages of different outcomes may be difficult if the outcomes are of quite different natures—for instance many people might find it difficult to decide whether they would prefer a million dollars or an extra ten years of life, if they could choose.

Several insights into the way logical decisions are made have come from man's attempts to program computers to 'play' games such as chess which require a series of decisions. Man's own thinking processes have been used as a model for these programs. The computer is usually programmed to select seven or eight possible moves for analysis whenever it is its turn to 'play'. It then selects seven or eight of the most likely counter-moves its opponent might reply to each of the computer's moves, and in turn, seven or eight possible replies it could make to each of its opponent's counter-moves. This projection of the course of the game may extend for four or five moves ahead, depending on the capacity of the computer. The computer makes an evaluation of the outcome of each projected series of moves by assessing the strategic advantage of each, and then works back again to find the initial move which would lead to the most advantageous outcome. Finally, it makes this move.

Human decision-making is essentially similar, although in most situations it is the world, rather than a human opponent, that is being 'played' against. Man's capacity to evaluate all the possible outcomes of his actions are rather more limited than a computer's. A person can usually only perform a complete analysis for three or four moves ahead. The sheer effort and time required to make rigorous logical decisions often encourages people to abandon this approach completely and rely instead on habit, intuition, or pure guesswork. On the other hand, through *insight*, people sometimes see useful combinations of actions that might not be picked up by a purely logical approach. This explains why champion chess computers are still unable consistently to beat chess grandmasters.

In some situations where decisions are needed, none of the possible courses of action appears to hold an advantage over the others. These are often the most difficult decisions to make. The mathematical study of decision-making and strategy, called *game theory*, has sometimes proved useful in helping people to decide on the most appropriate course of action.

Similarly, decisions that may at first seem overpoweringly difficult may be simplified by writing down the possible outcomes of various courses of action and assigning values, whether positive or negative, to these outcomes—in fact to help thought processes by examining on paper the 'pros and cons' of various courses of action.

Creative thinking
Thinking logically has long been regarded as the only way to arrive at the solution to a problem. But many modern philosophers regard this approach, requiring the processing of inflexible concepts, certainties and absolutes, as inadequate in dealing with the types of problem encountered in the modern world. In many cases, the data about the causes of a problem is insufficient to form a base from which a solution can be worked out by a logical approach.

Edward de Bono, a philosopher and leading exponent of *lateral thinking*, feels that because life does not fit neat logical equations, people have come to prefer feeling to thinking. Comparing the progress made in technology with the lack of progress in the human sphere (exemplified by the wide range of social and economic problems man has brought upon himself), he suggests that our thinking methods require a radical revision since the present system confuses information with thinking.

Dr de Bono's *lateral thinking* tool is designed to unlock peoples' creative reserve and enable them to make more effective use of the patterning behaviour of the brain. Lateral thinking has already been used to solve industrial problems and make education more meaningful.

The company whose office lifts were inefficient provides an example of lateral thinking. Its employees kept injuring themselves hurrying down the slippery office stairs. The firm's directors saw two alternative solutions: to speed up the lifts, or to install a new lift, both costly and lengthy operations. The lateral thinkers suggested a simple and more effective solution: install mirrors on the stairs. The employees became so preoccupied with their reflections that they descended the stairs slowly, and thus did not risk injury.

It appears that there are no rigid rules by which thought processes operate in finding satisfactory solutions to problems. Much of the effort involved in finding a solution goes on quite unconsciously. Many people report that after several hours of concentrating on the structure of a problem, the eventual solution only arrives after the problem has been allowed to incubate in the unconscious for hours or even days. The solution may arrive in a 'flash' or in symbolic form through dreams. How the unconscious sifts through the facts of a problem or synthesizes creative ideas is quite unknown. As Einstein observed: the mind has to make a 'jump'.

143

Hair colour and texture are determined by heredity. Whether the hair is curly or straight, blond or dark, is a matter of genes. These are not necessarily derived from the parents but may be a throwback from previous generations.

Index